Returning to the Lord

RETURNING TO THE LORD

Sermons for the Season of Lent

Bede Jarrett, O.P.

CLUNY
Providence, Rhode Island

Cluny Media edition, 2020

Book I originally published as *No Abiding City*, by Burns, Oates & Washbourne, Ltd., in 1932.
Book II originally published as *The House of Gold*, by The Newman Bookshop, in 1945.

Book I
NIHIL OBSTAT:
Hilarius Carpenter, O.P., S.T.L., B. Lit.
Richardus Kehoe, O.P., S.T.L., S. Scrip. Lit.
Georgius D. Smith, S.Th.D., *Censor deputatus*
IMPRIMATUR:
Bernardus Delany, O.P., *Prior Provincialis*
NOVEMBER 15, 1933
Joseph Butt, *Vicarius generalis*
NOVEMBER 22, 1933

Book II
NIHIL OBSTAT:
Georgius D. Smith, S.T.D., *censor deputatus*
IMPRIMATUR:
Edmund Canon Surmont, *Vicarius generalis*
SEPTEMBER 25, 1930

REVISORES:
Reginald Ginns, O.P., S.T.L., L.S.S.
Thomas Gilby, O.P., S.T.L., Ph.D.

For more information regarding this title
or any other Cluny Media publication,
please write to info@clunymedia.com, or to
Cluny Media, P.O. Box 1664, Providence, RI, 02901

VISIT US ONLINE AT WWW.CLUNYMEDIA.COM

ISBN: 978-1950970681

Cover design by Clarke & Clarke
Cover image: Italian (Neapolitan) School,
The Return of the Prodigal Son,
c. 1630, oil on canvas
Courtesy of Wikimedia Commons

CONTENTS

BOOK ONE

BOOK TWO

PART II: THE FAMILY

PART III: HOLY WEEK

BOOK ONE

PREFACE

by Bede Jarrett, O.P.

In publishing these sermons I ought to say that I am not altogether responsible for them for two reasons:

First, I did not write them out but was given them by Miss Ethel Lynd, who had patiently taken them down in shorthand when she heard them in Our Lady of Victories, Kensington.

Second, I think that the matter was in part suggested to me. Some time before I preached these sermons I had the good happiness to be the guest of the Dominican Sisters in Wynberg, Cape Province, for some days, and there amongst the books put in my room was one from which I took the ideas that occur in the first few sermons. I can remember neither the name of the book nor the name of the author, nor indeed to what extent I have borrowed from my memory of what I then read. It may have been much or little. But the ideas must have come from the book, I think. Then, too, readers of Bishop Hedley's books will not need to be told whence I borrowed the theme of the last sermon in the book here.

For the faults in these sermons none of my above-mentioned benefactors are in any way responsible.

SERMON I

We Are Travellers

If you were to try to summarize the teaching of our blessed Lord, and if, for that purpose, you made yourself familiar with that record of his life and teaching, which we call the New Testament, you would find in it perhaps many phrases which might serve this purpose, many to keep by you to help you in your life—to help you to understand your life. Certainly you would realize that what was evident in his life as of supreme importance was not so much what he did, but how he looked at what he did and at what was done to him. Indeed, in some respects his life was an ordinary life in its exterior. There were astonishing things in it, miracles, his very self, but the ordinary measure of his life was simple enough. The criticism made of him by the Pharisees was that he was a glutton and a wine-bibber; that he went out to dinner with the publicans and sinners. And, yet, he looked at life strongly. Hence his meekness, his patience, his practical confidence in God. It is his attitude to what happened to him that stamps his character on the New Testament, and the same character can be seen in every follower of His. It is not what we do, but how we take things done to us that seems especially to prove our right to call ourselves his disciples. It is not

the external life, but the way we look at that life that matters. We
4 Christians should take things differently from others. Our attitude
to life should be different.

Now one phrase can be taken to show this, a phrase which seems to describe this attitude of the Christian. It is that expression of the life about him, wherein it is said that we are pilgrims—travellers; that we have no lasting city here; that we have no home. We are urged to live, remembering that we are pilgrims—travellers. This will help you to explain your life to yourself. As you look at your life perhaps it seems unsatisfactory. It has no apparent continual growth in an orderly progressive fashion. True, for life is not really a growing up but a journey. You are a traveller rather than a growing child. The Christian is building up no permanent achievement; he takes a journey to life eternal. People are disappointed because they do not understand this. This life is not a business, it is a journey. Things will not fit in comfortably if you are trying to live the life of a Christian! For if you are travelling the whole secret of a happy journey is to remember always that you are a traveller. Otherwise you will find people and places pulling at your heartstrings. It is so easy to settle down somewhere and then when you move on find you have left half your heart behind you.

You are being driven by the relentless hand of God. You do not realise that you are being driven along and you try to settle down. This means infinite pain and great dissatisfaction. You are a traveller—you must not settle down. You meet people and come into constant contact with them and then you never meet them again. The secret that we discover after a while is to remember that we may not meet them again, and to remain heart-whole. All life is like that. These places and people cannot but have their influence—yet so often we are torn apart from them, by physical distance or some break of sympathy, or death. It is so easy to find oneself left to mourn and to feel torn asunder. This is natural. But supposing all the time we had known that we were just journeying, and had remembered that here was not the end, we should not so easily have been hurt by life.

Again, death unites us. If we had remembered this, we should not so easily have been hurt by life; it is life that holds us at arm's length and sets up misunderstandings. But there is no misunderstanding between you and your dead. Misunderstandings are conditions only of this travelling life. We are travellers. This explains these inevitable drawbacks. It explains God's action. His relentless action, always driving us. It seems that our life is restless. It must be. We are driven, at last, to our home. All that we learn as to how best to journey, we have to apply to life. Thus we shall realize that no place, no person, where we settle down, can be loved or longed for without in the back of our mind having the consciousness of our withdrawal from it one day. At first you travel with a great many things, and on each new journey you take, something is jettisoned. There is so much in life that you can do without. We learn to leave things behind us. Above all, we learn never to forget that our home life is outside time, altogether. Unless we remember what is the end of all our journeying—what it is and to Whom it is—we shall so easily get muddled and confused. Nothing here really matters,—whether we have it or lose it—be it a book that seems to be a lifelong comfort and then one day palls on us; or be it a helper in our spiritual life who comes in to help us and then goes out again. We find him comforting, inspiring; then, he drops out of life. We had thought that we should have him until we died!

Yet what you lose you will find again. Or what has been of use has already, served its purpose. You must realize that nothing but God is of permanent value. Even good things may one day fail.

There must be people to whom the sacraments once upon a time meant a great deal. Then their conditions of life, near to church, with frequent services, made religion easy and comfortable to them. Now perhaps they find that the outer manifestations of spiritual life are denied them. Distance or ill-health makes the sacraments almost impossible. But God is still theirs. Him they have not lost. Life is so easy until something goes wrong. Learn to do without things. You are on a journey. If you journey well, you will certainly reach home. It is for the guidance of our attitude to life that we should always remember that we are only pilgrims. The secret of a happy and holy life lies in remembering that.

SERMON II

We Need Courage

If we try to realise that saying of Scripture that we have here no abiding city; that we are here as travellers—pilgrims—it helps us the better to understand what life means. We are always planning and designing for ourselves what one day we shall do. As children we planned what we were to do when we had grown up—in youth we planned for our middle years. As we grow older it is always in the future that the great event, whatever it is, is to happen. We plan, at last, to settle down in old age. We cannot settle down—we never shall—we are pilgrims. Most of life seems just living from hand to mouth. We seem to be doing things that are not of particular consequence—but one day the thing, whatever it is, will come. Under such conditions the great virtue that is asked of us is courage. If you are to go on a long pilgrimage you must accommodate yourself to others. So life is an endless accommodating of ourselves to others. You say when you begin: This is only for a short time—later on I shall be able to organize my life as I want it." That will happen truly but not here. Life is not at our individual choice. No one ever here really has a chance of having exactly what he wants. Only on the other side of death will you really have a home. We belong to a great city, but the city lies over the far side of the river. When you go on a journey and meet with all sorts of difficulties, you must comfort yourself with the reminder that it will not be for long. You live, more or less, in a muddle. At last you think that you will be able to settle down. Again this is true, only not on earth, but in heaven. Nothing is exactly spread out as you would like it. We say life is in such a rush nowadays. It always has been from the beginning. Turn up any letters of ancient days. They always say the same thing of life, that it is so difficult to fit everything in. This must be so in every age. Where people misunderstand life is when they imagine it is home. This spoils all our judgments of life, even all our judgments of the God Who governs life.

Why is that child born blind? we ask, half-scandalised. Why has someone else grievous trouble laid on him? Why do those who love each other never get a chance of living in one another's company? Please remember this is only a journey. The child will not be blind, when it reaches life at the end of its journey. It is sad that it is blind, but nothing really to trouble about. To the pagan, if he thinks this life finishes things, it is dreadful. To us life's troubles are robbed of half their sting. Courage is our great need. And courage is Faith's child, not Hope's, nor yet Despair's, but Faith's. We need to be always pulling ourselves together and saying that our life here is not going on for ever. Children play at hide-and-seek—that is like life: it is a search, a finding, a coming home. The dreadful part of death is that we go into God's presence unaccompanied. Yet death is the ending of trouble—compared with what it ends, it is no trouble except the uncertainty of where it will leave us. So lay up treasures in heaven—not here. You will find that whatever troubles you in life, only troubles you because you misunderstand life, either because you cannot have what you want or because what you want is taken away from you.

Say to yourself then, "I am a pilgrim." That things should be wrong on a journey is right. The things we complain of are really only the little things that never matter. The only real trouble is how to get home. Courage, then, and the remembrance of what we are going to will support us. You think you cannot go on any longer? Of course you can go on, it is only a journey. Of course you can go on. It will have an end. When on a long walk in winter you see the light of your destination in the night ahead of you it helps you to go on.

"Have I always to be keeping back my own ideas and so being a peace-maker in the home? Is that my life? Always doing this or that?" No, that is not your real life. Your real life is to see God face to face. But that you may have to do these things during your pilgrimage may well be, only it will not last for ever. Moreover, all you thought yourself capable of here, there, at last, will be reached. You will stand as God meant you to stand in the place for which you were fitted. You are immortal. You are too great to find complete satisfaction in this life. You were made for bigger things. This life is too small.

God's blessed Mother—what a life she had! What monotony! Even Christ our Lord lived such a life as this, too. Always he lived it quietly. He, too, was on a journey. "Follow me," He said. He goes walking. We come after. That is what we mean by the following of Christ. The great thing is not to let yourself be too tired, but to remind yourself that at the last there is a home. You must gather your strength together. What is courage but the power, not of those who are eager and full of activity, but of those who tire, still to go on. It is not the untiring energy of the child. There is no endurance in that. The child does not find it hard to be moving. The child finds it hard to keep still. But tired and yet going on with our labours, that is endurance. Why should we not? These will end shortly. These will come to an end.

It is the part of the traveller to see this thing today and that tomorrow, to enjoy a thing while it lasts, to take life as it comes, not to trouble about the past or the immediate future. The happy

traveller becomes as a little child. His life has the beauty of a child's
10 life. It is living simply for the day. The past is only to be talked of in the evening when we rest comfortable because of the toil done. And the future? We should not talk over much of the immediate future—but take each day as it comes. Courage then! Remind yourself that this journey will have an ending. Do not let yourself be weakened by weariness. Instead, by the grace of God, renew your energies in the thought of his constant assistance and companionship. Look at him, speak to him. Go on!

SERMON III

Out of Courage—Independence

If we try and take as our guide that saying and suggestion, that comes more than once in the New Testament, that we are pilgrims and strangers, and that here we have no abiding city, it explains something, at least, of our life to us—the inevitable dissatisfaction that it must create in us, the inevitable sense that we are not and never could be thoroughly at home. It helps us to realize that the great virtue required of us is the virtue of courage—the virtue, that is, by which we go on doing what is our work. And, again, too, like all other travellers, as we pass through the various places, naturally, we expect to see things that are foreign and strange to us, but, also what is inevitable is that we, too, are foreign and strange to those through the midst of whom we pass. If you take ship and go on a journey, and visit places you are interested in, you find an utterly different life lived there—different types of ideas, different policies, different views of life. It does not take you long also to realize that you are as interesting or as strange to those people as they are strange to you—that their manner of dress seems rather unusual to you, and your manner of dress is unusual to them. Their views of life which are more leisurely or more efficient than yours seem strange, but no less strange to them are your views of life, which are less leisurely or less efficient than theirs. We are strangers wherever we travel.

Now if it is really true that we are followers of our Master, and if it is true that his ways were foreign to the people with whom he lived, it is not strange that we should seem strange to those amongst whom we live. Not quite so strange, for our world accepts some Christian culture. Yet gradually as we grow older and touch the circle of a wider world, it seems to us, at first, that these people must have curious minds not to see as we see the things that apparently are so evident and so clear.

Again, if you stay in a country you begin to pick up the ways of the country. You find yourself adopting their phrases. You find that it is a protection in some way to do that. They laugh at you because of your particular way of speaking and to escape this you try to accustom yourself to copy their ways. No one likes altogether to be unusual. Most people are content, even prefer, to lose themselves in a crowd. There is something a little awkward for a stranger walking through a city when men turn round and look at him after he has passed them, and the children laugh as he goes by. In this other life, too, there is something of the same strangeness, something that strikes others as unusual. To avoid the inconvenience of this it is very easy to surrender, to take the colour of the place. This is like the habit of the hunted animal that, somehow, in process of time, learnt to take the colour of his surroundings that he might hide from that which preyed upon him. So poor human nature, too, in this long pilgrimage is often frightened of appearing unusual, strange, and pretends to agree with others and to be as they. We talk a great deal about the value of independence. We claim it as a product of our time. We say of the young people—that is so refreshing about them—that they are so astonishingly independent. We profess our delight that everybody now is free—that there is a wide tolerance for everything and every one. There is tolerance for all sorts of things, but there is never tolerance for the undying truth. Truth is awkward—always awkward—not only in the ages when men do not believe, but in the ages even when men do. There was something strange about the saints, but they were only strange because they were sincere and whole-hearted. They never surrendered to their world. They are the great independent figures of history. Their Master, Christ, was unfaltering. It was that that was so magnificent about him. It was that that made him the leader of mankind.

People tell us that with all these new inventions the world has grown very small. Certainly it is growing to be very much alike everywhere. Is not that the danger? There was a period when, owing to circumstances, the local group *was* local. It took so long for news to reach it that it had its own ideas. But with all this gathering together of people, with this wide press, with the broadcasting, the individual man, thinking craftsman, is in danger of disappearing; and though men praise independence, few have courage enough to be independent. So true is this that you could play any trick you liked on public opinion. Every one is normally too timid to dare have ideas of his own. You could design a revolting statue and foist it on the public as a joke and someone would think it high art. You would be sure of finding someone who would see in it something you never saw. Folk would be terrified of denouncing it. It might turn out to be fine. We talk about diffusion of knowledge. You can diffuse ignorance as easily as knowledge, perhaps more easily. Is it knowledge or ignorance that is diffused in fortnightly parts?

We are strangers, and we must pay the price of being strangers in the world. I suppose, if we wanted to give a definition of a worldly man it would be this: that he looked here for an abiding city. Or again it would be true to say that he took all the views of everybody round about him and that he dared not contradict them. This does not mean that we should always contradict and prohibit evil. Rather, we should set out wherever we could our ideal of goodness and truth. We should really listen to his teaching, and understand it and even if our lives be faltering, at least, should pay homage to the truth.

No abiding city! Yet we be the fellow-citizens of the saints. That is our high calling. Then we should have something of that quality, strong, unmoved, free, independent, of that austerity that characterizes the follower of Christ. We should be careful in our ordinary ways of life. We should be careful that we do not consent to propositions that in our hearts we know are untrue, that we do not accept at once any popular philosophy where it opposes the simple things of faith. The science of yesterday is old-fashioned. The science of today will tomorrow be old-fashioned. Why worry yourself into swift acceptance of any popular scientific theory and chafe against the faith? It matters only whether Christ taught a doctrine. If he did, then it is true.

We are pilgrims. If we really follow our blessed Lord's teaching we must expect to be different, and our views will be different from what are called common-sense views. It must almost be a relief to us when we find that something is, in some measure, unpopular if we are sure that it is his, for what we need most to cultivate is the great virtue of independence. It is harder year by year for people to stand out against mere majority opinion. It will grow harder as new devices are discovered for avoiding duty and escaping for a time the incidence of Nature's laws. The only thing that can save us is to realize that we are pilgrims, and that we dare not take our ideas from the people through whom we pass. We have much to learn, of course, from others. "The children of darkness are wiser than the children of light." We have all sorts of things to learn from them, all sorts, except our doctrine. That we must learn from him and from none but him. May he help us to hold by his teaching, whether it be popular or unpopular, not only in public centres, but in our quiet homes! Many a time Christ has been denied at a dinner-table when he would not have been denied at a public meeting. The world needs the truth, and Christ our Lord came to give it truth, and out of his mercy we share his truth and must share it with others, it is a responsibility on us that we hold the truth in spite of all hardships—remembering that we are fellow-citizens of the saints. If other people despise us, what does it matter? Do we feel hurt that we have been despised? He who was greater than all was most mocked at, most hunted down, most set aside and for ever so it seemed. Yet there is no one who has so large a following of men who love him than this great pilgrim has, who bade us follow where he led. He led to a lonely death, and when he said to his followers: "Follow me," he knew where he was going. We do not know where our following of him will lead us in our earthly lifetime. We do know where a faithful following of him will surely lead us when time is no more and eternity has received us, that city whose maker and builder is God.

SERMON IV

Whither Goest?

In our pilgrimage upon earth the virtues that, in a sense, are most demanded of us are courage and independence—the spirit, that is to say, that takes its faith absolutely and unafraid. Our faith, our life, our ideals, our actions should be proof against human respect. We should prefer to obey God rather than man or man's fashion—the passing fashions of mankind. And, again, it is the perfect quality of our blessed Lord that he was staunch to all the principles that he came to teach. He would rather die than surrender them. He would rather the crowd drifted from him than change one jot or tittle of the message he came to bring it. After that dramatic sermon on his Body that he was to give, and his Blood, to be man's food and drink, he preferred to let men leave him rather than alter his teaching to suit their prejudices or their ideas. He was the living truth. Truth is unfaltering; and though it may be many-sided, it is changeless. It is of eternity, it is God. God is truth as well as love. We pilgrims, strangers on earth, in order that we may the better hearten ourselves for our pilgrimage, have to remember that towards which we are journeying, to remember that life here is a passing life, that, though now many things press on us, one day we shall be out of their reach, that life's troubles, perplexities and bewilderments, all that work, will at last be done and finished with.

If you go walking, often it is only by a distinct effort that you can keep steadily in front of you that towards which you journey. Yet if you do, even though you may be tired, the very sense that you are getting nearer, that there is an ending to your journey, will of itself give you courage to go on. In our life on earth too, it would seem that we need to remind ourselves of that towards which we journey, which is now the hope of all our lives. We should be the most miserable of men unless those things we set our faith on, unless those things were true. So holding them as truths and journeying towards them, there will always be comfort and inspiration in the memory of that towards which we come. As man grows older he cannot help the intensifying of his desires. Perhaps, in a sense, this may also be the purifying of them. Something of the material dreams of childhood and youth must fade as his own physical order and its energies diminish, but the dreams of childhood and youth are still there. These dreams are not false. Almost, we might say, it is the purpose of faith not only to explain God to us but to explain to ourselves the secret of ourselves, our old hopes and ambitions, their newer modes.

Our Lord comes and tells us that we were made for God, that he is our purpose, that somehow we fit into God. Since he is the object of our creation, though, perhaps, we did not realise it, in all our youthful dreamings and hungers it was really for God that we yearned, really God that we desired. Faith does not come and teach us things altogether outside the range of our ordinary human faculties. We could not believe unless our nature was designed by God to be able to accept the living truths. Faith tells us, indeed, of much that is beyond their range, but not beyond their purpose. It tells us of what can comfort us, perfect us, of what, without knowing it, always men hungered for from the start. We were made for God. Well, you know, if we are made for anything we cannot help hungering for it. Each child is made for its particular, personal vocation and hungers for it from the first. Pick up any biography and read it. You see the man already in a child, beginning to do the things he wants to do and is to do afterwards. See Walter Scott as a boy collecting such historical relics as he can find, relics that belonged to the heroes of romance. You will find him as a child listening to the old stories, to the stories of the people, of battles, adventures, defeats, hopes, dreams. You can see all that he ever was to become somehow already in his childhood; or you can find the future engineer in a little boy with his fingers itching for tools. From the beginning tools or wheels have interested him; he was made for them. We are all children, and God is the vocation or profession for which we all were made.

People forget what the Christian faith is. They often quarrel with the prominence given to heaven in Catholicism. They will sometimes say: "Is it not rather selfish to work for a reward? Is this not something degrading to mankind?" They forget the essence of religion: it is "Thou shall love the Lord thy God." It is not degrading to wish, at last, to possess someone or something that is the love of your heart. No man has been degraded by that; man has been lifted by it. Man is always at his noblest when he is in love with someone or something. With a person, a cause, an ideal. He is most unselfish when he is working for that. Heaven is not a reward in the sense that it is something for which we are labouring. God is our reward. That is what we mean by heaven. In our foolish way what we strive for is to love God. He is the reward for which we were made. For him every faculty is crying out all our time. We were made for everlasting things—for God, the knowledge, love and service of him. We are interested in many of our own particular interests, whatever they happen to be. But it is not hard to show how these really are but fragments that mirror God.

If you look in the history of mankind all the arts of man began in worship. All the dramas we first hear of are sacred dramas. The

first dance was a sacred dance. The first music was the praising of
20 God in unknown and no doubt clumsy manners. The first representation that we know was a representation that lifted man above himself to God. It is out of divine worship that has come everything that has helped man to rise above himself. But eventually each civilisation and culture becomes secularised because men so easily forget the object for which they work. The world is so beautiful that it distracts us. Even we are tempted to say to God: "Why have you put such obstacles in my way? Why have you given me such a wonderful world to live in? Why have you given me such attractive people to live with?" He has commanded that he alone shall be worshipped. It is the breaking of this commandment that ruins most human lives. For God they have substituted something less perfect. They see what is visible. They miss the invisible. Yet one should lead to the other. From the visible things the invisible are known. That is what our Lord came to teach us. He took the world and showed it as a parable that could lead man to God. He sees a child—"Of such is the kingdom of God." He sees the sower. That too is a symbol of the kingdom. Whatever he sees is not something which blocks his vision of God, but something which opens and shows God manifestly. This is the definition of life that he came to teach. Cannot you see that God is right up against you? "Because you did it to the least of my brethren you did it to me." That is the true view, the whole view of life for us. That is what should hearten us and should give meaning to our lives. "My life is small," you say. Naturally, but only because you are short-sighted. "I spend my life looking after this one or that one. I am at someone else's service always. I never am allowed to live my own life." Yes, but see—cannot you see? "Because you did it to the least of my brethren." See Whom it is that you are serving? St. Francis got off his horse to kiss a leper. He did not see the leper. He saw deeper than that ruin of humanity. The leper would pass. His leprosy would fall from him, but that which was eternal in him would abide.

We are pilgrims, strangers, and this is not an abiding city. Or, if you like, "All the world's a stage." That which appears is but painted canvas, the kings wear cardboard crowns. But there is a reality behind. We must rub our eyes with the fairy's eye-salve and see the truth. We must look on that which is eternal, remind ourselves of it, comfort ourselves by remembering that all the rest will pass. We are going to God.

You have intelligence. You like to use your intelligence. You will then be able to use it to its fulness face to face with Truth itself. You love goodness, real, generous goodness, not mere respectable goodness; you shall go to goodness, infinite and complete. You love beauty—how can you help loving beauty? Do not you know you were made for beauty? Well, you will see beauty unveiled to you, the beauty for which men have hungered unknown from the world's dawn. That is what you must remind yourself of if you live in darkness, in dullness, this ultimate fulfilment of your desires. "My life is empty of purpose," you may say to me. O, blind, blind! Your purpose is above, not here. Not here! To complain that your life is purposeless is to deny Christianity, God is what you are made for, not this busy little world below. God is kind. He has no need of us and yet he lets us serve him in a thousand ways. Even here we can come on him. He is not far from any of us. For all this business must pass away and he whom we have served will still hold us. This passes. Do not set your heart on it. Look beyond! You are journeying to a city—your city. The saints are there already and the saints are your saints. As you grow older, the city will seem more familiar to you. You will know so many more each year of those who have gone to walk its streets. St. Catherine of Siena, in the year of the plague herself laid her nephews and nieces to rest in the cemetery, and she said as she laid each in turn there, "That one I have not lost." The tragedy of living is that in this misty world you can lose the living. The dead you cannot lose. Remember then that towards which you journey. It will give reality to your life. All those other things, the troubles and the joys, they pass, but that for which we were made remains for ever. Whatever passes, that shall not pass away. Our Lord came with a message of infinite peace to humanity. He gave us a hold by which to steady ourselves in the turmoil of life. Your heart is restless? It must be restless until it finds infinite rest. All of us he has called to that ultimate purpose—for that all we were made. Our soul is so shaped that it will fit into God as a key is shaped to fit into the lock for which it is made. To him we belong: to us he belongs. We were meant to be one. We should remember our ultimate purpose. In our moments of misery it shall be warmth to us. Poor are we? Feeble? Tired? Yet we were made for God.

SERMON V

Why Have We No Home?

If we take, then, as our leading idea that saying of the New Testament that here, on earth, we are merely pilgrims and strangers, that here we have no lasting home, we might, perhaps, ask ourselves what really it is that puts us into the condition of being pilgrims. Why are we not perfectly at home here on earth? All about us is the wonderful world of God's creation, and everything on the earth fulfils some purpose of its own. Man, alone, on the earth's surface seems so restless. Something, as we believe, has happened to him. Indeed, something has been given to man. That something we call grace. We mean by this that through a gift of God the actual soul of man has been altered. The soul of its own nature, naturally, though immortal, is of the natural order. Something happens to it, which we describe by saying that God gives it grace.

Almost the whole teaching of the New Testament is devoted to showing the establishment in us of grace. Whence it comes and how it was won for us, and what it is and what it does. We believe that God has now given to the soul something kindred to his own divine nature, that by grace the soul is no longer left in the order of natural existence, but is lifted up, as we say, lifted up to a higher order—a super order, a supernatural order. Man is now, not only man, but has more than his humanity, has something of the very nature of God. So truly is this so that it is the ultimate destiny of man living here, as he should, on God's very level, to gaze at last on the supernatural beauty of God. Not merely shall man who has been faithful live this life hereafter and see God as wise men might, in some dim way, even on earth discern him, but he shall reach out to and behold something that eye hath not seen, nor ear heard, beyond our imagination, beyond the most rich and most splendid of our dreams. Man is so lifted to the divine order that persevering in goodness by God's own guidance, he will gaze at God almost as one equal to another.

Grace holds the roots of glory. The supernatural is at the level of God. We believe, that is, that the soul of man is fashioned through grace into something higher and more splendid than itself. This, of course, is why we are pilgrims, why also we are restless. Of course we can never settle down for long here on earth. If you think of the story of our Lord on earth, and of his complete acceptance of his Father's Will, you will remember nevertheless that in his heart there was something all his life long that was crying for that other life, for heaven. More than once his words show us what lay in the depths of his soul. Thus, when he told his disciples that he must go from them, he made as though he were almost astonished that none of them gave him the congratulation that should so obviously have been His. Here he was indeed, but he was not meant to be here always. His human nature was destined for the peace of heaven when it was made. Even he, accepting the divine Will, felt in his heart a cry for something beyond this earth, a cry for heaven, and he is not the only one Who feels it, but all souls, too. Every soul that cometh into the world, every soul, in some degree or measure, has been enlightened and is not at home here on earth. You wonder why people are restless. You wonder why people can so seldom settle down. You wonder why it is that people are always planning and changing their plans. There is something missing to them in life, and, foolishly, they imagine that it is some material circumstance lacking. They have only to alter this or that, and all shall be well. This or that? It would be dreadful if man were ever at peace here on earth. We must look elsewhere than in persistent change or desire, for the true remedy for our trouble. We are strangers because we were made for something much greater than the life we know; and because we share that divine nature, there is in us something that understands and longs for God. Man understands man, not because of some stored-up experience, but because he is a man himself. He knows what men are thinking, he is conscious of other people's minds, conscious because he is a man himself. He knows his own human nature, and knowing it knows the human nature of the world. People will say, sometimes with astonishment: "But how could Shakespeare know all that huge assembly of mankind? What chance had he to store so much in his life, to understand all those various types of human nature?" It was not obtained from outside, it was obtained from within. He has no education in knowledge of this or that. How does he understand life? It is not really by searching the heavens or wandering over countries and strange peoples that you understand human nature. It is not from education that this comes, though true culture should help it. It is merely by taking cognizance of yourself. St. Paul can touch every note of the instrument of the human heart, not because he knows mankind in any wide, general way, but only because he knows himself. Being a man you understand human nature if you have any quickness of intelligence or sympathy at all. No man knoweth a man but the spirit of man.

Sharing the divine life you know something of God already by a God-given instinct. There is something in you that gives you, of itself, an understanding of God. Grace has lifted you up to that level so that you share a common nature, and therefore so that you understand. Hence supernatural man shall always be restless like people in better circumstances who, as our saying is, come down in the world. They are always chafing against the circumstances in which they find themselves. They are restless because of their memory of better and happier days. A sorrow, crowned with a sorrow is to remember happier days. Something like that is in man always. There is a memory that he shares with God. Just as dimly, sometimes, in the winter, if you sit solitary by the fireplace, you can almost let your memory run back to prehistoric man. You can almost feel in yourself, as you watch the embers falling, you can feel in yourself all that man has ever felt. You can think of his dreams, varying from age to age, in the mere material expression of them. In such a mood all that man has ever felt you feel. You are human nature in yourself. Now you have been given a share in the divine nature. You, too, in some mysterious way, echo to God. You are sensitive to God because of this thing that has happened to your soul, as people, by instinct, know when those they love go by. "I felt it was you when you rang the bell." Something much more mysterious, but no less vivid, comes to the soul that chooses to dwell in God. What is asked of you is that you should dwell in God, There is already something established between you and God. It is there. It is fundamental, not by nature, but by supernature. Just as truly as you share something with all mankind, so you, too, share something with God. You have the very condition and foundation of intimate knowledge—understanding—sensitiveness to him. By his deliberate choice you are one with him. All that is asked of you is to keep that oneness.

Remember that you can lose your sensitiveness to human nature. Men can grow selfish and forget the instincts of man. You can lose all contact with beauty. Darwin tells us that, as a young man, he loved Shakespeare and music. As an old man these meant nothing to him at all. He had immersed himself in materialism. All his interests were material. The opposite would be true of religion. Would be true of our faith. Remember, always, there is in us something which puts us on a divine level, which makes God friendly with us from the start, which establishes a unity between us: "That they all may be one, as thou Father in me and I in thee. That they also may be one in Us." All that we are asked to do is to remember that there it is within us. It is not our doing. It is due to no merit of ours. It is his sheer establishment in us. Live your life remembering it, and you will find yourself set down in a wonderful world. It is the particular glory of the saint that he has found this. This is the wonder of his life. He lives sharing life with God consciously. We all share it, but the saints knew what life they shared.

We are told the world is restless because of the speed of its traffic, because of the noise of the streets. Do not believe so superficial a cause to be the real one. It is restless for some much deeper reason. It is restless because it was made for God and because it has forgotten God. That is why it is restless. That is why the married folk are changing partners because the One Partner their soul cries for has been put outside the door. They blame each other for this unhappiness. Listen! "I stand at the door and knock," said He. To your last day you shall hear him knocking. He will not open the door. It is opened from inside. That is your fatal power—to let God in, or show God out—consciously.

In another way, God is always there. We share life with him and nothing can alter that. But this is why we are pilgrims because we have been made citizens of another fatherland and wherever we may wander, here we shall never find a home.

SERMON VI

The Lord Is My Shepherd

It is that wonderful gift of God we call grace that brings us immediately into the very circle, the family circle of God. It is a saying, you will remember, of St. Paul, that by it we are made co-heirs with Christ, that we are set in such relationship with God as to be co-heirs with his beloved son who was of the same nature as his Father, who alone knew his Father, and ho was known by his Father with a knowledge which was exclusive on both sides. Into that intimate relationship of nature, of knowledge, and of life, so runs the New Testament teaching, we, by grace, have entered. Because of that, naturally follows the pilgrim state of each on earth. This makes us always restless because, perhaps even unconsciously, we are homesick for a country to which we really belong. We meet souls at times who seem to be haunted, haunted by religion. Do what they will, they cannot keep away. They denounce it, blaspheme it, try to forget it. It for ever returns. It seems to them almost an obsession. There are many souls really that in some measure are like that. How strange to happen on people, perhaps, dragged down by all sorts of evil ways and customs, and who would almost be grateful if they could finally be rid of this pursuing dream, and yet they cannot. It will not leave them. Is it not a blessedness that they have always this homesickness for a far-off country? It is an echoing inspiration. The only dreadful thing in life is to be content with life. The only souls who never could get anywhere would be those souls—if there be any—who are perfectly satisfied with life. It was the one dreadful sin that our blessed Lord dealt with so severely—the state of the Pharisee, the type of the man who is content. He had done all he ever meant to do or wanted to do, and he was perfectly satisfied. How sad that such a one can never judge human life otherwise than that!

Christ establishes us in the order of God, makes us a fellow with God, and shares God's life with us. We must never forget these articles of faith. As St. Peter says, we are "partakers of the divine nature." This is what grace has done for the human soul. Yet, though we be partakers of the divine nature, co-heirs with Christ, though we be, to use another phrase of St. Paul's, "living temples of God," God still asks something from us—the movement of our own will. When St. Paul himself was struck from his horse on the road to Damascus, where, as one might say, faith was not asked of him, but given him, since the vision was too overwhelming for him ever to deny or to hold back from faith, when this vision came, this blinding vision, literally blind with the glory and splendour of the majesty of the appearance of Christ, he answered the vision immediately: "Lord, what wouldst thou, have me to do?" Do! The vision is given him. Christ appears triumphant to him, St. Paul's immediate question is the practical one: "What do you want of me? What am I to do?"

Always something is asked of us, some doing, some action of our own soul. This grace lifts us to the divine level, but there at that level we have to live, and live precisely in virtue of this shared life with God. Lowly man lives at that altitude of God. This is indeed what he asks of us. But what have we to do? What can we do? Life! It is not action exactly, is it? Life is surely not, "What have

I to accomplish? What have I got to bring with me when I stand before the judgment seat of God?" Doing is not Christianity, but believing and loving. Action? Is it not that? True. But it is easy to be mistaken and suppose that when we talk about a vocation and a purpose in life this means we have to do something quite definite. It may be, perhaps, that some people, have something definite to do. For them life is simple. But many people have not. For them life seems strangely astray. Some people have a definite work to do. It seems quite clear to them, even to others, what God wanted of them—perhaps a cloister, perhaps an outward life, perhaps to be a leader, perhaps to bring comfort and consolation to a world or a generation. It may be hard work but it is simple enough. But ordinary folk? They are not like that! It is very puzzling sometimes for a soul to say: "Well, what am I doing? or, indeed, what can I do? Here am I, and the few gifts I have, and the narrow limits set to my experience of life. What do I achieve? What do I achieve that is worth achieving? It is all very well to talk about the grace of God and all this splendid life, but what have I to show for it? And what could I show for it? Nothing!"

Now please remember, such souls can do all that God wants. What do you do on a journey? Nothing! That is the whole point of it. You are waiting or you are arriving somewhere. When that is over then you will settle down and do your work. Well! Here we are pilgrims. That is the whole point. Here we do not do any definite work. In an absolute sense we can say that here we do not live. Apparently most people live just disregarded lives. These have beginnings and endings. But there is no plot in them, no drama. There is nothing sensational. There is nothing in them that a man can say definitely that they have done. We were not meant to do things. *There is another life.* There will be your real achievements. People pity themselves. They say, "I have gifts, but I have never had a chance to use them." They say this so often that others find it tiresome to listen to them. But tiresome or no it is true of all of us.

We have never had our chance, nor can have this side of death. Do
32 not measure the saints by their achievements; or if you must, not by their achievements of then, but now. All the wonderful things they did. Yes, but eye hath not seen nor ear heard what they are doing now. We only know of it that it is eternal life. Measured against that, this is not life at all. This is but the thin trickle of the stream of life. There torrents pour down.

"So, then, there is no purpose for me? I am just wandering?" Of course you are wandering. So were the saints. So, says our Lord, are all of us. So was He. That is the New Testament teaching. You are a pilgrim. You are a stranger. Shall I go on to the end with all the powers in me undeveloped? Surely your powers are far more magnificent than you ever dreamed; wonderful if you only knew. But this is why the saints were so perfectly content to let the world go by them. They watched "doing" taken from them, perfectly content. "What opportunities you are missing," people would have said, hating their meekness. The saints missed nothing. They were waiting for the greatest opportunity. Death was the call. Here—it is on earth that we are all idle in the marketplace—here it will one day seem to have been emptiness and idleness compared with that fulness of life which is to be revealed hereafter. It must indeed be full and rich on the other side and here life is unfinished, incomplete, "a mere passage" as that old ancestor of ours said when they brought the Faith to the Angles. The sparrow drifted in through the high hall where they sat round the fire in the winter time. "He comes we know not whence, he goes we know not whither. He goes. That is all of our life that we know," said the pagan priest. "But these people come to tell us something of what happens beyond." "The passage of a bird through a high hall"—not a bad image of human life as it passes with its seeming lack of purpose, its uncertain, darting flight, its spent, fluttering wing. At the best so little done! Of the best he said that they would be "unprofitable servants." At the best? His mother? Her life was rich and splendid? Not compared with her life now. As she looks back how small, how petty must seem to her now that life at Bethlehem, in Nazareth, or during the years that followed on Calvary with St. John. Not this life shall fill a man's hopes and dreams and assuage them! Such is the Christian contention. Not this life shall fill up our measure. It should be unsatisfactory. The dreadful thing would be if we could settle down to it and be content. "And so I am doing that for which God made me?" If you are, you shall not wholly know it. There is no one who knows surely. The external lives of others seem so perfectly rounded, beginning and ending, and with a perfect scheme between. As we think of them we say to ourselves in our folly: "I wonder why these people are not satisfied. Surely they have all they want?" We hope they will want more than they have—always. They were made for God. In this life we have faith in God, not the possession of God in Himself really. Darkly to know him as in a mirror, that is really all that comes our way. It is not the invisible made visible that we hold. It is just a veil, it is just the hem of his garment as he goes by, that we are touching. But virtue passes out of him, only him you shall never see this side of death.

We are journeying to a far country. And until we get that New Testament view of life completely, into our whole mentality we shall always be misunderstanding and even criticising God. You may even hear human souls saying: "God has never given me a chance." Wait! Cannot you have patience? This is a passing life. There is an eternal life later. It is not fair to judge the artist until he has finished his work. Did you see it in his studio, that great portrait?" "But," you said, "that is not a portrait of such a one! His colouring is not like that! You have not caught the expression." Wait! The artist will say to you: "Wait till I have done!" And this other Artist? He knows what he is about. Wait, you are God's masterpiece. "We? Is this all God can do? We so tired! We so feeble! What a poor achievement! We God's masterpiece?" Wait, wait—leave the stained glass in the fire and then it will glow. Not at first, not yet, but wait until the whole process is done, wait till the work is over! Then, if you like, dare to criticize the artist who made you—wait till then! Do not be unjust! Do not say his handiwork is not beautiful. It does not look beautiful! But then it is only in the process. The completion comes when this life is over and done.

This life is a journey. We are pilgrims. This life must pass before we reach that for which we are made.

"What would you have me to do?" So live that you remember whence you came, and whither you journey. Keep your eyes steadily fixed on the height towards which you climb. You are content with nothing? Why should you be? You have not yet what you were meant to have. Forget the things that are behind you—strive earnestly forward. That is the purpose—not what do I do," but "Whither go I?" Only one bowed his head, saying "It is finished." He that was eternal—the beginning—the end. But not you or I. Our life never "finishes." That is the glory of it. That is the promise made to us. On earth lies a doom because nothing here can ever content us. We get past one difficulty only to encounter another. That is right and proper. Indeed that is the very grandness of life. It is a roadway that leads to something magnificent. Cannot you be grateful for the road? Do not expect, that is all, do not expect to find here your city—the thing perfectly worked out, complete, that you desire, dream of, work for. Do not expect to be able to settle down for long to enjoy your life. You dreamt of a kingdom in childhood. You hoped for it in your working years. In your old age you will never find it. Pilgrims, travellers, strangers, that is all we be! But we seek a city, whose maker and builder is God—a city that is God Himself. We shall enter within it by his mercy. God Himself shall be our home. Cannot you be grateful for the road though it be rough and uncertain? It does all a road was ever made to do. It takes you home.

SERMON VII

Who Would Resist his Will?

In this pilgrimage of ours, in our life, we are taking our journey under the direction of God Himself. Therefore in our life we are receiving from God messages as to how we should walk. Often, both in the Old Testament and in the New Testament, often phrases and sayings suggest that to us, namely, that here on earth we are directed by God Himself. Somewhere in the old Scripture it is written: "Thou shalt hear a voice saying to thee turn to the right, turn to the left. This is the path—walk therein." I am sure that none of us but must often be aware of this divine voice directing us in life, not merely in the choice of a religious vocation, a profession or a way of life to which we are called, but, once there, once started on our road, still conscious of God's daily speech with us, directing us, sometimes to go back and speak to someone, to go where we had refused to go, or to take this rather than the other; moreover, we do, almost surely, know that it is the voice of God speaking to us. Not in the whirlwind, not with any overpowering of us as he overpowered St. Paul on the road to Damascus, but, with that still, small voice, that whisper of his, God has directed us none the less surely in our life.

Of course, what is asked of us is that we should be prompt in our obedience to this voice of God. Sometimes, perhaps, people may be puzzled or bewildered as to which of two possible choices is really the divine will for them. This is sure, that if when it is at all clear, you have always promptly obeyed God's voice you will gradually get to know by spiritual instinct, which is the voice of God of several suggestions made. If you have a friend, the better you know him the more quickly you know what would be his choice in any particular matter even where he has not yet told you his mind. You know the sort of play he would like. You know, instinctively, the book that would not interest him. You know him so well that you know where his will would lie. So to be able to know God's will, we must have been faithful to God. If we are faithful when we know God's will is manifest, if we are prompt in our obedience, I do not think we normally need trouble ourselves but that we shall know the will of God where it is not at first very clear. To live with God, to obey God is to learn what God is like, and knowing him we shall, instinctively, know which of two possible paths is his path for us. Prompt obedience then! No grumbling! No reluctance! Is it God's voice? Then obey, not troubling as to whether it is something that commends itself to your natural desire or no. We are here to do God's will. That, after all, is the purpose of our life; and in our faltering and inconstant fashion, that really is our will, too. We really want to do the divine will.

Promptitude is the first quality of our relationship to this voice of God that is directing us all the time on our road. We should be prompt in our obedience to whatever is asked of us because the voice that speaks is God's voice directing us, because we are on a journey, and because he is the ultimate goal of our journeying. Prompt in our obedience!

Again, it means not only that we must be prompt, but that we must be humble in our obedience. We must take God's view of life and not our own. It is often possible for us, we know from our own experience, it is often possible for us to confuse ourselves by laying down as axiomatic our own preconceived ideas. "This is what I ought to be doing. This is how I should be employed." Thus we persist in our own will, choosing beforehand what we should be about. We must be humble. We must empty ourselves of our own ideas. We must wait for the voice of God to settle things and not be determined on our own choice.

In the Scripture what is so evident is the way in which people who merely listened for the voice of God, get where you think they never could get. Look at Our Lady, she was marked by God to be the Mother of his Son, yet she had had the divine will, somehow, manifested to her—that she must vow her virginity to God. You as a spectator would say that she had thereby spoiled her chance of becoming the mother of the Messiah; that she could never be the Mother of God. All the maidens of Israel had always hoped to be the mother of the Messiah. It is a great dream that still haunts the hopes of Jewish women, that they may be called to be the mother of the Messiah. But, here was this voice of God speaking so she took her vow, knowing it should surely prevent, one might think, every chance of the ultimate fulfilment of this dream. Yet she is the Mother of God despite her vow. "How can this thing be done?" was immediately her question to the angel. "I who know not man, how can I become the Mother of God?" "The power of God shall overshadow thee.... The Spirit of God shall descend on thee, and he that shall be born of thee shall be called the Holy One, the Son of God." What seemed therefore to frustrate her motherhood actually helped towards it.

Put yourself in God's hands, and you will get where God wants you to get. It seems to you that if you obey God's voice you may be spoiling your ultimate chance of success. How can God's will be hurtful? Rather be humble. Not your wisdom but divine wisdom will best guide you. God likes, sometimes, to play with souls asking only from them complete acceptance of what he does. Go his way and you will get what he wants you to get. Be prompt and humble.

38 Another quality required is to be brave in doing the divine will. We require courage in the service of God. You would think, really, if you listened to the people about you who are always disapproving of religion, you would think that what was wanted in religion was fear, not courage. Submission of our will, fear and reverence for the majesty of God, are certainly asked of us. That is true, but courage, undying courage, that is no less asked; and if anybody really sets out in life to look for the divine will and do it, he will need all and more than his mere natural stock of courage. He will need courage reinforced by divine grace, divine power and divine help. Courage? Surely courage to go the way God wants him to go. It must seem at times to us that though God must be wonderful in his knowledge and complete and sure in his wisdom, his ways of guiding us and others are not the best ways. You say to a child, "Don't touch that!" "Why? Why?" asks the child. A grown-up person often seems foolish to a child. "Why must I do this?" it asks again. And you try patiently to explain why it must. Yet what child really understands? If the ways of grown-up people, especially wise grown-up people, puzzle a child, will not God's ways be likely to puzzle us? If the gap between mature wisdom and the opening of the child's mind, if that small gap produces bewilderment, what shall not the immeasurable gap between divine wisdom and human wisdom at the best, occasion to us of bewilderment and dismay? Trust him absolutely and go on, right on, to the very end. Often enough we are not afraid to look for God, but we are afraid, sometimes, of God looking for us. We are not afraid, sometimes, to search out the divine ways, but it does terrify us that God shall be searching out ours, that God should be watching and directing us, and that we should have to commend ourselves absolutely to God. We are the children of compromise and what we dread is the full courage that accepts everything unafraid. A child needs courage. It is made to do all kinds of things that it shrinks from. It requires, above all, courage

to obey. Well, courage too is asked of us—courage to go the way God wants us to go. But if we are obedient, that is prompt, humble and courageous in our obedience, God will make us into what we are really capable of being made into, that which he discerns in us.

There is, naturally, I suppose, in every one's heart a desire to be independent, to be let go his own way, indeed, to be himself. We all, at some moment in our life, late or early, feel ourselves capable of something, and our lament often is that we have never really had our chance to be it. We grumble that all sorts of things have interfered with us, first this, then that, so that we were deprived of showing the excellencies we have. Away back in childhood we were chafed by authority which hindered our desires, hindered our dreams; and we said to ourselves: "When I am grown up, I shall live my own life. I shall be able to settle things for myself. I shall have freedom." Yet, somehow, we never got freedom. Our desires we have never had fulfilled. We never secured our thorough independence. Are you independent? Are any of us? Is your life according to your choice? Dare you even live the life you want to live? There are conventions to be followed, and other people's opinions to be respected. We must follow fashion. We must dress as others dress. We must talk as others talk. Do we brave popular prejudices? Criticize honestly what our contemporaries curiously approve? We cannot bare our inner judgments really to the world we meet. Thus in the end we never really dare to become ourselves, except the saints, except the saints! They were fearless—that is what makes them stand out against the background of their time, that is why they are so, fine and striking, and why round them eddies still perpetual discussion. How clearly St. Francis stands out! Not because he chose his own life, no! That was the very last thing St. Francis ever dreamt of doing. He sought and followed the life God had planned for him. That is what made him great. The others did not achieve greatness, only because they were afraid to go all the way God led. If you and I listened to God's voice directing us and obeyed it, we should be great characters, unafraid of opposition, unbroken by the world's despite. We should be able to scorn mere popular ideas or theories, or the gossip chit-chat that mists human doings in uncharity. We would seem, perhaps, at times to go against our best interests and deny ourselves the use of our own talents and our own gifts; and, yet, we would never more fail to make use of our possession of them. We should live the life God meant us to live and be ourselves, God alone knows what we are capable of. God alone knows why he made us. We do not know, really, which way we should go, nor what we should do, nor what gifts we have hidden deep within. But God knows; and if we are only obedient to God he will make of us that which he had in mind when he first designed us. We shall fulfil all his purposes. We shall have room made here on earth for the due employment of all our gifts. To go our own way is to go the wrong way, the undivine way. Yet we would never choose a way deliberately that we knew God never meant.

If you want to be independent obey God, and you will be truly independent, of any one else. God is afraid of none. By his side, of none will you be afraid. The hour of darkness will come, it will find you fearless and unafraid. We shall need to be fearless in these our days. Poverty, the hard ways of life, look as though they would grow sterner; the road seems not to be lightening but darkening; for all we know the worst is not yet. To listen to God's voice is always to go on unafraid into the future. Indeed, it is our only chance to do that. Panic, suspicion, dreadful rumours will else threaten us all our life! We shall be questioning ourselves. Is this God's world? Am I created by God? Is life but a journey that must pass? Is there a city towards which I journey? Is there someone directing my path? Do I believe that? If I do, then I must listen to his directions; I must promptly, humbly, courageously obey and be truly free. If I am obedient to the divine word I shall achieve the divine ideal. Once you dreamt of your own future, you had your own idea as to what you would do and be in the world, you had your daydreams. Now it may be they seem all impossible. Whatever your dream of your future was, it cannot equal his dream of you. All your hopes of youth, so wild, romantic, extravagant, are nothing like as romantic or as splendid as God's designs for you. Lay your own aside. His vision is more richly peopled, his knowledge truer of you, his knowledge, that is, of your capacity, of the place you still could take in life. Leave yourself in the divine hands. Listen for his voice with humility and promptness and courage, and you shall reach at last to the very stature of Christ.

SERMON VIII

Go We Must

We live our lives as pilgrims and travellers, but directed in our journey by the voice of God. God, when he created us, had a definite purpose in his mind, and created us in order that we might do this work of his in the world as we journeyed through it; and all our lives, since it is his will for us, God is always speaking to us as to where and how he would have us go. All our lives then he but asks of us that we should steadily listen to his voice, and by listening become aware of it, know when he speaks. Every time we either ignore his directions, or deliberately act contrary to them, it means that we have missed subsequently the turning of the road he desired us to take. It means further that only very painfully shall we get back to where he meant us to go. If when you were journeying you ever missed the proper turning you will have found that later on you had to make a long detour to recover the road again, that is what seems to happen in many human lives. Looking back, sometimes, we can see where we took the wrong turning. Perhaps out of negligence, or perhaps sheer indifference, or perhaps deliberately we refused to enter on it. It was rather too hard at the time. It may take us a long time, perhaps, to get back to where we should have been when we faltered and refused. Since life is a pilgrimage and we are always on the move, since we are travellers and have here no lasting city, it means that every mistake we make can only be recovered from after a time. Sometimes the call of faith comes—and people deliberately refuse to listen to it; and, all the rest of their lives this still affects them. At last, in much more difficult circumstances they have to go back and again face the cost of buying truth with pain. In all sorts of ways God speaks to the soul and we refuse to listen, or are merely so foolish that we do not hear him, or hearing we refuse to obey. Thus are we endlessly hindered and our life made far more painful spiritually than it need have been. To obey instantly is to recover the ground quickly—to find, at once, really where we should be, where we belong. Our Blessed Lord came for the purpose of helping us to realise the greatness of the journey, and the importance of paying attention to the directions given. His Father was a city towards which we journey, and he Himself was the way. It is one of the Christian heritages to realise that the road, for us, is something in itself holy; and that life here need not be something mean and sordid. Indeed, life cannot be sordid if it is lived in obedience to the divine command. Life itself, here on earth, though it be a pilgrimage, though it be just a wandering, life itself, here on earth, can still be extraordinarily great, but it is great only on the terms that we dare listen to the voice of God and set ourselves to go by it deliberately. After all, God is so strong, so overwhelming that we never really can escape him. We must, at last, come into the very hands of God, There is that ultimate meeting between us and him whose voice has so often spoken to us. At last, we must stand facing our judge. If we have listened to that voice on earth whenever we have heard it and tried to go the way God wanted us to go, then all that while we shall have been getting nearer and nearer to him, and, when we meet him at last we shall meet him as a friend. But to meet him so then, now means listening to Him.

You know a great artist is not only someone who gives you a

beautiful picture, but someone who teaches you, through what he gives you, to see beauty that you had hitherto missed in life. He gives you, perhaps, a picture of the light falling through a window on a common scene of work, like in those Dutch pictures where the light streams through the window on the red tiles, or a woman cooking, or a jug of milk. You begin to realise from the picture the beauty of that in life and recognise it when next you see it. By isolating it, he has made it more apparent to you. Once having seen it in a picture you are able to see it again as you live your life. Whatever else artists do for us, they do that much for us, they help us to appreciate the things that are actually before our eyes. All the world is in front of us; of ourselves we look at it and miss its beauty as it goes by, "A cat may look at a king," says the proverb; but the cat does not see him as a king. You can look at your world and miss the beauty of it, but the artist comes to show you the beauty that is there. He shows you the beauty of the evenings over the Thames valley—the grey, falling shadows, and the long row of glimmering lights. Until you saw that beauty you never realised the exquisite shimmering, of the river, but after that, the river, for you, is never quite the same. It was always there, that clinging beauty, but you missed it. You were looking at it, but you never saw it. Because of Whistler, you will see it till you die!

Our Lord comes to show us the beauty of the life we live in. He takes, one by one, the things of life. All his parables are just so many paintings to us. Now, never again can you look at them without remembering what he said. He came to teach us the beauty of the world—to show us how through our life God is calling us. We are never far from God at any time. God is speaking and calling to us, and what we have learnt to realize from his teaching is that it is God calling, so we go gladly, not reluctantly, however hard the thing is or painful which we are called to do or bear. He will never leave us alone. He is pursuing us always. Because he has clearly in his mind where he wants us to be. He is urgent with us. If we attempt to take a short cut when he calls us, we shall have to take a long way round to reach the place to which he has called us. If we be patient, even so, we shall get there in the end. Though we sometimes act against his will. He is too much for us. We shall gradually find ourselves shepherded wheresoever he wants us to be.

Over and over again in the Scripture we have put before us two, of whom one listens and the other is deaf to the call. The good thief and the bad thief were equally thieves, villains, folk who had broken the law. They are both in equal circumstances and he hangs evenly between them. One sees him, and one misses him. We do not know why it should have so happened, where they were, how they stood; but all we do know is that one saw and had his ears open to listen, and the other who had no less in front of him than his fellow had, missed the beauty and the call. Or you have Paul called on the road to Damascus and leaving all to follow Christ, while Judas, who lived side by side with that wonderful life for three years, betrays him with a kiss and then despairs. The life of our blessed Lord seems to be of incredible beauty, its charm, high spiritual teaching, its delicacy, tenderness, strength. Judas lived side by side with that for three years and missed the exquisite teaching of it. Whatever it was that led him astray, we can hardly guess; yet somehow he went wrong, somewhere missed the turning. He missed it. Did he ever come back? Right to the very end, right up to his very betrayal and beyond and after, he could still have come back on the road to the turning, Peter did. What do they tell us? "The trembling of a leaf between men's choices"—just that by which you may see or miss. The child Samuel recognized the voice at last and begged: "Speak, Lord, for thy Servant heareth." The rich young man knew the voice but would not heed it. Perhaps he came back when he was no longer rich or young. Perhaps he had to be beggared of both youth and riches before he would hearken and follow. God in our lives and God calling; if we miss his voice he will call again, we may still have a chance to follow, still get where he wants us to be, only much more painfully shall we now find him. A nation, too, can live like that, can ignore the signs against it on the road, and be brought back again only after infinite pain. So is it true of souls. Some would not obey God's voice until, at last they had to.

God then has his will for us, his high designs. Of these we are capable. Finding them, we shall find the real solution of ourselves, our hungers, failures, hurts. If you listen to God, he will make of you what you are capable of becoming. If you will not listen, then you must be compelled against your will to do what he requires. Blessed are they that have served him from their youth. It seems hard at times to be called so early to his service, yet, in the end these are seen to have gained. They are saved so much. The service of God is surely harder when the soul has grown stiff with its habits of evil. Easier is it to go when we have all the energy of our nature to help us. A sad pity when we have to limp in tired fashion, worn out and weary a long way behind. Yet God's grace is marvellous. With his own wonderful power he can rebuild broken lives. He can compress labour that should have been spread over a whole lifetime into a short passage of years.

It is one of life's marvels to find souls who have lived in extraordinary softness, who have faltered along the road and wasted youth's fragrance, suddenly seeing themselves to be face to face with God and overcome with it, living ever so brief a life afterwards, yet having it so crowded with divine understanding and divine suffering that they have been made perfect in a short time. So it is never too late to find the road again, though it is only rediscovered with much costing search. Moreover, it is a pity to give God merely the scraps of life when you have already had all the pleasure out of it. Better is it to give God your life while it is the fresh and eager thing. But give God whatever you have. It is all you have.

God calls us; if we do not hear, or miss it, we shall spoil our life. He will get us back at last, but we shall have got hardened in the process. We shall need to have our limbs broken and set again.

Perhaps, only so can he mend us and make us walk again so as to go his way. Though it looks to you hard, whatever it is that you know to be God's will, remember that it is easier to accept it now than to let it slide. Easier? To say that is to use a poor argument. We shall not merely say that it is easier. Our call is to love him. that is why he made us—that we might love him because he had first loved us. So that is the only way in which we should look at life. Not that to do his will is easier in the end but more loving. He who calls me is my lover. He is my friend. He knows me as I never know myself. If I do what he tells me, when I know it is his voice that is telling me, then I should give him all that I have—not much, but all.

When you are in love you realise then how humbling love is. You realise when you are in love what a very little you have to bring to the one you love. Friendship, while it exalts you, makes you realize the poverty of your own heart, the emptiness of your own soul, you wish you had much more to bring, more of yourself, a finer character, a worthier gift. This humility will be found in divine love too. Once you awake to the knowledge of what God is you realize how very little you have to offer him. You want to give him at least all of the little that is yours, not because it is easier, but because it is more generous to go God's way when he calls you. He is your friend. So we ask him (because it needs his own gift to do this) that we may know his voice. We ask him to help us to listen for it, so that we may know it as his voice when it sounds to us; and then that we may have courage to follow the voice wherever it call us, not with reluctance because the road whither it calls us is hard or painful, but gladly because he that calls us is our father, our lover, our friend: "You have not chosen me, but I have chosen you." What is love but choice, the choice of a friend? He calls us, because he loves us and he is always calling us. May he give us the silence of heart that will listen, and the discerning wisdom that will recognize, and the courage of love that will obey.

SERMON IX

Our Eyes Are Holden

It is this life of God in us that makes us pilgrims and strangers on the earth. Earth is too strait a home for us whom God has lifted up into the circle of his own life. It is only because we share that divine life that earth and all it has to give, must of its own nature be insufficient for us. What he has done for us entails the giving to us if we be faithful the reward ultimately of Himself. To make men for finer things is really to give them a very desperate hunger; and all the world was made for God, God in his infinite variety. God's absolute truth, goodness and beauty—man must inevitably and essentially pursue these things, though he may think them hidden under many disguises. The grace of God that is in us, as our blessed Lord said of it, works in us while the man sleeps.

So often, in the parables, our Lord compares it to the seed that is cast into the ground; and through these parables, followed one after another, we realize that this living thing, the seed, is not us, but something divine, and therefore of its own nature inevitably fruitful. What we are in the parables is the soil. So that what fructifies and opens in us, is none of our own doing. The life in us is not our action, but is something beyond the reach of our human, created action, something spiritually above us, something divine. As our Lord phrases it, this divine life falls into us. All that we can do is to minister to its growth. All that is alive in us is his life not our own. He compares it, as we have said, to the seed that is scattered; now the seed everywhere is vital, the seed everywhere is the same. What makes it here reach a rich harvesting, what makes it there fail and drop, what makes it here dwindle and die, and there grow luxuriant, is not the seed's fault or favour; everywhere it is fruitful, alive. It is the soil that is helpful or harmful to it, enables it to produce its own natural fruit or hinders it from becoming what it might. Again, our Lord speaks of it as cast into the field and growing through daylight and darkness while the farmer sleeps. True, he prepares the soil for the seed, he cleanses the soil, he breaks the soil, he scatters the seed, he scares away the birds from injuring it, but while he sleeps as well as while he works the seed will grow. So with us. Our Lord's teaching is that the same law of spiritual growth continues while we go about our business as well as while we pray. Life grows or dwindles. The life is within us; it is a divine life, a seed cast into the soil, nothing of our own production. It is not the result of evolution from within. It is something thrown into the soil by the divine hand, not of our making or gathering, divine in itself and given by divine choice. We are just sharers in its efficacy, ministering to this divine life such virtue as our soil can give. It grows of itself. And, as is true of all growth, it grows, not only when you are actually attending to the growth, but so long as you are doing nothing to hinder it. A child grows fastest at night. You have seen a child ill, and then when he got up from his bed of sickness again, you suddenly found he had grown very swiftly. Indeed, lying in bed will set him growing, walking will not let him grow so fast. In our Lord's phrase while we sleep the seed grows.

So in your life, when the divine seed is thrown into you, when this divine grace, this share of the divine life, is cast into you, do not imagine that its growth will be visible to you while you watch it. You do not imagine that you can hear it grow. Up, up, through the tree, comes the sap mounting. You do not see it pushing its way along the branches to the softening tips. It is hidden. You never hear the ebb and flow of that tide. Life is silent. Always, growth as we know it, is silent, only to be noted afterwards. Silence and the darkness alone can measure the mounting height of growth. You do not watch things growing to see them grow—not in nature, not in life, God's seed is sown in our hearts; shall we know that it is growing? Shall you know whether you are growing holier in life? Certainly not. You will never know. The seed is growing by itself. You minister to it; you cannot measure its growth. Silence and darkness are its needed conditions and the thing grows of its very nature. You can help it and you can hinder, but you do not really make it grow. Our prayers, are they improving? You will never know whether your prayers are getting worse or better. Prayer is not a measurable thing. It is something invisible, something that no eye can ever reach, that even no intelligence can ever watch flourish or decay. Do not imagine that if your prayers were better you would know they were better. You will never know. Do you think a saint stops and says to himself: "Now my prayers are better." Sinners may do that, not saints. Do not suppose, we cannot suppose, that the saint, as he grows in sanctity, suddenly awakes to the fact and says: "I am a saint." Sinners—oh, yes. Sinners may be self-complacent, perfectly self-satisfied, but that is dreadful, not reassuring. The saint, as he grows in sanctity grows in self-disesteem. When you think your prayers worse they are likely to be better. Likely, that is all that can be said. They may be worse, as you think them worse. They may be more distracted. There may be less comfort and inspiration in them. But whether they be better or worse, you will never know this side of death. Darkness and silence alone can measure a thing's growth.

The most beautiful prayer, so the Church teaches us, and the highest, and the noblest, is the prayer of absolute silence. Not in this silence can a man stop and think of any such desperate self-measurement. Any examination in the midst of its prayer to see if the soul is progressing, would be either mischievous or fatal. You can never know. It is hid from you and always will be hid from you. Not when you are striving can you stop to remember. Not when the child is running about is it growing. Not when you think, not while you are working at your soul will your self-examen help you here. Probably you are only thereby torturing your soul. What God asks is simplicity and confidence in him. Leave your moral worth alone to him to be judged. We are so small minded that of ourselves we are encouraged only by what our eye can measure in the spiritual world. If we live at all in the spirit, we must live by faith. We live by not troubling over whether we know or not. We live, really, by ignorance. We live by making no effort to discover exactly where we stand in the divine judgment. We live by absolute trust. To that we are always reduced as the final principle of our perfect serenity. You would be no happier if you saw you were better, at least, you would not rightly be any happier. All that can make us happy is the consciousness of the compassion and care of God. Never can happiness be based on self, never on our knowledge of our own growth, but on God only and always. It is foolish here to be looking at ourselves. Only to be looking at him is wise. Let us go back almost to the first thing we ever learnt in our catechism. God "made me to know Him." Never fully shall I learn that lesson until, at last, I see him. Till then I must go on learning. But no command is laid on us that we should know ourselves.

So the essential business of the soul is prayer, prayer always and not action. Not what I do matters, nor so much how far my virtues are cultivated, nor my sins gradually laid aside. All that must be attempted truly. Yes! But that is a lesser work. Watch and listen to the saints! They will tell you, one by one, that all the great work of their souls was achieved in prayer, while they were not thinking of self at all. Is not it a phrase of one of the saint's: "You are only truly praying when you do not know that you are praying." Prayer should be something unconscious in itself. Perhaps on a spring morning when you feel life coursing in you you may be aware of it, but ordinarily you do not stop to think you are alive. Life is natural. With us the supernatural should be like the natural. Thus will the soul be growing best in its prayer, when it is thinking not of self, but of God. Its gaze should be riveted on God's wonderful goodness, God's haunting mercy, God's untiring forgiveness, God in Himself, the marvellous truth of God.

"How interesting!" we say when someone gives us the explanation of something we have seen repeatedly but never found an answer for, noticed but never understood. Every little bit of truth is interesting, but truth absolute, complete, must be fascinating above all else. Endlessly, too, goodness attracts us always. How marvellous to grow in the knowledge of God's goodness! The better we know him the more evidences should we find of his goodness. They only see God cruel, who see him not at all. The more they know of God, the more will they know of his infinite goodness. The answer to, "Is there a God?" is to know him. He is his own answer. That riddle you will only answer on your knees. And beauty! God is that infinite beauty. You grow more cultured as you gaze on beauty, more holy as you gaze on infinite beauty. We reach goodness by knowing goodness, by loving goodness, that is, by prayer. By prayer we are brought nearer to God. Prayer is getting somehow into touch with God, but not necessarily at all being conscious of knowing him. You are not conscious of being alive, not in the daylight, nor conscious at all when you are asleep. Yet, we are as much alive sleeping as waking, as much alive, as truly growing. So is it with our souls and God. It is foolish to attempt to measure our spiritual self. It is foolish to worry about securing a true judgment on ourselves. So is it foolish to say to ourselves: "I am no good at prayer. Therefore I had better lay prayer aside." Prayer is trying to know God better. Then persevere in prayer. There is no other rule than that to learn how to pray. There is no measure for prayer in prayer. There is no measure for prayer except constancy. There is no reward in prayer except to those who hold on. There are times when you feel more alive, but at those times you are not necessarily more alive. Even when they are dying, folk will sometimes tell you they never felt so well, and that they know they are improving. Yet you know that the doctor has given up hope for them. Still they say: "I feel ever so well today." Feeling is a poor judge in this court of human life. It is a poor judge equally in that other court of supernatural life. Just as of the body it is true to say while we sleep the growth goes on, so remember that all the growing of the soul is done by him, that all the transformation of our soul is achieved by divine action. All we can do is to help or hinder that action. We cannot do anything else at all. "I can do nothing of myself," that is the everlasting Christian gospel, I must be humble and remember that I can do nothing. Whatever is done, is done by God. "Paul may sow, and Apollo water; but it is God who giveth increase." Paul and Apollo deal with the conditions of the seed's growing, but the growing is of God.

Or to vary again the metaphor, we are pilgrims; and we are pilgrims because God has made us pilgrims by the greatness of his precious gift, because he has given us a share in his own reality, because he has lifted us up out of creation and set us by his side. "I have come that they might have life, and have it more abundantly." Whose life are they to have? His. We are pilgrims because he broke our relationship with earth, because he dusted away the soil that clung about our feet, because he fitted us with wings. You remember, in the Scripture, how with touching beauty he compares the way he deals with souls to the mother eagle teaching her young to fly. If you read the story of the eaglets, you will read how the mother eagle teaches her young to fly by making them dare the great depths and heights. Nearly always out of every brood there is one that grows timid, that has not the courage to flutter off from the rock where the nest lies. Then the mother bird takes twig by twig the nest away from the ledge. She will make its ledge most bereft, desolate, lonely. Meanwhile, the others go sailing by on their newfound wings of flight. There is always one that is timid, that stands and twitters and cries, and will not dare. Do you remember how the prophet describes that, at last, but not impatiently, only with exquisite and disciplined affection the mother eagle will beat the little one off the ledge with her wings. Then as it falls, crying with terror she dives under it and catches it between her wings. Then she shakes it off and again dives under and holds it between the spread of her wings until at last what of itself it would not dare do, it is made to do. It finds that flying is not so difficult as it dreamt.

In our life whatever is done is done by divine action. Does this better explain your life to you? There are souls God treats like that. He gets rid of their home about them stick by stick—the nest that might give them some comfort and that makes them cling to the rock from which he wishes to free them. Stick by stick is their nest broken up. But still they will not dare to attempt what he asks of them. So cowardly is human nature! "How should I learn to fly? However should I?" It is the cowardice of the man with only one talent. It is the coward that falters. "But, I have so little, I was never intended to do this wonderful thing. I—to go praying? You do not know me, if you think that. What do I know of prayer? I cannot pray at all." But, you have never tried to pray properly. You have never ventured out into the depths. Some cannot walk much, who yet could fly well. Birds can walk but little, yet they can fly—wonderful is it? Nay, not so wonderful as souls! There are souls that are as small and yet as great as that. If there be such, God will beat them with his wings. Only because he loves them will he un-nest them. If they will only dare where God wants them they will find they can do it; find that the free open spaces are nothing to be afraid of. Oh, yes, if we thought merely in terms of human power, these would be something to be terribly afraid of! If you think yourself of the depths below you, you will never dare the immeasurable flight. Think instead of God's wings under you, of the divine action. Beneath us are the everlasting wings. It is not what we do that matters. It is only and always what God does. That is why in this world, we can be so great; though they try to discourage us by telling us that we are descended from animals and by insisting to us the immeasurable distance of the stars. They say, "Look how little man is." But man can look at these wonders; and these wonders cannot look at man. We can measure the stars though they be right beyond us. No star has measured us. Little? Oh, yes, we are but "earthen vessels," still the treasure we carry is immeasurably great. We but carry it. It is not ours. With us it cannot mingle. It grows in us. We, in a sense, never grow.

We are pilgrims, we are travellers. We are meant for finer cities. We are finer than this life we know. This will perish and we shall abide. We need always to remember that what is done in us is done by divine power through prayer. Thus can we help or hinder. But what is living in us is not ours but His. It is the thought of this that makes us great on earth with a greatness no eye can measure. Rest in his power perfectly content, without attempting self-measurement. Do not look down, look up. Do not look within, look outside of you. Do not question your soul but pray.

SERMON X

Yet Shall I Trust in Him

There is something subtle and strange in the way in which nationality or race produces sympathy or antagonism of itself in us. We are often at a loss to discover why, or to set out the reasons or motives that produce it. Something strange, we repeat, about the way in which people of the same nationality understand one another, and, again, strange in those antipathies that race or colour produce. A curious knowledge! A curious hostility! If you go across the Atlantic where from many nations emigrants have gone out, you soon realise there how strangely their original racial characteristics often continue under utterly different circumstances. How people of the same nation, of the same racial origin almost naturally gravitate together, how they drift into the same trades. Thus there are certain racial capacities that very quickly establish themselves. People from a common country not only gather together, but adopt the same trade because they have the same capacity for this or the other craft or form of business. It is as if there were something really running in their blood. Thus there are certain nationalities, which emerge and take possession of government or the organization of the arts, as though in the blood was an heritage—a sympathy for it, a knowledge, a capacity, a strange magic.

My brethren, the same is true of that inner life of grace. Which constitutes us pilgrims here on earth, and fellow-citizens of the saints. There is something about it that produces a strange, unexpected knowledge, a certain sympathy of understanding, a certain capacity, a certain strange magic by which the world can be transformed by those who have it and by none else. It carries with it a certain knowledge, a curious sympathy. Sometimes people are astonished that some book or other, that deals entirely with the supernatural, or some spiritual aspect, becomes, as the expression is, "a best-seller." And, they say, "How unexpected that a book like that should have so great a sale." Books that appeal to, or exploit the lower portion of man, works of that sort, that are deliberately written to excite the lower passions, it is easy to understand why they are popular. It is difficult to understand that this, so spiritual in its outlook, yet can sell, and be popular almost everywhere. It is not really strange: "He enlighteneth every man that cometh into the world." There is something in every one, which can be roused into sympathy with God and the supernatural. There is a hidden root upon which this growth can be grafted. He does not destroy our nature when he shares life with us, but fulfils what is already there. It is sometimes a surprise to come across people whom we have known for a considerable period, and to be told of them, "So and so has become a Catholic," We say, "But how strange!" It is not really strange. There is in every soul something that connects it with the God who made it. There is a subtle sympathy begotten by a unity of blood. Man is no stranger to God, at any time, any how! How can he be? He is a child of God. Essentially and necessarily there is in the soul an incomplete understanding of divine things, not dominant necessarily but always there. It can be surprised into quickened life under stress of some great emotion. A man who has forgotten all about God, yet, in a moment of great pain, may be found calling for aid, invoking almost unconsciously, the God Who made him. Or, at times, another, surprised by some marvellous blessing, almost in spite of himself, will say, "Thank

God." It is not merely a phrase; it is deep understanding; something so deep that the man is hardly aware of its continued existence; it is something that forever remains. For man is fashioned after the divine likeness. There is in man always an intimate relationship to God, the relationship of child and father, and so always a sympathy, always a strange knowledge of God, reasonable but not reasoned.

Again, the beauty of our world is a divinely fashioned beauty. Between man and it there is an everlasting sympathy, overlaid by custom, by ignorance, by baffled powers, not used, yet, in stress of great emotion awakening again to life. Not only has man sympathy and knowledge of his fellow-men, but a capacity to deal with them or with created things. Men, women and children suddenly find themselves, unconsciously, an instrument of divine action, unexpectedly, suddenly realizing it they are carried away by it, feeling just at that moment that they could do almost anything. It is their hour. In such a mood they can deal with any souls. In such a mood they will say something that is of help, inspiration, of a wisdom larger than their own. They suddenly awake to the fact that they have a capacity they never dreamt of; the consciousness of it carries them triumphantly along. They find themselves able to deal with a particular situation that has hitherto baffled them. Of course, it is not really surprising; all of us are children of God, all of us have the capacity of our race, which is a divine race, a supernatural race into which by God's grace we have been reborn. We are sharers in his divine life. What is there then that we cannot accomplish? What is too great for us?

Nothing! We are the very children of God. Generation after generation seems to have felt in itself at times this mysterious wisdom. So is it with each of us in our day. We carry the infinite wisdom of God. We carry it indeed in an earthen vessel. There are times when it seems to overcome a man or play through him as though he were just a harp with a divine wind playing through him; or as though he were a tool moved by an artist's hand. God is always with us. Moreover, we have our divine origin. Unexpectedly at any moment the power of God may break through. That hidden magic, of which every soul is capable, may find itself suddenly turning its old world into a new world.

That this should surprise us is because we neglect these hidden things, or push them out of sight; it is because of our utter forgetfulness of these deep things of the spirit that in our time so many freak religions are born. They are the feeling of ill-taught souls towards their full manhood, which holds traces of the faith. They get the truths they stumble on only in part, a fragment; and without complete, rounded knowledge they let their imagination run wild, run to extremes over it. But they have felt some portion of that which is spirit moving indeed their spirit. For the truths of faith are not ours only, they were meant to be the inheritance of all mankind. All has been fashioned, all has been redeemed by God. All is loved by God. All has sympathy of blood with God. All the world is God's child. It is because we are hardly aware of our own relationship with God and because we are still less aware of our responsibility to others, that these spiritual truths are but half known in our world. What we need is to deepen our own supernatural life so as to keep ourselves in more or less continuous relationship with God. What we all need is a deeper sense of prayer. This does not mean that we need to devote ourselves to something that would take up more time than we have leisure to give. Already we say our prayers, but what we need is a greater intensity in our prayer, a deeper sense of God's nearness to us. And this not only when we are kneeling down, but when we are going about our work or duties. What a pity it is that so much of our reading is of material things, that we read so little of the high, spiritual things of God! What a pity it is that men and women, as they go about their business, do not hold themselves quietly in the tube or bus and say their prayers. Why must they needs hold in front of them the record of the world's sins, and be content with it? Murder, violence, court cases, gossip, scandal, shame. Is it not possible to say to ourselves: God is here, and all these people have need of the consciousness of God? Cannot I sit in my place and pray for them one by one? Cannot I realise that God's immensity fills all of it? Cannot we live with God and share our life consciously with him. Shall we not then be able, all the better, to help the people we meet? To say the right word when we should speak, or keep silent when we should be silent? We do not learn this tact out of books. We learn it from God. Somehow we must keep close to God if we are to be moved by him, like the planchette on which you put your hand and which then writes your thought. So must we let ourselves be moved under the divine movement. We must let ourselves go. We must put ourselves into the divine power or recognize, rather, that we are there. This involves a life of prayer, not necessarily, though perhaps also, of church-going, for instance, a daily visit to the Blessed Sacrament. But it does mean that we live our lives consciously in touch with him. Then will come to us a knowledge of God, an understanding of him. That is why he said: "Thou shalt love the Lord thy God." You must have sympathy to understand. Once you say: "I dislike such a person, race, or type," your knowledge of them is finished with, it will never be true. If you want to know God you must love him, and that means prayer. Our life should be more consciously full of God; it very easily can be. It is to help us to achieve that that our Lord came. The beauty of his life is not his love for his fellow-men, but his conscious relationship with his Father.

People are always telling us what religious people ought to be like, forgetting the essential thing. All that is asked of us is to love God; the rest follows of itself. Without that religion becomes mechanical and cannot be realized. Religion is all begotten of God, of our conscious relationship with him. We are God's children; that we must never forget. That fact establishes a certain root of sympathy on which is grafted all our faith, everything that is supernatural in our life. Every one has it. No one can utterly get rid of it. No one, therefore, is beyond redemption, no one is outside the capacity of faith. If it were something of our own making, yes, it might lapse and die. But it is not. It is something God has planted in us. It can never be done away with. It is essential to us, it is rooted with our nature. It can never be laid aside.

What is true of us is true of the whole world. None is outside his kingdom. All could be nearer than they are to God. We must begin with ourselves, and try and keep ourselves in that divine company and realize what an effect such a consciousness would have on our life, this conscious relationship with God. It means a new life. The ordinary life, but now crowded with God's company. To sit in the tube or while walking and to say to ourselves: "God is infinite power. Nothing can happen to me except God lets it happen." Now knowing this, let me look at the world! God's wisdom is governing everywhere. I can never have cause to feel a panic. The infinite wisdom of God guides all I know. Let me read about the distresses of the world and see these from the right angle. Who is the Lord of the world? What was he like? He was most compassionate, was our master, but absolutely at peace always within. There was nothing frantic or fanatical about him. He was exquisitely gentle, full of the sense of the fatherhood of God. He saw suffering; was touched by it; knew God to be its Providence.

People are either passionate and impatient with God or pious and careless. I must say fragments of the Lord's Prayer as I go up and down, and round about. That will do. Anything will do that can be repeated over and over again. Here we shall find the immense value of the rosary for keeping us in touch with God. If we can only do that our world will be richer, and his magic will transform it. We shall grow larger—to the fulness of the stature of Christ.

What a width of vision there was in the saints! It is the width of vision that must most matter, not a width that is a tolerance which does not care, but a tolerance which cares so absolutely, because only out of faith can souls see what is right and true and sane. These are the children of God. What we need is this deeper, supernatural sense, consciously awakened, this steady and daily increasing consciousness of the nearness of God to us in life.

SERMON XI

Faithful in Little

"Receive not the grace of God in vain." That is a warning of the apostle showing us that it is quite possible to receive grace in vain, that is to let it be without result in our life. In some measure, perhaps, we have had experience of that. Perhaps, we can go back to a day when things, good things, came more easily to us, so easily that we hardly valued (as we should have valued) this gift of God. Then, because in little ways we laid aside our former habits of self-discipline and a delicate fulfilment of the divine Will, gradually, by laying it aside and neglecting it, we lost our sensitiveness to it. We grew not to be quite so responsive as once we had been. You must keep your faculties active if you are to keep them sensitive. You must be always perfecting your gifts if you are really to keep them alive, alert. Whatever gifts you have, if you lay them aside for a while, they will lose something of their activity; they must lose something of their power. This is true of everything we know in life. It is true of man's natural gifts. It is true of things material as well as immaterial. To let a power die down is to let it die out. So, too, in the spiritual world. What we need through all our lives long is a daily addition of grace. This means not so much doing more than we are doing, but doing what we are doing better than we do it. It does not mean more prayers, but prayers said better. It means that I begin my prayers with a great effort, putting myself deliberately in the presence of God. It means that when I attend mass I try deliberately to get from mass what it has to give me. I should try, during the most solemn parts of the mass, to rivet my attention on what is happening; thus, that the priest is holding at the altar something for me to adore. We go regularly to our Sunday mass and yet, what very little fruit we obtain from it; yet we need to get from it everything we can. There is a danger of just settling down to life, taking ordinary, everyday views, losing our perception of the supernatural in life. It is a danger of which we are all aware. What alone can keep us free of it is this daily, almost hourly, infusion of the grace of God. This grace of God that has been lavished on us so freely, we gain in proportion to the way in which we use the small opportunities of life. If you ask someone who has come to the Church from outside, why he has become a Catholic, nearly always he will tell you that it was something small and trivial that finally brought him to the faith. The sight of someone's obvious belief in Catholicism, some chance faithfulness, some surrender, that had this extraordinary reward, and brought him, at last, to his home. Always, it is true that in proportion to my use of what has been given me shall fuller use and fuller gifts be made. He that is faithful over little shall be given greater things to rule.

A man may say: "I am not going to trouble over little things." That will not do. It will be followed shortly by this confession: I am losing my power of observation. I am losing my familiarity with divine things." Half a gardener's proper work is done upon his knees. The work of the cultivation of our soul is done humbly, in prayer and service, in quiet moments, and through the use of what we have. You and I are not fit to have the greater graces. We must be content with a very little. All the more, therefore, so that we may use the little things that come our way, must we value them, must we try to secure from them all that they have to give. Prayers, ordinary, everyday prayers, must be used faithfully. We shall not be treated even to little things, if we lay these aside. We shall be even less responsive to graces than now we are. What is asked of us, then, is a steady faithfulness to divine grace, realizing the greatness of our need and realizing that this need is daily, hourly urgent and realizing that grace comes to us through apparently insignificant ways. Thus God's revelation, apart from his revelation through our Lord, is a daily revelation to us as to what is his will. This will, we have said, comes not in a thundering fashion. We shall not be struck off horses on our road to Damascus. That is right for a great character like St. Paul, not for us whose dramatic value is so much less. We must go much more quietly, and use the things we have not dreamt of, only because they are the things that are actually at our door. We have no cause to imagine that our call is to serve others in some wide way, but be perfectly content with home; not dreaming of a vast work which we shall one day be called upon to administer, not taking things merely in quantity, but in quality. Every little thing can be made great, great because of the power we put into it, because of our faithfulness, carefulness in the use of what we have. Our Lord, Himself, dealt so patently with the little things of life that to many he seemed no great saint; He showed no great life lived patently to the world. The chroniclers of the world in his day are silent of him. An apparently small life His! Yet it was charged with an affluence of divine greatness. His human body seemed so ordinary in spite of its radiance. That tiny child! To kneel in front of that! You know what a child is like?—so pitiful, so small. Must I kneel in front of that and say: "This is the God who made me. This wee child is the Creator of the world. This he who set star by star in its place!" Is it possible to believe that this child is God? Faith gives that vision to us. In the little things of life we shall then learn how to find the infinite greatness of God. To despise nothing, to use everything, to realize how near, all our life, we are to the infinite power of God. We have only to take our life as it is, the people we meet, our work, our prayers, and use these to the full. If only we used all these precious things that he has set in our way! To pay no regard to them is to lose our due sense of perception. To shut our eyes to them is to lose the nearest we shall get to the beauty of God. Carefully, deliberately, with a sense of responsibility, not torturing but inspiring us, shall we try to live a life closer to this infinite friendship of God.

Yet, we must realize the solemn warnings of the apostle. To watch our Lord dealing with people is to realize that there must come an ultimate moment, a last divine grace, though the mercy of God is in itself without end. He is infinite, endless. It is we, we who have an end. God's mercy shall go on for ever, but we, at last, close down. There must be a last grace. What shall we do with it when it comes? As we have lived, so shall we deal with it. In the life of grace you never stand still. You go forward or backward. You move the whole time. You are a pilgrim, you are being hunted, driven by God across the face of the earth, but you can halt and go back: He that looketh back is not fit for the kingdom. He cannot reach it if he is turning his back on it, going the wrong way. As long as we realize what is asked of us, as long as we try, out of our store of small things, to gather the good things given, we must trust to the infinite mercy of God that all shall go well with us. Our need is then to use daily the grace of God. Grace is given often; all we need is to awaken to the fact. Use his grace, trusting to his mercy, that we shall be led where he would have us go.

SERMON XII

In Sorrow's Company

Since our blessed Lord has set us out on our pilgrimage, it is inevitable that we should feel, all our lives, the discomforts necessarily connected with travel. We have only to watch his life to see that he also suffered in the same way. He left his Father's side, he came on earth. He lived his own life of pilgrimage. It began in a ruined stable under a rock. It ended, lonely, desolate on a cross. All the while, He, too, was a pilgrim and a stranger here, not like the beasts which have their nests and their holes, of the earth earthy. He, being a pilgrim, had nowhere to lay his head. So, all his life long sorrow went as his companion. There, in the shelter of the rock, when he was only a child, sorrow stood by his side. He was the innocent one of God, and, yet, from the very beginning. He was ushered into the earth with crying—children slaughtered, and mothers crying because of their loss. Thus his very birth was the occasion of dreadful suffering owing to the fear Herod had of what his coming would mean to him. When he was born, then, he was born to the sound of cries, and, from that moment until at last his eyes were closed in death, from that moment his unfailing companion was sorrow. She walked always by his side. It was she who went in company with him. Down into Egypt he went, exiled even from his country, such country as he had, and she went with him in his company. In his company she came back. She was there in that house of Nazareth, where his boyhood and youth were spent. She was there watching all his toil. She saw him grow up in his poverty. She saw him when he was else unnoticed by men. He was royal, with the royalty which was older than the oldest king. He came of a lineage which stretched back and was rooted in God Himself, yet no one paid him reverence. "Do we not know him. Is not his father the carpenter?" That was the way of his fortunes through the wandering pilgrimage of his life. So, too, again, it was sorrow that went with him when he left his home and began his work of preaching, journeying up and down through the provinces of Palestine, Galilee, Samaria and Judea. Sorrow went with him always. Whoever failed him, she never failed. Some might walk no more with him and leave him, not she. Some might desert him in his hour of need. She never left him, he was a pilgrim. Those who go on pilgrimage have sorrow always by their side and discomfort and the burden of travelling, never really having what they desire. So, she went with him in the days when he took his place among his people, even when he worked his miracles. Was there a miracle that he worked that had not its ill effects on the crowd? On the Pharisees? On somebody? They said he had done all things well, but what did he do that did not meet with challenge? Everything he did was mistaken by those who watched him or even at times by those on whom he lavished gifts. No act of that compassionate heart was done but someone was troubled. The Magdalene was at his feet in sorrow, but the Pharisee that was his host was scandalized at her repentance and return. He but laid his healing hand on someone, and at once his enemies were aroused. Had he not broken some law? Some Sabbath? In all he did there was always something not apparently as it should be. So, when it came to the end, those days of which Holy Week is the everlasting memorial, sorrow still went by his side. Palms there were, acclamations, shoutings there were, the echo of the hosannah, the beast carrying him in triumph, the children triumphing, and, yet, there were some who disapproved. "All the world has gone out to Him," said the Pharisees. "Yes," answered Caiphas, "but, remember, one must die for the people." Sorrow never left him. even when he rode in triumph into the city of his love, she rode invisibly by his side. Sorrow sat by him when he was with the twelve in the upper place. It was a family gathering, that should have had a mellow happiness but over it the inevitable shadow was cast. "What thou hast to do, do quickly," Sorrow listened, sorrow understood. Out he went, that other, into the darkness. Still there was sorrow that stayed behind. He spoke and they would not understand. He took them with him out into the garden. He went to meet his suffering, and they slept. They left him, she never left him. She was with him still. He went out by Himself, and knelt in the darkness, and yet sorrow still held hands with him. At last the angel came to bring him comfort and now you would think sorrow would leave him. But at once they heard the sound of men marching, and watched the advancing shadows cast by the swinging lanterns, and one there was who stepped out of the trees into the open and betrayed the Son of Man with a kiss. This was the beginning of newer depths of sorrow. Now was he led like a lamb to the slaughter. He was denied. There was hardly one who stood faithful to him out of all those who had followed Him—hardly one; and even those who stood by him and were faithful had slept. Of the others he had to watch their sorrow. This could not lessen his own. The mother was faithful, but he had the more sorrowfully to watch the mother in her pain. He who knew everything knew the dreadful sorrow she was undergoing. He carried her sorrows as well as the sorrows of all the world, as well as his own. What was her pain but his pain? What was his pain but hers? Sorrow went with him. When his arms were held she still went with him. Lifted against the sky-line she stood by him, she was also lifted up to his embrace. Though he was desolate of the

Father, forsaken, sorrow, though she made him desolate, did not forsake him even then. He was a pilgrim, and he faced, one by one, the difficulties of all pilgrims. He was a wanderer. To be a wanderer was why he came. He lived his life of pilgrimage, and he ended it, as pilgrimages have a habit of ending—on a hill. There, at last, sorrow left him, but only when he died.

Now, you know we are taught by St. Paul that the Father chose us before the foundation of the world. That means that we are chosen in the Man of Sorrows. This is our greatest grace. By this are we his brethren. It must needs be that if we are really his brethren, we have been chosen before the foundation of the world. If we are to go with him we must share his pilgrimage, and share the companionship of that sorrow that went by his side. It is a part of the very price that we must pay for his company. We are not only going with him. but in him only are we sanctified. Our good works, our life, our actions are only of value in so far as they are in him. in so far as we live in him, in so far as we are not merely in his company, but in some mysterious way one with him shall we be brought into the fulness of his blessed vision. It is that to which we are called by our faith. What is faith but his knowledge that he shares with us? Of course you pay for your share of all his gifts. Are you sensitive to beauty? You must pay for this by your pain. Are you sensitive to beauty? Why, then, you must be sensitive to ugliness. While others less sensitive have none of the appreciation of beauty that you have, none of the joy, the pleasure this brings you, therefore, have they also but little of your pain. You pay high for every gift of God. For faith?—you must pay very high indeed for faith. God calls people, as he called Abraham, out from house and family. You must leave all to follow him. You must dare something if you would go his way, for he would see you part of his own mystic body.

You pay not for faith only, but even for hope also, for that too you share with him. Our courage is but a sharing of his courage. Remember that to lose hope is to lose life: "Unless you eat my flesh and drink my blood you shall have no life in you."

Love even. Must we pay for that? Love it is that makes you a pilgrim. You are a pilgrim because you love something that you shall not see here, because you are seeking after that which is invisible, which "No man has seen and lived." That is indeed what makes you a pilgrim—love! It is love of something that is not to be found here, that is on the other side—love also is the prize. For love it was that he gave his body and blood. For love went he to Calvary through Good Friday's pain and all the Passiontide.

We are pilgrims here—we are strangers. The only dreadful danger that assaults us is the danger lest we settle down. We are pilgrims on the march. Always beware of comfort! Beware of being content with what you have! Forget the things that are behind and stretch forward. There ahead is your comfort; and this also shall comfort you, that you are not a pilgrim alone. "You are not left to yourself." He is your fellow. The fellowship of his sufferings is the fellowship of his pilgrimage. "I am the way," He said. What does sorrow matter? His company is there too. You may not see him. Their eyes were held, and they never saw him. None the less to Emmaus he went a pilgrim by their side. He was a pilgrim with them, talking with them, and they never knew it was He. "Did not your heart burn when he spoke to you? You did not know it was He" But then, they constrained him to stay with them. "Stay with us for it is now past daylight and the evening comes." When will our evening come? None of us knows. They could see the light failing. They could see the shadows lengthening. They could see the great, hot sun sinking and the darkness widening, widening. When it is our evening, we know this, that we shall have no need to constrain him to remain with us. Always is he by our side. Had they known who it was they would have remembered that he said: "I am with you always." That is why he came, to give us his company always. We are pilgrims, and yet. He comes with us. That robs the pilgrimage of any real pain. "This day shalt thou be with me in paradise." He was only a thief, and he hung there in agony, but it was honour and paradise to hang by the side of Christ. Would not you wish it also, to share the privilege of the good thief? Would not you wish that you too when you are dying should die by the side of the dying Christ? Well—that is always possible. If you live with him you shall die with him. You shall die with him if you wish to. He will be there. Death means only that you step out of your pilgrimage, that it ends, that you come to him face to face.

May he give us all the courage that we need to go the way he shepherds us. That when he calls, we may go unfrightened. If he bids us come to him across the waters, that unfrightened we may go. And if he bids us climb the hill, may we not notice that it is a hill, mindful only of the happiness of his company. Even if he calls us to a last desolation, though he seem absent, he will be there. If he calls us to bitter agony, that too would be an honour and a privilege, since our agony would be still only a sharing of his agony; He would have lifted the coverlet of suffering and brought us in to lie by his side.

He made us for Himself, that we should travel with him and see him at last in his unveiled beauty in the abiding city where he is light and happiness and endless home.

BOOK TWO

Part I: *Life's Temptations*

DEDICATION

by Bede Jarrett, O.P.

Dear Msgr. McMahon, to whom else than to you can I offer this book? Your kindness these twelve years has been constant and generous and I cannot see how else I shall be able to show you my feelings of gratitude and friendship. Yet even this book that I offer you owes its existence to yourself. It was you who invited me to preach once more during Lent to your people, and it was you who asked Miss Adeline Porter to listen to the sermons and to take them down in shorthand as I preached them; It was you, too, who helped me by your discussions over the problems that even these simple sermons raised and at whose hospitable board I was privileged to meet others whose views might stimulate and clarify my own.

However, such as these sermons are, I offer them to you in their original form as a thank offering of affection.

May I thank, too, that delightful hand of younger priests whom you have had with you and whom you have inspired by your large-heartedness, your humour, and the nobility of your ideals to carry on to later generations the fine generous traditions of the American priesthood?

Your people, too, I thank for their friendly welcome, their alert attentiveness, and the edification they gave me by their devotion to daily Mass, their wonderful frequenting of the Sacraments, and their love of the liturgy.

To that *Domus Aurea* then, as you love to call the Church of your heart, with all it stands for in your memory, to you as its founder and the inspirer of its spirit, to your assistant priests as the joyous abettors of your designs, and to your devoted people I offer these sermons as a sign of unforgetting friendship.

SERMON FOR THE FIRST SUNDAY

Power

It is good to realise that one of these various temptations, my dear brethren, to which our blessed Lord was made subject by the Spirit of God, was the temptation of power. Indeed in some degree it ran through all three temptations. We call attention to it because we don't always remember that power can be a temptation. Power, that is, can be abused. For our Lord the temptation to power was a real temptation, and yet it is strange that it should have been. It was a temptation to our Lord even though there could not be any indecision in his will. Remember that he came for power: "I must be about my Father's business." "I come to do the will of him that sent me." "Art thou a king? For this was I born. For this I came into the world." He came to be a king, and yet, somehow, the offer of the supremacy of the world was a temptation—a vision and yet a temptation: the high mountain, the low world.

And if you think of it, it is the temptation that comes to the noblest of humanity; or again, the temptation that comes to humanity in its noblest mood. If you think, in the history of your own country, of the great names that stand out, they are all of them men who sought power. There was not necessarily any hurt in that. They were men who didn't just by accident find themselves compelled to accept power. They were men who quite deliberately sought power. No one becomes a president by doing nothing or by accident, but by submitting himself to the votes of his people, for even when a vice president succeeds to office "by accident," his vice presidency has been sought. Fine, noble men they were, and yet they looked for power. Of course they looked for power because it seemed to them—we must suppose it—because in some degree it seemed to them that by power only could they individually give the nation what they had to give. They saw their people, perhaps, suffering some hurt and thought they had a remedy; so they sought power that they might heal it of its distress. Or again, they saw that there was something lacking to their people, and they felt perfect confidence in themselves, that they could give that something which was lacked. Or they saw their people enslaved and wanted to make them free. Or they saw their people in poverty and felt they had it in them to give prosperity. They saw their people degraded and wished to lift them to great heights; saw them dominated by an ignoble faction and wanted to give them the power that was theirs.

So men begin finely, but in time there comes a moment of temptation—not one moment, but a series of moments. This happens to all men who take great place. The politician becomes intoxicated by his own power, and longs to hold power, not because of any purpose, but just for the sake of holding power, that's all. He has been flattered by people who want something from him. They have applauded him. They have pointed to him as the saviour of mankind. He has become a great figure in world history. Men have sung his praises as the man of the moment, a great outstanding force. Now human nature highly placed is still human nature. Howsoever austere, after a while, men grow to love praise, to love power and forget what it was that led them to it, what ideals they had, what ambitions, what dreams. They forget that. They only remember, they only think: "Now I am in possession," and they are not great enough to be willing when their work is accomplished to let their power go, or while retaining it to keep unforgotten before them the reason that once impelled to want power.

A man seeks money perhaps, as a means to an end. It is not a purpose, but something that leads on to a purpose; but later the confused mind fixes on it as a definite purpose in itself. He wanted money, for he was poor. He wanted money, for he loved comfort. He wanted money, for he had a dream which money alone could help him to fulfil. Later money became a passion. He forgot all about the purpose he had in wanting it, forgot. A confusion invaded his mind. He forgot that it was intended for a purpose. He had wanted it for something else; he forgot what he wanted it for; now he only wants it for itself. This is the danger. This is where power gets astray. It is a means to an end originally. It becomes an end in itself at last. A man desires power at first because it is a condition of action. That is the use of it. At first he says, "It will help me to something. It will give me an opportunity. With it I can do the fine things I want." And then, oh, then it is just power, loved for its own sake. Irrational, but desperately human! Now it has become a temptation. It is more than a temptation; it is a sin.

Again you find it in the builder-up of a newspaper. He had a purpose once. He had a policy, or there was a person that he wanted to assist, set up, give opportunity to, and he used the power of the press for this perfectly definite purpose. After a while that is forgotten. All he wants now is to circulate his newspaper. He wants to sell more copies, that's all. He has forgotten his dreams. He has forgotten the real thing that justified to his mind the existence of a newspaper. Now he is only anxious to break a record, to sell more copies than his neighbour or his rival does. He has forgotten his purpose. The paper has become just an end in itself; not why he began it, but what he is doing with it has become tangled up with the paper. Confusion reigns now over his reason. Greed now masters him; his dream is forgot.

Or the writer who had something he wanted to teach people, something he felt they desperately needed; and he begins to write his books for a purpose. Then the writing becomes a passion. He can't stop. He is writing and writing, because his publishers ask for more. It is always like that, power beginning nobly and then gradually opening out and becoming something that is merely vulgar, a mere vulgar love of power. Nothing more than that. Not what can be done with power, but power for itself alone.

You get it again in this age of transport, of speeding up. We want to go from somewhere to somewhere, and we want to get there more and more quickly. That is rational; but at last it is not to somewhere or from somewhere, but only we want to go quickly. We have forgotten why. We do not know why we are going, or where we are going. We are just going. The purpose is forgotten. Again it is a confusion of mind in regard to power.

Indeed, my dear brethren, we can all see it in everybody else, but we have got to realise that something like this is probably happening in our own hearts. It isn't only in politicians and the makers of newspapers, isn't just writers or people like that. It is all of us; and it comes to us, not of course because we are the noblest of humanity, but it may come to us in our noblest moods. We all have got some power, each of us. To us therefore our Lord's temptation is the suggestion, reminding us of our need to be wary. If he was tempted, I must be tempted somewhere. Somewhere in my life where I have power, an evil spirit is coming and tempting. It is suggesting something to me now. What? That is where we have got to look at ourselves. We must say to ourselves, "Now where am I being tempted? I know I am being tempted. He wasn't left untempted. Surely I shall be tempted. Surely, I. Now where?" In the family—father and mother must think of this. To aspire to be father or mother is a noble ambition. That is all right. You want power. You have it. But why are you given power? What is fatherhood? What is motherhood? For what have you that power in the home? "They won't obey me," parents complain sometimes. Why were they taught to obey you? Why is there an obligation on them to obey you? Why are you given power in the home? Not just for power's sake, since power is given only for a purpose. Fatherhood, motherhood, are fine things, but they are not just yours to give you power; they are yours that you might be in a position to use your power. Fatherhood is a man's relation to his child. Motherhood, again, is a relation to children. Neither parent has the right merely to say, "But they don't pay any attention to me." Have you deserved attention? How do or did you use your power? The children were very little once. How did you use your power with them? Did you really train them, teach them, lead them, inspire them? You were older: you should have been more wise than they. "I have done everything for them." But you shouldn't. That was wrong, surely. You were given power to train them, not to do everything for them, but to make them do things for you. If you never taught them to be unselfish, you have no business now to cry out because they are not unselfish. You never taught them to be so. You did not use your power wisely, hardly used it at all, and now of course they disregard you. Parents must seldom blame their children. They must only beat their breasts.

Childhood is a power. Youth is a power. It is a power, isn't it? A power of doing wonderful good. Youth has its health, its energy, its activity! It is the age of visions. These so quickly pass. Middle age knows nothing about them; it is much too sensible for visions. The old, they dream of the past. There is no future to them. It is youth that has its visions. Youth has its activity. It should use it surely as a power for a purpose, not just something to exult in, as a man might exult in his strength. There is something splendid in youth.

But in God's world there is nothing splendid for itself, other than God Himself. All other goods are for a purpose. Youth has its purpose too in the home. As Christ was tempted, so surely is youth being tempted. Let youth ask itself: "How am I using my power in the home, in the family? Is my activity of youth, are my visions, for the comfort of mankind?" In business, trade, each man is tricked out in some little brief authority. Everyone somewhere rules over another soul. What are you doing about this? How are you using it? Merely to strut about and take large place? That won't do. Service is the purpose of power, service of others. That is why the Master came. To be waited on? There is nothing fine about that. That is the desperate penalty of old age, to be waited on and served. That is what we shall all come to if we live long enough. Before that helplessness comes on us, we must use our power to serve mankind, serving while we can serve, and realising that we are—were meant to be—men's servants. To serve men was almost the highest thing that he claimed. Who are we to claim more? No disciple is above his Master. A disciple cannot be above the deep humility of Christ. He girded himself with a towel and washed the hands and feet of the Apostles. He fed them with the blessed body that was to be broken for their love.

Power? He rejected the power that was the mere power of splendour: the high mountain, lording it over the low earth. "All these things will I give thee, if thou wilt but worship me." He didn't come to be a king like that. He was no king to be given the world. No man is given anything that is worth having. The only things that are worth having are the things you buy, the things that have cost you all that you have to give—your life's blood, even. Those are the things you will always find worth while, and not the things that you come into easily. "Easy come, easy go," says the proverb. Easy got, easy lost again. There is no stir, no fun in such a life as that. But Christ would be a king. For this he came. For this was he born into the world, but not the kingship that gets to its place through evil, through the worship of evil. Not the power that you get by flattering those higher than yourself. That power is not worth having. It is not noble. It is something that degrades both him and you.

We come, don't we—we should come—with noble ambitions.

We have something to do in the world. God made us for that, each of us separate, unique. If the work we are sent to do isn't done, no one will do it; there will be something missing in the plan of God. There will be an instrument silent in his orchestra. There will be a voice hushed in his choir. God made us to do something, each of us, for God is wise, working always for the purpose. We are a purposed work in his world of work with power enough for our purpose. Each of us must ask then, "What am I here for? What is my power? Who are the people I am set to rule? What is my position over them? I am here not to hold power merely, but to help by power. Should I now let my power go?" Sometimes there is wisdom in letting go, in not holding on too long. Haven't you watched people building up some cherished work and then, because they don't know when to let go, strangling with their growing blindness and feebleness the very plant they reared?

There are such unhappy things in the world. Fine people even (if we can trust biographies, religious people) have done that sort of thing, and forgotten the purpose of their actions and remembered power only as it came.

You see, for him it was a real temptation. Then from such an experience we are not likely to be exempt. Looking at our hearts, at our lives, experiences, we must say, "Whom am I ruling? For whose sake? Why?" "We," says St. Paul in the Epistle, "should so act that our ministry be not blamed." We are all ministers. You are a priestly people. Every soul alive is a priest. You have got something to do for someone. "Now act so that this ministry of Christ be not blamed in you. You are all ministers, remember that, for by minister we mean someone who serves. We, if we are great enough, can make ourselves the servants of the servants of God.

SERMON FOR THE SECOND SUNDAY

Quiet

It might seem strange, my dear brethren, to put as one of the difficulties of life a desire for quiet. It would be, perhaps, unthinkable as a temptation, except for the gospel that you have just heard read. Wherever, I suppose, you go, to whomsoever you speak among those that are living, you will find almost everywhere the longing and desire for quiet; and often people, in this desire for quiet, hardly realise what it is that they are asking for, hardly realise that what they are desirous of may not be a good thing for them.

In one of her very beautiful and human letters, St. Catherine of Sienna, busy always, almost the most busy amongst the saints, interested in politics, wandering over Italy and southern France for the achievement of her political visions—St. Catherine, mystic, writer—St. Catherine, that inspiring friend of the young men and women of her time, her letters crowded with chaff of the would-be poets, writes in one of them to say that she has stayed with cloistered nuns, and adds, "It is a great temptation for me to linger on here." A temptation, mark you, for this busy saint to go into a cloister and find rest and quiet! A temptation for her! In our day too very often we hear people clamourous for quiet, even religious women lamenting they have so little time for God, telling us that their days are so full and busy that they have hardly time to pray.

Those sayings, of course, show a complete misunderstanding of life, and again, of prayer. Prayer has nothing to do with time or leisure. Prayer is something outside all borders of time, like every other great thing that lasts. There is hardly a masterpiece in the world that is not unfinished, or was not unfinished when the artist died, hardly one. Time, completeness, the finished object—the desire for these here is the misunderstanding of petty minds. Quiet? You will find, I think, nothing in the gospel urging quiet. Peace? Christ came not to give peace, but a sword. There is no requirement of our Lord urging on us that we should go out into the still places of the earth. You don't find that laid on us. On the contrary, he preached and practised the gospel of work. The great saints who were the masters of prayer, by whose teaching the world has ever since been largely influenced on matters of prayer, these saints were the busiest of mankind. You can hardly pick up a book on prayer without finding in it some quotation from St. Augustine. Yet there is hardly a saint in the calendar more busy than he, the greatest of the fathers, great in everything that he touched or attempted, theologian, preacher, biblical scholar, bishop, writer—hardly anything that he touched in which he did not reach the highest point—a man whose days were crowded, whose nights were spare of sleep. Yet he is a great master of prayer. St. Gregory, Pope for fourteen years, St. Gregory, always in ecclesiastical politics even before he became Pope, his torrent of letters surviving to us, the vast volumes of his sermons surviving, who though he was all his life a sick man, and obliged to spend half the day lying down, converted Europe, who organized and re-organized our liturgy and music, was yet a master of prayer. Prayer has nothing to do with leisure. It has nothing, to do with the busy-ness of life. It has nothing to do with any desire for quiet. It can be at its best without leisure. St. Bernard, again, was the arbiter of Europe. Everything that was done in his time he was consulted about—every philosophy, every political action, every crusade, every dream. These men were busy and yet lovers of God. They were, full of activity, they had hardly a moment to themselves, and yet they realised that for them work was the way to God.

It was all very well for Peter and the others to go up to the hills and to say, "It is good for us to be here." The untroubled beauty of the still air, perfectly serene, is wonderful. To appreciate and enjoy it is all very well for the moment. But it is not life. Up on the hills it is so easy to despise humanity in the valley; so easy a danger can refinement bring to the soul. There is a danger, isn't there, for the Catholic rather to despise the rest of men because they haven't got the Catholic's freedom from worrying about the articles of faith? We are given our articles of belief and religion, that is true, and these others are out there searching and seeking, but we were given the faith, not to do nothing, but to work with it and for it and to pray until he come. It is true that we are given our mysteries with a clear knowledge of them that is withheld from the world; but we were given them that we might work and live, not rest. Heaven is our resting place. Here, we must work till we die. He climbed the hills, indeed, our Blessed Master, once or twice to get a rest between his labours. But even the hills were no place of resting for him, except when on a hill in utter agony he died. Work is our portion and not leisure, not the way of ease, not the lifting of temptation, not a prayer that all the busy-ness may cease. Not that; that is not religion as Christ taught it. That is the foolish dream of the leisured shirkers of mankind. It is the dream of the idle woman who imagines religion to be like that. It is the so-called mysticism which can only be lived in boudoirs or drawing-rooms. It is not the life instituted by Christ. He came to bring not peace but the sword. The life he came to teach could be lived in the market place, a busy life, in warfare, not at all in shirking the busy toil of men. It is very natural to long for quiet, of course, but to give way to it is a misunderstanding of what the Incarnation means. The Incarnation is the philosophy we must learn in our own lives.

90 Temptation, how we hate it, loathe it. Why should I be tempted in *this* way? Why should this particular temptation be mine? Why not something not so coarsening, not so lowering; why not something higher for me? Isn't this the very cry of St. Paul? "Why this sting of my flesh, this angel of Satan to buffet me? Why to me should this come, who fourteen years ago had that intimate vision of God?" The clamour of the soul, I want to get rid of it all. I want to go into quiet, still waters. I don't want this bothering temptation. I don't want to have to follow all these dry and barren trials. I want emotion and thrill and stir and all the fun in religion. Why, why temptation? "Thrice I besought the Lord, and he made answer, 'My power is made manifest in your infirmity.' Gladly, therefore, will I glory in my infirmity." The peace comes not from without, but within. It is not the circumstances of your life that you should ask God to smooth out for you. That is not his way. It is not things that interest him. It is the soul. He doesn't, because we pray to him, lift the obstacles that surround us. He doesn't for that, smooth down the pathways of life. He doesn't lay the road for us perfectly even. He does something finer. He deals with us—He doesn't lift temptation from us but he pours in power and strength to meet it. He doesn't rob us of our greatness. He would have us men, meeting life, meeting whatever life stirs against us, brings against us. In trouble, he would have us serene. Not his way is the lifting of the burden, but the straightening of the shoulders with which a man walks erect, unbeaten, unbowed. That is the way of Christ, he that carried our griefs, carried them as a man should, not whining, not complaining, not moaning. So he would have us follow by faith—believing God to be within us, God over all.

So, my brethren, when they tell you of Russia, when they bid you pray for Russia, pray for God's blessed will to be done. Whether he lift the persecution or no is his business. God knows what the world needs. God knows whether or not we that live in quiet and leisure, in protected lives, need some fine example of a great-souled people that loves and will suffer for its faith, be persecuted and emerge with brighter eyes. It may be that the trial of Russia is a message for us to straighten our souls as though with steel. Not perhaps will the temptation of persecution be lifted from them, but through it souls will be made more strong. Persecution winnows out the weaklings. Persecution has its own purpose, under the hand of God. One of my own countrymen, travelling in Russia not very long ago one autumn, went down into a little village that he might learn closer at hand the spirit of the people, not in publicity, but in their homes. They were starving and there came one day through the village a train, bringing wheat to the people, grains of wheat, and there came with it one of the Komisars. The villagers gathered in the station around the train and he stood there at the open doorway with the peasants in front of him. He didn't step down. He stood there at the entrance, of the carriage, and spoke to them for a while. This was the burden of what he said to them: "We are bringing you grain. Now you can do what you like with it. You can eat it. Only if you do we shall have no more for you next year. If you eat it your children will die. For next year, there will be nothing for them. So if you eat it now, they will die. But if you sow it, with this long winter, you indeed will die yourselves but your children will live. Take your choice. Sow and die and give life to your children, or eat now and let your children die in the future year." The train moved on. Never a word, never a protest rose from the crowd of peasants, yet they were men and women. They must have felt something of the hard choice before them. They must have felt it. "What did they do?" I asked him. "Oh, they sowed the grain," he said. You see, they are a great people, and always God has his own destiny for the great. It may be because we are little that he stoops to our pettiness, gives us the riches in the world to share because, perhaps, we have not the greatness that would withstand unbroken the rattle of the sword, the sight of it drawn from the scabbard, the feeling of it cutting us through. It may be because we are so petty that he stoops to our littleness. It may be these others are great and he shares with them his own cup of pain. Nerved at least by the sight of their suffering, be more patient with your own. Realise that an infinite wisdom guides all of us. Beneath us are the everlasting arms of love. Let him deal with you as he wills to deal with you, not asking him to lift the sorrows from your path, asking, rather, that you may have something of his greatness that walked out and met sorrows unbroken, unbowed. Quietness, peace, serenity—ah, yes, surely—not in our lives without, but within, not at the mercy of circumstances but created by the soul under God.

SERMON FOR THE THIRD SUNDAY

Place

In this Sunday's gospel, in the passage that you have just heard read, my dear brethren, you have had put in front of you by our blessed Lord his view of the relationship between Himself and evil in the world. The world was held by evil. Evil was the strong man armed, who kept his court in peace. Our Lord was the stronger one and he came to despoil the evil one of its possessions. He was so strong that evil could not withstand him. compared to him, the evil one was weak. So our blessed Lord showed us what he would have us believe, that he Himself is stronger than all evil, and yet he goes on to add that he may be dispossessed by evil if the soul be not loyal to him, if it still cling to the evil which it once had. When he has driven out this evil spirit, He, by his power, strips it of its possessions, of its strength wherein it trusted. In his picture of it, the evil spirit goes out wandering, and finding nowhere to rest comes back again, knowing that the soul is still at heart in its possession. "I will go back to my house, mine, whence I came out." It is still his soul, his dwelling place; so, gathering other evil spirits, he comes back and dwells there, a long stay, a dwelling—and the state of that man is worse than before. As our Lord would have us see it, human souls were possessed by evil, the evil was dispossessed by Christ, and yet the evil spirit may find its way back again if the soul is not loyal to Christ.

This had its lesson for the Pharisee, a type of man who undoubtedly followed religion, undoubtedly stood strongly for good things. He belonged to the nationalist party in politics, the puritan party in religion. The nationalist, the puritan, in their way are moved by fine things. But our Lord is repeatedly pointing to a weakness of the Pharisee. He is a lover of place, the first places in the banquet; he wants men to salute him as he passes through the market place. The Pharisees were men that sought to be acknowledged. And these that love place and position are meaner, don't you think, than those that love power? The man who loves power has something strong about him, something real. Perhaps he has an idea that he wants to get established; perhaps he sees inefficiency and he thinks himself efficient. He wants to control a situation that has got out of control. But these place-lovers who are always out for position, have got no such dreams, no such ambitions, no ideals in reality. They just want people to acknowledge them. Whether they are worth acknowledging hardly troubles them. They are not out really for the esteem of others. They only want position. They are not out to establish their worth. They want to be shown the first place.

In the days of an older world, of an older organization of society, days that we speak of as the days of aristocracy, the problem was never of that kind. Positions were regulated, were settled by rule and custom. Everyone had his place. The only disturbance possible was someone getting out of his place and trying to go somewhere else. There was never any trouble for long, for each man's place was known; so that no one fought for pre-eminence. It wasn't personal. It didn't go with worth. No one thought of it as that. This one had a higher place; he walked first; he took precedence. It wasn't the man that mattered but the position; it was his office that gave him his place. About the man no one troubled. This had its obvious disadvantages. You got inefficiency often coming to the top, not always, but often enough. You had the efficient person who was lower down, who could never have the chance to control, getting impatient with a state of misrule. Then followed a revolution—people breaking up from below. But despite its disadvantages, in that age place was separate and apart from personal worth.

Then you have the world of democracy coming after. For it there is no such thing officially, as place or position into which a man is born. Democratic folk tell us they are not going to trouble about that. A title is something hollow. It is pretence. They are going to judge a man only by his worth, his native human dignity. They have abolished all the nonsense, all the snobbery of position. This sounds beautiful. But how are you to know a man's worth? Everybody is to be acknowledged and his place found for him in exact proportion to his value in society. But who is valuable? How on earth are we to know which man is valuable? As a result, they appeal to us, each of them to acknowledge what fine fellows they are. They parade their wares. If only my worth takes position, then I must impress my worth on the world. I must. How else is anyone to know my worth? So democracy becomes obviously an age of advertisement. Everybody has to cry his own value to a hardly listening world. Once upon a time, all worth was settled objectively by birth or other tests. This had notable disadvantages. But at any rate no one had need to advertise. All the world knew who were the great. Their titles proved it. All the world acknowledged his pre-eminence, not because of the man, but somehow because of the place that he held.

But now who cares for the man of worth who doesn't blazon his worth? With democracy you get a scramble for position, everyone desperately afraid of being looked down on. You get it even in Catholic life everywhere, the strange snobbery in which men must fight for their position, must show their position, otherwise no one will believe that they are really worth anything at all. So I suppose you find, the world over, the strange attitude to the world about them of the man or woman who is beginning to get on. Shall they help the priest by work in a parish? Once upon a time, perhaps, they were quite willing to work, to come down and work with others. Come down? No, they were already down, for all were on a level. You see it is a democratic world, and all the world is democratic in language. They worked in the parish. Everybody worked in the parish. Then these people became a little better off. Circumstances helped them. They managed somehow to rise above the others, by their intelligence, worth, or whatever you will. They became a little better than the fellows. Will they still go on working in the parish? Oh, no. "People won't realize I am better if I work as I did before. I will help, yes, but not as I used to. You see I am now a little better off. I am further up in the scale; but unless I let people see where I am, nobody will ever know it, and so—No, no, I don't—I can't do that now. Generous? Oh, yes, I will subscribe, indeed I am most willing to subscribe to your charities, but come and ask me, please. You must ask me for my subscription. And not just anyone shall come for it, but the better people or the priest himself shall come and ask me. I shall be made an exception. Oh, yes, I am generous, surely. What I have, I give." But you see this is show, pretence, advertisement. Unless he can impress on them his importance, nobody will know how important he is.

Or it is the neighbourhood in which he lives. The neighbourhood? "Oh, this is no longer my neighbourhood. I must move out a little. You see, if I stay here no one will know that I am better than I was." It is not worth he is troubling about, it is esteem. It is not even esteem, it is position. It is place. All the world over, I suppose here as well as everywhere else, people are vastly sensitive to establish their social position. They move away to a better neighbourhood because they want to show what has happened. These are the paradoxes of democracy which proclaims so splendidly the value of a man's life and worth, and then has to fall back on the "title" of neighbourhood to prove it. Again, it is Catholic education. Once they were, of course, in favour of it and they are so still, but, well, not quite with the same enthusiasm. You see, everybody has got to go to a Catholic school, and that means, of course, that in a Catholic school you will find all sorts of rough people. A Catholic school does not trouble very much about social position apparently, neither does the Catholic religion. It is all-embracing; it takes in all sorts. "But now that I have got on a little better," these people seem to say to themselves, "of course you know, it won't altogether do for me to send my children to herd with the rest. The boy or girl won't get quite such a good position later on if they go there. Those Catholic schools are not exactly well known." Oh, yes, from the point of view of intelligence, of education, of the scholastic training the Catholic schools are admitted by these people to be as good as the rest, but they don't give quite the same social distinction, and, somehow, these people want social distinction conferred upon them. Evidently they haven't got it themselves. It must be given them by the school. They are afraid to stand on their own worth and value, in spite of all this talk of a democratic world. They are afraid, really, of reality. They just want to impress their position on their neighbours. All they care about is what other people think: "A rough school, and my boy or girl will be hurt by it." You see, there is no home influence to set against the rough element in the school. There is no real culture at home, no background. Wealth is their only claim to respect; this is the shifting of values in our day. Worth doesn't depend on place or culture, but on rising a little higher up in the financial scale. What scale? Some scale of betterness? No. Just a little more money at their bank. Their business is doing better than it used to, and so on—so off the children go to some other school or college or university. And the result? Well, if all the people, once they get better off send, their sons elsewhere, how can the Catholic school ever have an opportunity to improve itself socially? How can it begin to improve? If as soon as people get a better standing they take their children from the school, if they empty the school of the people who could give it, perhaps, social distinction, what will happen to the school?

Christ, our Lord, came to teach his own blessed doctrine, the value of the human soul. He came to teach his own blessed doctrine that faith mattered, and nothing else beside. Other knowledge, says St. Paul, is fine, but he sets above every other knowledge this knowledge which is more excellent, the knowledge of God and Christ and the eternal things that abide. It is not these fashions which alter, not these positions which move up and down with the rise or the fall of stock, that matter—not really. We need something worth more, a real democracy that judges by the value of a human soul. When St. Agatha, the virgin of Syracuse, was led before the proconsul, he said to her, "But you come of a noble house. Will you associate with these mean-living Christians?" for, as St. Paul said, there were "not many noble; not many wise amongst them." She said, "For me it alone is true dignity to follow Christ." It was worth more to her than crowns of gold could be worth, the fellowship of Christ.

We are living in an age of advertisement. It is an age of impudence, of the loud speaker, of the big noise; an age in which everybody proclaims his own excellence, and obtains possession, in consequence, of high place. As you go to your business and you face the swing door of its entrance, there you find the motto of the world, "Push," written there to greet you, the first greeting as you cross the threshold. It is an age of push. As you leave your business it is the last thing you see written again on the swing door, "push."

"Walk," says St. Paul, "as children of light," that is his gospel. Choose which you will, but this is the gospel of Christ. "Blessed are the meek," he said, "the poor in spirit." "Blessed are the meek."? Is this a world for the meek? Is this a world for Christianity? Are we Christians really followers of Christ? Do we worship meekness? Would we follow meekness? Would we dare be meek in this world? We are all of us sinners; all of us falter here. Blessed are we, at least in this, that we know the truth, and in our wayward way, remind ourselves from time to time of it by tasting the refinement that comes from a following of Christ. We should not so much worry ourselves over an outside, impressed refinement, but over that refinement which springs native from the soul. Refinement—how often in the peasant, in the poor country dweller, is it to be found, rather than in the rude people of the town, with their strut and their struggle, their lack of meekness! Hardly in the towns will you find, in the people you meet as you go about your business, the refinement of the soul the sacrifice of the Mass, symbol of our following of him, in order to watch Infinite power putting itself at the service of mankind. That is our doctrine of true greatness; that in a world of darkness was the light he came to bring. "Walk then as children of this light."

SERMON FOR THE FOURTH SUNDAY

Common Sense

It is undoubted, my dear brethren, that the atmosphere of the New Testament is full of the miraculous; that however you interpret the New Testament, however you try and understand it, you are always faced by that very definite fact that both those that knew and watched and listened, and our blessed Lord Himself, thoroughly accepted the miraculous as something which was constant and no doubt inevitable in life. But that, of course, is a point of view that not only disturbs but even distresses a certain number of people. There are people who, in their way, would like to serve God, and do serve him, but their great danger and difficulty lies in this, that they accept almost as their test of everything whether it fits in or no with what they call common sense. Their great criticism of anything or anyone is to say that it or they are unreasonable. And by saying that somehow or other they imagine that they have produced an argument. It isn't an argument. It is merely a label. Unreasonable? Faith is unreasonable, not in the sense that it is against reason, but in the sense that it is more than reason. So, of course, is art. So, of course, is love. Because a thing stretches beyond the measurement of reason, it doesn't follow for a moment, it doesn't prove, that a thing is untrue. Art, in the loose sense in which they use this word, is also eminently unreasonable, but it may be beautiful, and being beautiful must be true. So again is human love or human patriotism, or any of those great passions of mankind that end as all passions must, in death. Of them all it is true that they are eminently unreasonable. That is to say, you can't calculate about them. They are beyond the measurement of reason. Or again, you can't calculate about them because they are alive. Reason for us is never the framework within which you have to fit our lives. Reason is rather the springboard from which we take our leap into life. Reason governs the beginnings, but it cannot govern the endings of things. You begin on the earth, but you end in the skies.

That is why, I think, sometimes it may happen that people become—all of us perhaps are so more or less, from time to time—desperately insincere. We would all of us be horrified if anybody suggested to us that we didn't believe our faith; we would be horrified if people said that we weren't really true Catholics. Yet in some measure I am sure it is true of all of us that we are not true Catholics; in some measure we are insincere. Perhaps the supreme test of it would be for us really to say to ourselves: "I am seeking God, yes. I am looking for God, true. But would I like God to seek me?" That we should look for him, yes, that we can attempt indeed. But if he proceeded to look for us in life, should not we get afraid? Or, putting it round another way, doesn't it often happen that, when we are confronted with difficulties that make the practice of faith for the moment really impossible to us, we are not at all sorry, but almost relieved? That we are sometimes glad to be confronted with difficulties which prevent our doing something that we feel in our conscience is good? We are satisfied with all sorts of good excuses—really good excuses. But it would be a mistake to suppose that a good excuse is necessarily a good motive. We may have all sorts of plausible reasons for not doing things, and yet perhaps it would be finer to do them. The mind, our way of judging life, seizes on some plausible excuse which truly and really justifies us in not doing our duty. Yet we can do it, and it would be a great deal finer if we did do it. We may have thus insincerity in our life of faith.

Or again, to put it perhaps a little differently, we find ourselves defending ourselves to ourselves. We are doing things, we are half conscious that they are not quite right, but we can excuse them. I can invent a reason for going on reading a rather unclean book. I can invent a reason for going to this play, for going to visit this person whom I know to be dangerous to me. I have all sorts of excuses for doing what is dangerous, and yet I know, in the heart of me, that I had better put them aside. It is better for me not to do it, though I may be justified in doing it. Unreasonable? Common sense?

And again, sometimes it happens that when people use the word unreasonable about the action of the Church or the Pope or their parents or some priest, when they say some one is unreasonable, they mean he is not ordinary; that something is being asked of them beyond what is usual.

Well, that is true, of course, always about faith. Faith is always asking people to do things that are unusual, and out of the ordinary. This must happen if men deal with God. God can never be ordinary. He must always be outside of order as we know it and can see it and can measure it. God is within his own limits, which are limitless. He is not within any other limits. Therefore God is always breaking in on things that men have settled—not really settled, but only observed. "This is the law of nature," they say, by which they mean "this is what we have always noticed that nature does." And God one day does differently. God must. That is his way. All we know is merely what we observe to have happened so far. What God does is sometimes outside what has been normally noticed. That must be allowed him Who is God.

Thus it is unreasonable, people say, to ask us to believe in Jonah and all those stories of the Old Testament. It is unreasonable to ask us to believe in them. It doesn't really matter, perhaps, whether we take them literally or figuratively, but the argument implied in this objection people raise is foolish. A story may be unreasonable, but to say it is unreasonable is not to say it is untrue. To say it is out of the ordinary is not to say it is untrue. Children are surprised, of course, by all sorts of things in life, but they never get to the point when, because they are surprised, they therefore argue that a thing isn't true. You tell a child the most extraordinary and fantastic story you like, a ghost story, and directly you finish the child says to you, "Is it true?" That is the only thing they are interested in. Is it true? However apparently unreasonable, if it is true they will take it. They don't mind. Now we, of course, shouldn't go about just believing anything that is told us, but there is something in the heart of a child which it would be well for us if possible to recapture. To be surprised, yes, but not to cease to believe because of your surprise, because you learn of something new. The longer we live, the greater is our danger of being worn down into accepting merely what is usual, so that anything unusual strikes us at first as being untrue. Thus at first we refuse to accept or believe not merely religion, but science. When it comes in front of us with something new, we say it is impossible, by which we mean we haven't yet noticed anything quite parallel. Now a child is very different, for a child is always fresh, always eager, always alive. A child could go on being surprised all through its childhood, and still be able to believe in extraordinary things. We get dulled by age. Our education, to a large extent, stifles our fancy. It destroys our power of believing. We begin with the charm of childhood, and when education has finished with us it has robbed us of most of our charm. Often education is deliberately destructive; very largely, as it is at present conducted, it aims at the obvious and the denial of the unusual. It brings us all down to a dead level, to accept only what ordinarily happens. We forget the "Once upon a time."

A willingness to accept the unusual, the unexpected, something, a little different, is required as a condition for faith. Faith gives men and women the everlasting youth of a child. It doesn't make them believe everything, but it does prevent them from saying about new things that they can't possibly be true. We begin with reason. We don't end with reason. We begin with those nearer things, and we go out into the far distant places. We are not the children of the bondwoman. We are the children of the free, with the freedom wherewith Christ has made us free. The old law held people down. Christ broke through that, so that under his spirit St. Paul is simply alive with a new sense of freedom. He is like a boy that has burst out of school. He lives on holiday and with a huge sense of freedom, of running wild. The high winds of the spring, all life tingling, and St. Paul caught by the atmosphere of escape. So he reminds us that we are not the children of the bondwoman, but the children of the free.

When you go on a voyage, my brethren, when you begin to leave the land, for a long while after you will still see the lights of the human dwellings, or of a lighthouse or the lightship. You see for a long while after as you go out in the darkness, for a long while after, all these human lights along the shore. But if you go far enough, you lose them. They die out, one by one. They have guided you, these human lights, they have guided those that navigate your vessel. By them these judge their distance and position; they judge their dangers by the lights men have lit. But there comes a time when they have to cut free of these human landmarks, when all they have to guide them in the darkness is the stars. They have left the human lights. They have left the little measurements of reason. Not the things man has made, but what God has made alone guides them in the wide waste waters. Even the compass may fail. Yet though their compass fail them, with the stars above them they may yet guide their ship safe to its port at last. Is not this in some measure true of reason, though it be a gift of God? Reason may fail you. If you are going to do anything with life, you have sometimes to move away from it, beyond all its measurements. You must follow sometimes visions and dreams. "He has," say they perhaps of some great man, "a genius for business, for commerce." What they mean by genius is something beyond reason, a flight away from that which measures things for ordinary folk. We have all of us to have a genius for God, something beyond just ordinary human measurement. We have got to leave these human lights and dare the waters lit by stars. Even the stars are not eternal, but they will last our lifetime. They will last all the lifetime of mankind, then they will disappear to give place to something finer—the lesser lights will give place to the full day. For us, reason and common sense and those lesser measurements have a value. They enable us to begin, but not to end our work. They help us at the start to avoid the normal dangers, but then we must have larger courage and a nobler faith. We must guide our life after we have broken away from all human measurements. But then we must guide our life by the stars set by God in the sky of faith. These are the lights that God has lit. They will last our lifetime. Then Faith will pass into vision, darkness into day. But following them we shall find our way to him, by the stars of faith, to our port of safety, to our harbour and our home....

SERMON FOR PASSION SUNDAY

Haste

In that phrase of our blessed Lord, "Before Abraham was made, I am," He claimed, as the whole context shows, the eternity of God, that he was before all time, and that the remote period of Abraham was something which had happened within his own vision. First, then, it is a text which shows us unequivocally the claim to the Godhead made by our blessed Lord, but again, it has something too which lifts the veil and shows us the character of our Lord Himself. Perhaps more truly it explains to us the character that he so evidently possessed.

It is because God is eternal that God is infinitely serene and patient. It is because Christ our Lord was eternal that he was patient and serene. God is eternal, and therefore God is never in a hurry. In the parable that our Lord told us about the man that woke to find that his enemy had oversown cockle in his field, the people labouring under him said to him, "Let us go out and pull up the evil weed while it is yet young, before it is strong." But the master's answer was the answer of someone whose strength was absolute and who was never in a hurry, who had exquisite patience: "Suffer both to grow to the harvest." If you try and interfere with evil, you may hurt the good. Suffer both to grow to the harvest. It is all to be cut down then. That is why God is never in a hurry. God is strangely patient with a world that is oversown with evil. But God is patient because he can afford to be. All must come to him at last.

Our Lord was patient, yet man is impatient because man has a boundary set him within to work. Man lives in time. Man is always in a hurry (or there is the danger that he is in a hurry) and therefore man is impatient. Nearly all the mischiefs of mankind have grown from impatience. The great heresiarchs, the leaders of heresy, were heresiarchs because they were impatient of the Papacy or God. They saw evil. They saw it leniently dealt with or perhaps not dealt with at all, and they grew impatient. If you are ever in a hurry you are in no mood to weigh and ponder justly the things, brought to you to decide: "I am in a hurry. I cannot deal with it now." A beggar who then begs of you will get scant mercy: "I am in a hurry. I am already late for something I have to do." Man is normally lying under that anxiety—I have got something to do immediately and therefore I am in a hurry, and because I am in a hurry I am impatient. Then people wonder why, when they are in a hurry, everything goes wrong or breaks, whatever it is that they are using, a bootlace, whatever it be. Of course it breaks, because you are in a hurry. Exactly! Because you are in a hurry, you deal roughly, unfairly with it. There is no steadiness in your action; you pull by jerks. And when you are in a hurry your mind moves by jerks also. It is not patient, not serene, not just. It is in a hurry. We have so much to do; all our world is so much in a hurry, so eager for work but is not eager to think or ponder, not eager really first of all to secure perfect serenity of mind. Yet greatness requires that as a preliminary to action. All great work requires it. The great leaders have always insisted upon the value of silence in life. Silence is a condition out of which great thoughts have come to mankind. By this we mean silence of spirit, rather than mere silent conditions of life. Busy people can yet be serene people. A convent is full often of immense activity, and yet has a prevailing sense of serenity and peace. What a change, what a contrast to the world without! The religious don't work less, but they think more because they pray more. There lies the difference. Thence comes their quietness, serenity, peace. An age that is in a hurry cannot do great things. It can produce big things, and mistake bigness for greatness. Greatness endures. What is done in a hurry is done impatiently. It can't last.

Our world inevitably, because of the enormous increase of the power of mechanics, has produced an era in which people really have more time on their hands than they had before, more time for leisure. They haven't got more leisure, only more time for leisure. Leisure is not the absence of work. Leisure is an attitude of mind. People can have far less to do, and yet lack leisure. Leisure is a condition or a state of the soul. In the old country days so much more work was done at home than is done today. The housewives made all the jam, were busy from morning to night, hard worked, were over worked and worn down by work. Now they have time on their hands. They don't work or make, they buy. The danger is now that they get unhappy, not because they have got time on their hands, but because they don't know how to use it. They cannot do anything to occupy themselves. Hence you get that steady drift from the country to the town. It is not because they have got too much time to themselves, but it is because they don't know how to use the time they have. They are not happy. They have got nothing to do. Yet this should give them opportunities for thought, for leisure—indeed is not one of the purposes of education to teach people how to use their leisure moments? St. Philip Neri said that one of the great arts of life was to know how to waste time wisely. Time is on our hands but the spirit of leisure in which to deal with it is lacking. Our world gives men and women and children a far greater opportunity than ever they had for thoughtful leisure and yet the spirit that should benefit thereby is in danger of becoming hurt by it. People are unhappy. It isn't work that makes people unhappy. It

is the way in which they look at life that makes them unhappy. Now
110 the way a man looks at life depends somewhat on his capacity for thinking, and very often the power to think has dwindled through lack of practice. Men now can merely receptively watch and listen, and that is all; so that if there be nothing for them to be amused by, no place of entertainment, they are tired because they have got no power to interest themselves from within. There are children whom you can leave to themselves because you know perfectly that they will amuse themselves, and that with a minimum of material. There are other children who have always to be amused. The children who need always to be amused are not happy; they are restless, the provokers of trouble in a home. They must do something or annoy somebody. They must somehow fill out their time. They have no incentives, no power within to create interests. It must come from outside. They can sit and listen, or they can sit and watch, but they can't do anything unless it be provided them. What a troublesome lot they are! Now their fault is the lack of the power of contemplation, of quiet pondering. We grown-up people cannot take (so few of us) a railroad journey without a book, else we should grow bored, tired of our own thoughts, or the absence of them.

Thus the danger of speed is that it leads to mere haste and not to any deeper thoughtfulness. It is labour-saving but soul-losing, so that the symbol of modern life is a wrist-watch. You must always have the time in front of you so as to ensure your fulfilling your next engagement, regardless of whether it is worth going to. People feel they must go on, they must fill up the time somehow. Hence the day becomes crowded with obligations to go here and there. This has to be done and that has got to be done. Over it all, too, broods the heavy anxiety, "shall I be able to fit it all in?" Lists of things and people and places to be seen or visited. But what is your temper over it all? What is your attitude of mind to these? Is it hasty? If so you are losing the sense or the power of proper proportion. You will be irritated; you will easily be made angry. You will be easily hurt.

What we want is a greatness of soul which comes from contemplation; one means that has created this in the past is a love of the liturgy. The liturgical age is the age of thought, always. The return of the liturgical spirit is always the symbol of the return of the faith. It has always been so. If you study contemporary history at the time of the Reformation you will realize that the power of contemplation and the love of the liturgy were going. They are coming back in our own time. The missal, for instance, is a book of prayers. The missal is now displacing other prayer books. The missal holds great thoughts, great words, a great pageant, devised not by human instrumentality merely, as so often the prayer books are, but the long drawn thought of the Church, standing watching the dreadful sacrifice of Calvary, eternally aware of the majesty of God dwelling in her midst. Short, succinct, admirable are the prayers of the Church, brief, for she is ever busy, but they show no sign of haste. The liturgy evokes a spirit of leisure, secures for us quiet, serene and just judgments, unrushed by panic or popular outcry or an unreasoning spirit that may break over a people or a race.

Moreover, forever in our midst there is an abiding proof of the spirit of strange serenity and the power of ritual to create it—namely, the enduring parable of the Jew. He is clever, quick-witted, a lover of gold. These should have drowned him. But his religion is essentially contemplative, for his religion is full of ritual splendour, of quiet ceremonial and of chant. Hence the Jews have held their own as a people. They have preserved their individuality. They have impressed others, themselves little affected by others. They have dwelt alone and apart. To do this they have had little else left them but the majesty of their ritual, with its immemorial tradition, its fast days and days of high solemnity. This day perhaps they celebrate the memory of how they were wrested from the hands of the Egyptians and that day from Assuerus, and again on another day the feast of Esther is kept with its royal memories. They have endured all these centuries with nothing else to hold them but a venerable tradition and the majesty of a ritual. Of course they have been persecuted, and that has given them a unity and a fire. We should learn from them something of that devotion of theirs to the majestic ceremonial of the Old Law. But we should be strengthened and made permanent beyond them who have a mere figure or type—we who no longer have a symbol by way of worship. We actually show forth "the death of the Lord until he come." Thus the pageant of Holy Week will bring Calvary to us in order to set our minds to see the awfulness of God, the dreadfulness of the world we live in, and yet the serenity of a man of prayerful heart. Thus the mass becomes a doctrine and a lesson and an example, something that we believe and watch and copy. We witness it to recover something of its hidden spirit. Thus by contemplation we rise from mass leisurely quiet, serene, and therefore patient and just.

We men are in a hurry to finish our work. You won't take your work with you when you are dying. You will only take your soul when you go. That you have left your work unfinished when death summons you doesn't really matter. If it is good work, someone else will carry it on after you. If it is bad work, it is better it should go. You won't take work with you. Death ends it for you. It is only what you are that matters. What you do is left behind you. What you are abides. We have said God is serene because God is eternal, God is eternal. But so are we. In this sense are we eternal that we never die. Also are we immortal sharers in his immortality. Though at the last everything we have done will go, yet because of God we have a duty to be more careful of ourselves, of our thoughts, of our attitude to life, much more careful of the way we take things than of the things we take; much more careful of the spirit in which we do things than of the things themselves that are done. Are they great or small? We are too near to judge them. Are we great or petty? Our Lord says, "There is One that seeketh and judgeth." Leave all judgment to him. Seek greatness, if you can, within your life. Be never in a hurry. Love speed, if you will, but never haste, for speed and haste are separate things. A fast driver is not necessarily reckless. A slow driver may be more reckless than a fast driver on the road. It is not speed that we dread, but haste. It is the spirit, alert, eager, looking ("watching," is the phrase of our Lord), but perfectly self-possessed that we need to cultivate, because we are grounded upon the vast mysteries of faith, eternal and undying, because we rest securely upon God.

BOOK TWO

Part II: *The Family*

SERMON FOR ASH WEDNESDAY

The Home Fires

In speaking tonight, my dear brethren, and during these evenings of Lent, on the subject of the home, naturally and necessarily that subject has been chosen because it seems to be the subject most vital to us at this time; and the opinion that it is so will be confirmed in your minds by what you have read in your newspaper this morning of what the Pope said to the Lenten Preachers whom he blessed in Rome. It was the subject that he ordered them to preach about; the subject of the home, of marriage, of human love and human offspring, of the old and the young and their mutual relations each to each. The reason for its importance I suppose everyone of us perfectly realizes, for it is round this particular subject of the family that the war of the Church with the world now centres. The war there has begun. What is this war? It is the defence by the Catholic Church of the sanctity of human love and marriage, of the sanctity of the home against its enemies, because the Catholic Church with her divine mission comes not merely to speak to men of divine things, but to show them that human things, through Christ in human nature, have been made divine.

We are all of us aware of these attacks made on the home. We have noticed for ourselves, those at least of us who are midway towards their century, how the whole conception of the home, of marriage, in public estimation, in the public press, has vitally changed. Divorce, an older thing indeed than our time or our generation, has yet within our own memory been pushed forward with an impetus that increases year by year. Nor is it divorce only that has developed in momentum, but that which has always in human history immediately followed it, the custom or practice of birth-control. Once marriage has been followed by divorce in human society, then immediately this further step has always been taken, namely birth-control. For it is nothing new, nothing fresh, nothing modern—to use a word that for some reason people think to be a compliment. The conjunction of the two is something that occurs regularly in human history. Divorce has always been followed by birth-control. You will also find in all human history that birth-control in turn is followed by open immorality. Those are the three notes which have echoed together in harmony. Their arrangement is inevitable. One follows the other. For it is seen that divorce bears hardly on the children. So an age of sentiment and emotion forbids the little ones. Henceforward let no public stigma follow immorality; no public shame; let there be no children to go through their lifetime pointed at, begotten out of wedlock. That, men say, is now ended since there are no children. Thus to prevent hurt coming out of adultery its results are removed. Immorality follows. It is followed by no disadvantages. No one now need know about it. Round it is a hushed mystery of silence. Later it will be public, unashamed. Then along with these, this also has always followed a vital attack upon moral education. Children must be brought to believe that there is no certain truth. These things are inevitable, my dear brethren. They follow steadily upon the heels of divorce.

But for all that you must not scorn your fellows in this generation. It is true that they have forgotten the teaching that was customary among them. They have lost all sense of dogmatic principle. But then no moral doctrine has been taught them. Every man has been told that he should be a law to himself. Ever since the Reformation they have had that idea hammered into their minds. Its creed was the formula that there must be no church with dogmatic utterances. Man needs only his human conscience and the written Word of God. It sounded magnificent. It sounded as though men were breaking out of slavery. What it meant really was the dissolution of all society. Every man a law to himself. Then there can be no teaching outside of him greater than himself. No Church of Christ can tell him what he must believe or what do. That has been the fundamental idea of Protestantism. It has ruined all notion of a definite teaching of Christ. So do not blame the people of your own generation. They are going where they have been led. The only difference between this age and its elders is that it is fearless where they were hampered by prejudice. These are more logical, they are carrying out unashamed what their fathers covered in their hearts but didn't dare believe. Hence we have about us a pagan generation. But Protestantism must breed paganism, it must breed eventually a creed that denies all creeds. It must demand that no law of Christ should be imposed imperially. Its faith is the faith of the rebel. And a rebel has no lot or part with Christ. He gave the law. He taught the law. He loved the law. Law is the way of Christ. What we witness in the present generation outside the Catholic Church is the inevitable result of the new Renaissance paganism; the inevitable result of Protestantism, namely the destruction of all law, of all authority and the individual left entirely to himself.

Now, my dear brethren, to meet this ill the Catholic Church comes with a remedy. It is not her remedy, but the remedy of Christ. First she lays down definite principles on the subject of the home, of marriage, of the relationship of child and parent, of the relationship of parent and child. She lays down certain definite obligations which are not of her making, for of herself she imposes nothing.

She does but carry the message of Christ. She lays down her law, which is his law. She teaches merely what she has been taught. Christ, our Lord, spoke often of marriage. His first miracle was at a marriage feast when he turned water into wine. It is a subject which is often to be found in his parables: "The Kingdom of God is like to a marriage feast." For him evidently there was something sacred in the relationship of woman and man. It is not guesswork to suppose this, for in each of the four Gospels we are given his teaching on the sanctity of marriage, on the unbroken bond of marriage, that "they two shall be but one flesh." He laid down the law for us on this as on other subjects, and the Church does but echo it. What is revealed to us is the law of Christ, God Incarnate, he who knew man, whose hands had fashioned man, who knew therefore what was for man's good. But people say to us, "But those principles are impossible. No human power can obey them. You are asking too much of men." They say to the Catholic Church, "What do you know of love and marriage, who forbid it to your priests? What do you know of the capacity of human nature, to keep these rules of yours, you who know nothing of the lot of human kind?" They say that the law of Christ is impossible for human nature. But of course it is impossible for human nature. That is exactly why Christ came. He came not only with a law, but a sacrament. He came not only to teach, but to help. He came not only to say, "Thus shalt thou live. This is forbidden you." He came to give to human nature a divine aid to carry out the new commands. Thus he gave men a sacrament instituted for the family. Now this sacrament itself supposes that human nature is not capable of itself of the high things of Christ. But then we are not left to unassisted human nature. You must remember, when you hear men denouncing Catholic teaching as narrow or impossible, that the Catholic teaching on marriage is incomplete without the Catholic doctrine on the sacrament of marriage. The two fit in, one with the other. They are needed to explain each. The law of Christ is not complete without Christ's sacraments.

Thus Protestants, having abolished the sacrament of matrimony, of course in their own eyes find that the way of matrimony which Christ taught is impossible of man. Our Lord began with human nature. Here in this sacrament he supposes human love. People say to us again, "Your doctrine of marriage is impossible. It is wicked. It would link together reluctant people." But we are not in favour of linking reluctant people. We wish to change their reluctance. The Church echoes the voice of Christ. He came not to destroy, but to perfect human nature. He supposes a human love. If you find a generation which hardly cares about the sanctity of human love, is merely interested in human passion, thinks of marriage as a thing that comes and goes, builds it on choice or fancy, reconciles men to it or bids them separate because the two who have come together say their natures are incompatible, they are looking at it as though it were merely a contract, as though it were a mere business relation. In all our theory of it we suppose as its basis human love. Christ supposes that, builds his fabric of marriage and the family on that solid, flaming foundation: love and marriage and the sacrament, and the Catholic home.

For the Church, the ideal of the Catholic home is something which is no less sacred than the life of the cloister. It is a life which the Holy Family chose for its own. Those three, One supremely good, and the others only less so, those three whom we follow as our great leaders, were joined in a Holy Family, not a cloister, but a home. The Catholic home should be built as carefully as the cloister. The vocation to it studied as carefully, as prayerfully, as the vocation to the cloister, for it is a state made sacred with a sacrament whereas there is no sacrament consecrating religious life. Just as the Catholic home as an ideal is something sacred, so those that enter it should view it through holy eyes. Just as the cloister is built, arranged, adorned, to enable the individual religious to live his life more easily, so in Catholic concept, should be the Catholic home. There should be in it emblems of religion, especially the figure of the

Crucified; that supreme emblem of unselfishness should adorn the
122 walls of the home and be set over the marriage bed. There should be figures of the saints, prayer books, Catholic books, Catholic newspapers, holy water. People may laugh at these things. They may say: "But we have parted with all that. That is no longer possible. Why will you force on us the superstitions of an older age?" We say, "Well, has it changed for the better? What is your married life like after all? Have you now found happiness? Has the world found happiness by removing these sacred things? Is the married life easier because they have forgotten the Holy Family? Is married life easier with Nazareth forgot?" "Holy water and the other old-fashioned gadgets, what have these to do with us?" Well, their purpose is to remind you of the sanctity of the room where you live; to see it as a shrine of human love and affection; to enable you to realize the spiritual side of its responsibilities, its pain, its joy, birth and death and childhood, gathered within its four simple walls. You see the Catholic ideal is something which you cannot despise in practice without losing all the beauty the home has to bring you, for the Catholic ideal is ruined only by selfishness. These symbols help to peace and unity. Selfishness is the individual against the group. I for myself, whoever I am in the family, mother or father or child. I for myself. Family? That is forgotten. My own rights, not my duties. Not others. Myself. Ideals are always ruined by selfishness. They must needs be. An ideal lifts a man. Selfishness must drag him down. Those emblems of the faith have then their own purpose, to remind each member of the family that there is a holy purpose behind it, that they are to help one another to God. Wife and husband are united for a blessed purpose, namely that each might lead the other nearer to the ways of God. A child is given them, that a child might be led nearer to the Father over them. The child should be got ready for his ultimate home. Now selfishness wrecks this. What is the trouble in our time but selfishness? The old are selfish and the young are selfish. Neither is to be acquitted of blame.

Now here is a strange thing. People say now, "What a blessed thing is frankness! How wonderful at last to say what we mean! In the old days they did things roundabout. They weren't open-hearted. Now we say what we mean." But they don't. For instance they hate being questioned, the young by the old, or the old by the young. "Let's be frank," they say, yet they hate someone to say to them, "Where were you last night?" "Frank, not afraid. Utterly fearless." These are the things they prate about. "Let us put all our cards on the table, and let us talk quite openly, above board." But they hate frankness where it unveils them, so they curtain it about. Interference, they call the questioning, these people that preach frankness; somehow we wonder if it is because they are ashamed of what they are doing and won't be frank? Anyhow selfishness is really at the bottom of the trouble on both sides.

Of course there are homes that are real places of sanctity. There are homes which are homes, indeed. There are mothers and fathers and children who somehow make a success of family life against all the laughter of the world. There are quiet homes, full of joy and happiness, radiant. There are mothers of many children, whose home is a blessed success, and whose children, like pigeons, come homing to them long after they have left their home. Authority? Oh, yes, authority, but somehow made romantic, lit, somehow, with the flame of love. A mother can hold them and a father can hold them. Impossible? It is not impossible in a Catholic home.

You know, you owe it to the world, you of America, to rebuild the home. Divorce is older than your time, I know, and birth-control began outside your borders, but you have practised it and preached it more widely than all the world. You, don't you lead the world? Aren't your fashions the world's fashions? Aren't you the nation of progress? Don't men look to you, bow to you, and say that you hold the sceptre and the gold of the world? What will you do for it, you that are leaders? It carries responsibility, don't you think? Doesn't it mean something to have the foremost place in the world? Those that broke the home knew how to break it, they alone have the power to build it again from the beginning. You have that power. What we called a "house," you called it a "home." You spoke of one of your cities as "The City of Homes." You and the home! It was you that sang that song that is undying wherever our common speech has gone. Men gather in loneliness in far places under the quiet stirring of the stars and sing it; men in ships, bored with their life on the sea, have whistled it one to another in the watches of the night, pioneers and adventurers sing it, exiles have hummed it, your song which is "Home, Sweet Home." It is your song. You sang the beauties of home as no one, I suppose, has ever sung them. Surely you can find a home for home. "Do you remember after your Civil War was done," an English admirer wrote to Robert Lee, to offer him an estate in England, wanting to do something for him, for who could not admire the heroism, the exquisite courtesy of the man? But he wrote back, "I only want a quiet home in the woods," he said—"A quiet home in the woods." It is the old American ideal, the ideal of your fathers, a thing they fashioned wherever they went—a log cabin or whatever it might be. They had some such ideal as that. They had an ideal of a home, of some shrine that was sacred. Amongst you it still survives. No one can look on these great cities as America. They are indeed the places where is shown the splendour of your great architecture. But they are not homes, they are not you. All the while there are all sorts of people pouring in at your ports, who are not your people, so that the life here that men see is not your life. But beyond these cities there are wide plains and homes elsewhere, real homes, where the faith lingers, where men love and are not ashamed of love, where they look upon love as something enduring, where a child is welcomed, and no one forbids. Even in the city places love still lingers under the ashes. The fire still burns. Under the ashes it burns.

But the home of today must be a new home. That is the trouble of it. The old ways won't do. It must be something new with a new fashion about it, for the old ways are impossible—at least I suppose they are, with modern life. The common prayer of the house, the prayers of the children, heard by father and mother, the family together at home every night. What home in this city could you enter in the evening and be sure of finding the family there? Do you know any such home? There must be a few homes like this still left: yet they are not typical. On the whole I suppose those old ways are finished with. Nothing can ever bring them back again.

Moreover, in our time the many unmarried, the bachelors and spinsters, have introduced a new element into city-life. Thus, in the organization of modern society new forms of social life must be formed and met. So there has always to be something new in the world. You can't bring back the old fashions. That is not a matter of great concern. There are new forms to be invented. Who shall invent them but you. You were adventurers always. You are never afraid. Just as you tear down an old mansion and rebuild something more glorious in its place, can't you do it with the home? Can't you show the way to the modern world that will always follow you, imagining all you do is something greater than their own, holding some secret of your progress and success? Can't you fashion some new way of home under the faith, you of the New World that have it? Can't you rebuild it again? You had a Revolution, and out of the ashes of the cities and the homes that were charred you rebuilt the nation. You had your Civil War and you destroyed a civilization and remade it more wonderful than the age that had gone before it. Now here again, this is what men ask of you, those of the household of the faith, they say, pointing to your nation, "What you do, the world will do after you. Now give us a leadership here. Show us the new way of the home, under life's new conditions: human love blessed again by faith." Today ashes are on your brow. Under the ashes with which your brow is marked, was once a flame.

If you could stir the spent ashes, they could be reillumined, not now from beneath, but from above. With God helping, you may do such a blessed thing; not for your people only, but for the whole wide world, you can bring into fashion again the Catholic home, with its wonderful piety and its wonderful warmth of love, a home with God set in its midst. You can do it. Perhaps no one but you can do it. Perhaps if you don't do it, the thing for many generations will not be done. Others may come after you and show the way. Don't leave it to them. Do it while you have the power of leadership. Show the world, you that see it, the beauty of the home.

SERMON FOR FRIDAY AFTER ASH WEDNESDAY

Two in One Flesh

When Christ our Lord became man, he came to sanctify all the world. Not only was God made flesh, but through the blessings of the Incarnation flesh was to be lifted to the heights of God. Our blessed Lord came, partly at any rate, to tell creation that it was the creation of God, so that it might take a nobler view of the world about it, esteem others more because of their divine origin, and give us also a greater respect for ourselves. It was prophesied long before he came that when he came all flesh should see the glory of God, which means to say that our blessed Lord came that he might help men to see the goodness of the world they lived in, that he might take the hurt out of those things that were hurtful to human nature, and rob of their sting all the ministers of death! He came to teach each living soul that followed him to see life nobly, because it had been nobly planned. In a vision on a housetop to St. Peter, he showed him just such a vision of the world. Henceforward there should be no division between the clean and the unclean of creation, that division of the old law that forbade men to eat unclean things. All things that God had made were blessed to the eye that was blessed. All things were clean to the eye that was clean:

"What God had made, let no man call common or unclean." Such was the vision on the housetop, a vision of the grace that faith has to give to every soul alive.

So he took bread in his hands and blessed it. Food had hurt mankind. Food is needed by man's nature, but man can be intemperate in food. He took bread and blessed and broke and gave, and ever since that moment he has sanctified all human meals. Banquets have hurt man often. This is the hallowing banquet that has made sacred to the eyes of faith every meal. He took the wine cup. Oh what a deal of hurt the wine cup had done to human nature! What evils, what hurt, what degradation ever since the days of the pagan! How he had worshipped it, worshipped its very intoxication, as though in some strange fashion it lifted men above the earth. They saw the grape growing, but its power over men was so extraordinary they could not believe that its power was really begotten of earth whence it sprang, and so they wove their story that it was a god who had brought it. Yet that myth of theirs couldn't rob it of its hurt. But he took the wine and he showed all men that they should see in it not merely the blood that he gave in his real presence, but a choice emblem of Himself. Since his day man can see it no longer hateful, it need not be hateful; no longer hurtful, it need carry no hurt. "I am the vine," He said, "you are the branches." Can't you look at all life along this mystic way? Can't you take the things that, yes, might easily hurt souls and lift them and see them nobler because of him. The noblest things, the finest things that the world has to give, or heaven for that matter, are the things also that are necessarily dangerous, because they are great. Even the sacrament of his love may carry hurt to the unloving: "He that eateth and drinketh unworthily, eateth and drinketh judgment to himself." Hurt? He has robbed the world of the power of hurting humanity, if humanity will look at it through eyes that God has cleaned. "Become as little children," He said. There is no guile in the world to the clean eyes of a child. You see hurt. They see none. That is what he wanted us to learn, that the evils of the world are the evils we let hurt us. We need not allow any hurt to come. He took human nature, Himself, to his Divinity, and from that moment he lifted human nature to a new height. He taught man that flesh was not something evil. That matter was evil had been taught by the pagan philosophers that had gone before him, austere teachers, noble leaders of men. They said that man could only become noble by suppressing his body. Christ said no, flesh was to be sanctified, not suppressed. His flesh was sanctified, because it depended upon the spirit within. The body was fashioned by the hands of God, and the spirit of man dwelling in the body, could mould it, fashion it after the model intended by God. That is the secret of the saints. They fashioned their body, moulded it, controlled it. They were masters of themselves—their bodies were not a hurt to them, but a help to them, once they were mastered, once they were under control. If you let anything escape your control, however helpful to man it may be, if you let it escape your control, what can it do but hurt? Fire: How it has civilized mankind, so long as it is dominated! Water: It is something which carries life to the parched earth; yet something, that can get so much out of control as to be terrible, causing ghastly destruction as it goes. You have read in your paper today of that broken torrent in France.

God became man to lift man Godwards, to help man, somehow, to find God even in himself. He showed that the radiance of the spirit can dominate the flesh, helping it. That has been shown often since in the stories of the saints. Do you remember in the story of Bernadette, how she came, a little child, and knelt at the Grotto? How her neighbours told her mother all about it? How the child knelt there and seemed in conversation with someone, and how they were convinced that something was really happening to the child? At first the mother wouldn't believe them, but at last, on one occasion of the apparitions, she came and watched her child, and what she saw frightened her. There was the child, kneeling. Her

child, and yet not the child she knew. There was a light in the child's
130 face; in it was a radiance, the reflexion of the glory of God! From this splendour she turned shuddering, the mother turned from the child she had begotten. "That is not my child," she said. "That is not *my* child." Bernadette was transformed, lifted. It wasn't the child she knew. There was a radiance through her: grace, the spirit of God in-dwelling. What the mother saw was more than the child.

And long ago, what a hush in the crowd when another mother followed listening while he preached to the crowd! "Blessed be the womb that bore thee." "Thy mother waiteth for thee." They knew his mother. Was it because through her shone the glory of God?

That is the fruit of grace; that is an effect of the Incarnation, namely to take human nature, not to deny it, not to say it is evil but to say that though it can be evil it can also be charged with God, and so ennobled, made wonderful and splendid, a tabernacle of God. He took the things of earth, bread and wine, and made them forever blessed to us; and he took human love, which is also a danger, and he made of that a blessed thing. He blest the love of man and woman for he came of a woman and he was born in a human home. It was a home because a mother was there, and the mother's husband, and he, the mother's child. A Holy Family. If you look back in the records of the paganism that was just before his coming, you can see evil, even, in the family of those days. To us now, the family is blessed, sacred, but to read the story of Rome is to read of the terrible power of the father of the family, an awful power. In Rome the father had the power of divorcing his wife and selling his children to slavery. The power of the father of the family brooded like a menace over the whole social life of Rome. The mother, the children, were his possessions absolutely. With these he could do as he would. The family was ruining mankind when Christ was born in its midst. He sanctified the family and renewed the beauty of family love. The love of mother for child has always been thought beautiful and the love of father for child, beautiful too. A more beautiful love than that he taught man. "For this cause," He said, "a man shall leave father and mother, and shall cleave to his wife, and they shall be one flesh." And therefore he adds "not two, but one." He had bidden his followers leave father and mother. He had called them, he said, to a higher life, and he had said to his followers, "You must come out of your father's home. You must leave your folk behind you, else you are not worthy of me, not worthy of my following, of my fellowship, not worthy till you step out of your home." He said it not only of his own following, but of the love betwixt woman and man. They also must leave their home. They must, you know, else there will be danger. They must go out from their father's dwelling. They must live alone. He gave husband and wife power each over the other. He was lord of her. She was his queen. He set them in that strange, topsy-turvy world of his, that Kingdom of heaven let down on earth as a bride; in that strange kingdom there were to be two monarchs and each of the two was to rule the other with absolute sway. He gave power to the husband over the wife, yet he was hers, power to the wife over the husband, yet she was his. All his love was for her, and for none other. All her love was to be for him. Around about them he built a garden wall; they were to be garden-enclosed, intimate, fragrant, dear. He built a wall about them, the power of each over the other. This is his concept of human love: "A man shall cleave to his wife and they shall be one flesh." "Not two," He adds, "but one." He taught the power of each over the other, and of course the duty of each to the other, and of both to Himself, soul and body, body and soul. In that old form of marriage, ran the phrase: "With this body I thee worship," as though there was something sacred about it, and of course there is, or should be. It should be sacred, blessed, the reverence of love for the body, of the beloved. This is the teaching of the Incarnation. It is something that he came to give mankind; a new relationship of marriage, of power and duty, and of love over all. His view of it is of an intimate, personal relationship, their mutual knowledge intimate and their love.

132 It should be a great help to peace, that the intimate relationship of twin human souls is to be based on the fact that each knows the other. Why? Each should know the other that each may help the other. For that reason was woman created in the world. God made Eve that she might be Adam's helpmate. Helpmate in what? Surely in God. What other purpose have we here, we Christians? What other purpose is there in life; what fine noble, ultimate purpose but God, and God always and God only? And why are we here as a multitude, but to help one another to faith and hope and love? What is the Church for? Why the Pope on his throne? Why the priesthood? Why men and woman, and the children about their knees? The purpose of everything is that man should be helped by man, lifted nearer to God. If he falls and he is alone, there is no one to lift him. Why have we fellows? That in our fellowship we should lift each other, if we can, nearer to God, help one another. God-wards, to God.

Well, husband and wife are for that. To help one another. Their intimate knowledge of each other should guard, protect, inspire one another. Knowing each other's defects, even, should show them how they can help. This will not demand grudging human service of them. This means it is a privilege to help. For the Son of Man didn't come to be ministered unto. He came to minister. That is divine love; and human love has to follow the same road. The soul, too, must learn the ways, the customs, the courtesies of human love in order to develop love divine. Help one another then, lifting one other Godward, be you husband, be you wife. Husbands, have you helped your wife Godwards? Remember for that you were linked with her under the blessing of God. Wives, you, are you helping your husbands? Helping, not merely pointing out their evil, but helping them against their evil, not hurting, not hindering, but helping them nearer to God?

You see that this intimate relationship of man and woman in

love and marriage can be either a very great help or a very great hindrance. It brings them so closely together. Through it they are so intimate, each to each, that it is easy to jar nature on nature; character on character. It is so easy not to help, but to hurt. In the beginning the love ecstasy carries them forward, and then the fire of it dies down, and real life has now to begin, real life that forbids all pretence: The bandage is lifted now from the blinded eyes of love. The two made one are so close together that naught serves but the truth. After a short while, all their memories have been told to each other, all the stories of each other's childhood have been learnt by heart. Each one knows the other almost to tiredness, knows all the other's stories and familiar witticisms, hearing them over and over again. They may come to dread like a nightmare, when they entertain their friends, those things repeated which they have heard told so often, heard till they are sick and tired of them. All the element of surprise, the unexpected, which brings us such laughter and joy in life, all that, it would seem, is ruled out from their lives after a while. They know each other well, too well, through and through. They know each other's pet phrases and they know each other's weaknesses, each other's vanities, each other's virtues to the extreme point. They can see each other's vanity being played up to by others. They know where the flattery is to lead. They may easily let themselves grow weary of each other, till life becomes dull, dreary, drab with drudgery added to family responsibilities and cares.

You know even in our relationship to God there comes a period like this. We have experience of it in prayer. At the beginning there is a sort of love ecstasy, the wonderful beauty of the prayers of the child. There follow, more touching than a child's prayers even, the prayers of youth, threatened by danger, stirred by temptation, real, alive. The prayers of youth are beautiful, emotional, touched with the exquisite colours of the spring-time and then—well you know, what follows, the utter dreariness of prayer. All emotion gone, everything of that sort. If you pray you just pray because you know you should. There is no pleasure in it. There is no stir or uplift. There is no vision of the glory or the beauty of God. It is just the will, holding for us obscurely now, the friendship of God, feeling nothing though believing all things. Something like that happens not only in man's love of God, but the love of man for man. There is a danger of it, anyhow. All men know it and recognise it. Every priest has heard it over and over again in the confessional. A soul grown tired, weary, dreary: "Can I ever go on?"

My dear brethren, there is this in every mingling of human love; there is this because they are not two, but one. Two in one flesh, human nature so intimate and so united, yet so dangerously near its quarrel because made from the moment of marriage, one. It begins so joyously but the ecstasy of it passes. Unless it is based on something deeper than mere physical pleasure, the love that they call love will go. It isn't an animal passion, this thing our Lord is speaking about, a thing so blessed that he bids men leave their homes to find it, "come out from your father's house." To him it is something which is not of the earth, but is of the heavens: "It was said of old that a man could give his wife a bill of divorce, but I say to you, No." He is teaching the world a nobler way. He wants men to be more than men, to walk on the height of the hills where God is. The love he preaches is not mere passion; it is not of the earth! This love has wings. It lifts. It flies. It is something that carries men upwards. It stoops indeed only like the fairy prince who stooped over the sleeping beauty and wakened her from her slumbers to life again with a kiss. It is a love which is not just of the earth, but somehow touched with God's glory. A wonderful love, this, which Christ came to teach!

Not very long ago, a young man came to me whom I have known from boyhood. For almost every sacrament of God it has been my privilege to prepare him. Because he had some reason to suppose I knew him, he came to me with one of these stories of human love: how he thought that he loved and found that he hadn't; that it was just a love of the eyes, not of the heart, of the soul. Someone had attracted him; her external appearance held him; he thought it was love that fired him. It wasn't. Happily he had found that out in time, so he came to me with his story. He had spoken to her. He had told her what at last he had discovered for himself. He had found for himself that it wasn't love, but just the stirring of passion, so he said very simply to me, "Father, I know this will never last, and I have tried to explain it to her." She was not of his faith, she didn't believe as he did. She was taught other ways, in another faith. He said to me, "I have told her as well as I can tell her, that for me what alone can justify the intimacies of human affection, the embrace of marriage, is something deeper than physical pleasure. Spirit must be married to spirit as well as flesh to flesh. It must not be a mingling merely of flesh and flesh, but of spirit and spirit as well. There must be something deeper, higher, if this marriage is to last." He said to me, "I can't persuade her to see my point or believe me. Will you speak to her? Will you tell her what I really feel? Can you put in front of her something of what it means to us Catholics, this love between a woman and a man?" I did what I could. She listened but I don't think she understood me. She couldn't believe that a young man really could have such ideals. Unbelieving she reluctantly let him go. It is hard, isn't it, to explain such a view of love to someone who has never had the glory of our light, to whom these things have never come as a revelation, who are pagans in their outlook on marriage, who are easily reconciled to divorce, to whom love is but a thing that comes eagerly and is part of the joy of youth—something that they can conceive as not only begotten in the youth time, but lasting only with it, going when it goes. Not real, you say; just a dream, a romance, something that is not higher than earth but like one of those mirages, when as you look across the level desert you see city which is no city, but just a reflection of the earth. For us love is nobler, finer, "a mystery," says St. Paul. By which he means that it shows us the union between God and the soul, as intimate, as wonderful, as splendid as that. For St. Paul it was a sacrament, because it showed forth the union between God and the soul. There we have something in common with him. The soul is after God's image. The soul was made for God. Real love therefore will always hold, but this other love that is begotten in the eyes and dies in the eyes, that love must pass: "Fed by gazing, fancy dies in the cradle where it lies." There must be something in love besides this. Spirit must be mated with spirit; spirit must be in love with spirit as well as flesh with flesh.

He came, did our blessed Master, to take hurt out of hurtful things. He came to take that intimate relationship of husband and wife—one flesh indeed, "not two but one"—He came to take that, with its possibility of jar and danger, and make it something which should be always full of life. He transformed it into something which was divine and therefore unselfish, in which each thought of the other. Not the power given to each over the other was to be remembered so much as the duty that by each should be given to each: not the power they had, but the duty they gave. He showed love robbed of whatever might hurt it, showed it something that would ennoble mankind. But who is sufficient for these things? What human love is capable of these great heights? At the beginning of love—yes, then it is possible. Again it is possible here and there in moment of crisis, but on the long, level stretch, that dreary dull passage of the road, the difficult places, familiarity palls on human nature. "I have said all I can say. I am tired and weary. How can I go on, Father? How can I go on?" "She is so flippant." "He is so tired in the evening. All the burden falls on me." Oh, that ghastly self-pity! "I am the victim. He or she rides free. I am the slave. It is I that am serving. It is I that hold the home together, and no one but I." Self-pity. Are you not his follower, and didn't he come for service? Don't you realise that service is noble? That is where you rule. That is how you are a queen. A queen is not someone that walks in majesty wearing her jewels. A queen is someone who serves her people, at their beck and call. A king that is worth his kingship is not someone that domineers, not someone who only rules. To rule only is absurd. God on his throne is our servant. God is at our beck and call. Speak and he hears you. Cry and he answers you. He lifts you as a man is wont to carry his little child. "So," He said to the Prophet, "have I carried you, oh you children of Israel!" God ordains us to service, not self-pity. Let there be none of that which cheapens the heroism of mankind and dwarfs man to being a god merely in his own eyes. Let him be a servant in his own eyes, and glad to serve where love impells him. That is love, not of the flesh, but of the spirit, the love that Christ blest by coming and wearing human flesh.

SERMON FOR THE FIRST SUNDAY

The Unbreakable Bond

Sometimes, my dear brethren, we Catholics are asked by those outside the Church why it is that we forbid what seems so reasonable to them, the practice of divorce, and we must remember in any answer that we ever make to them that our sole reason, really, is the word of Christ. We forbid it merely because he forbade it. We forbid it because we believe him to be God.

We can, of course, afterwards, after we have realized that it is precisely his teaching, we can discover all sorts of other reasons which seem to our mind to justify it, to justify his action. We can bring in the experience of mankind. We can show, merely by pointing to the pages of history that wherever divorce has entered—and it has come not unfrequently in the history—wherever it has been introduced, society has fallen. You could show this from the records of the past. You could show the little value of divorce as a social institution. You could show the hurt it has done to the child. You could bring all sorts of other arguments, based on experience or social science, but those are not our reasons. Our reasons are the words of Christ. He forbade it, and we, believing him to be God, who knows all things, knows human nature, planned the destiny

of man, we are sure that his advice—indeed, not advice, but com-
140 mand—is of obligation on all men, that all who know it should follow it because he is God. He knew quite well, when he was laying down the doctrine that marriage could not be dissolved, that he was teaching something severe to human nature. He says Himself, "It was written of old," referring to the legislation of Moses, "it was written of old that a man could by a bill of divorce put away his wife, but I say to you, no." He knew he was teaching a higher doctrine, something harder to mankind, but he did not merely teach it. We know it to be a principle of divineProvidence that God never compels any human being to do anything without giving him the power to do it. God is just. God does not say to man, "Thou shalt do this," and command him to do what is above him. If God lays an order, God gives power. If it is God's will, God wants it done. He won't leave it to mere erring humanity. He gives grace. He brought in more severe legislation, but he gave a sacrament to enable man to fulfil his law.

These people outside the faith who would introduce divorce, do so because they have denied the sacrament of marriage. It doesn't appear in their religious code. They retained, or they did for centuries, the mere blind law and denied the sacrament. They have found the observance of this law at last to be a thing impossible. Why, yes, having denied the sacrament of marriage, of course it is impossible—to give a law and not say there is extra help for the soul of man. Christ knew what he was about. He was giving something more austere than the world had known until his time, a single wife, an unbroken bond of marriage, unbreakable except by the fingers of death. And yet he knew man, for he had made him, and so he established that blessed sacrament of marriage whereby he gave men grace and women grace to fulfil the law that he laid down. He laid on men, then, the obligation of an unbreakable marriage, and he bade mankind go to the sacramental sources of grace and so live with the help of that.

Now we, looking at divorce after the event, can see the evil that it has wrought in the children of men. We can see for instance that, because divorce has now been made popular, accessible, cheap, as they say (Is it cheap, do you think, or dear really to society?), none need hesitate in choosing a helpmate. There is no need to trouble over the choice or to take care of it. If the partnership does not work, the partners can separate and begin again. It is only a passing engagement. It is something that finally doesn't matter to human life.

If you know when you have been given change at the counter that unless you look at it at the moment and report a mistake immediately, no errors will be acknowledged or corrected later, that no one will listen, to your complaints or pay any attention to you—well, you are careful to count your change. It is now or not at all, so you take pains to see that you have been charged correctly. But supposing you knew if you came back next day they would still listen to you and correct errors you asserted they had made? You would hardly trouble about counting at the time. If it is so easy to change later, why bother about being very careful now? To introduce divorce is therefore to open a flood gate. A torrent will follow. "Divorce must be allowed only when it is necessary." But once established it is an ever-widening breach. Once possible for any reason, it will soon be made possible for many reasons.

And again, we know, too, another result of it. We know quite well that supposing people know they have got to live together whatever betide, they have in that fact a very potent reason for making up any quarrel they may have; since they can't separate, they have thereby a very powerful motive for peace. They must live side by side; the same walls must enclose them; well, since it is so, what is the use of quarrelling? Thus they will more easily find a way out of their strife. Men agree to be patient when they see that they can't alter something, and that there is no better way of dealing with life. Any other way weakens man. Thus if he can be sure of getting divorce, he has little motive for trying to reconcile differences that

must inevitably arise. He just drifts with the tide.

And again we know, for all men who have studied the society of our day tell us so, that divorce has made sin easy by making adultery easy. There is less motive for not indulging in it. If a couple does not get on, they can therefore separate, and since adultery can but result in a new marriage why not make a trial of it? The door thus is opened in all sorts to other crimes.

The Catholic Church, indeed, allows the possibility of separation. Supposing married people can't get on together, supposing that it is absolutely impossible for them to get along together, supposing they have tried their uttermost and best? Very well, it is a pity, and it is plain that they must live apart; only neither can remarry. Isn't that hard? Yes, but the Church claims no power over the word of Christ. She has no power to modify his teaching. It is strange, isn't it, of Christians to say to us, "But surely you will alter the old ruling to meet the times and new demands." Times? Demands? We live by eternity, his unbroken Word is eternal. The heavens, the earth may pass. No word that he spoke shall pass. These words which we echo he spoke.

Hard? You see it is perpetually an appeal to sentiment. If any man attacks you on divorce, his argument is always sentimental. He will say to you, "I know a case—" "A case," mark you. Not your reason, he is not appealing to that. He is appealing to your heart. He is getting away from the principle. It is not the teaching of Christ that he is looking for, but merely a way to ease the difficulty of man. But you know that any principle is hard to live exactly. To be just, to be generous, to be always truthful—are you asking these of us? Why surely. Christ did. "But I shall lose by following justice, generosity, truthfulness." Oh, yes, you will lose but you gain, you know, something even greater than you lose. You and I have got to live by faith. Hard? "I know a case—do you expect the woman to be faithful? He is shut up in an asylum for the insane." "He is a criminal. Are you going to tie them together until death parts them?" Yes, Christ thinks even thus nobly of mankind. He thinks a woman's heart or a man's heart can bear even that strain. You see how wonderful in his eyes is human love. Indeed, lit with the divine grace of the sacrament, even such a love, constant, enduring, unselfish, is possible to mankind! It is not we who despise men; we lift them. We believe in their power to endure. We say that love is really enduring. It can be enduring to a heart that wills to think it so. Hard? Why yes, it is hard, but to be always truthful, or always to behave like a gentleman in life is hard: "I know a case—" You are going to get hurt by it over and over again. Of course you are. People will just jostle you in the subways of life. They will just fight over your head for the first place. You can do what you like, of course, jostle as they do or be ready to be courteous in spite of all. Supposing you say, "Well I have my own idea of what a man should be like. I believe in trying to behave like a gentleman whatever betide," then you have a principle to go on and if you suffer on its account, you know really you are conquering. Your principle is worth more to you than the inconvenience of being left behind. Your ideals are finer than those of the people who trample on you as they go by. They, they are just beasts fighting. You, you walk serene like a man.

Hard? Why, of course it is hard, and so is all of Christ's teaching. "Blessed are the clean of heart." That is hard. "Blessed are the poor in spirit," "Blessed are the merciful," "Blessed are the meek," "Blessed are they that hunger and thirst after justice," to hunger and thirst after justice, that is too hard. It is so easy to watch the little injustices of human life untroubled and to use your influence merely to get yourself out of difficulties. But blessed are they that hunger and thirst after the justice of God.

It is hard, this teaching on divorce, but it is Christ's word, and that is our comfort, and that, indeed, is the very root of all our faith. We have got no other motive than that in forbidding it, that it is his teaching. All the social arguments are arguments that pass. They are good arguments but they are not the real arguments. They are the arguments brought in afterwards to justify the doctrine to those that need to find an external justification of it. But for us the words of Christ are enough. We can easily let all the rest go.

Again, the union of love is the oldest and strongest union that we know in the history of man. Yet the State claims all sorts of powers to deal with marriage. We answer, "Yes, you have got a perfect right to deal with the civil effects of marriage. That is your power. You have a right to regulate all sorts of things dealing with that aspect of it, to legislate on them as you will, but not to touch the bond of marriage. It is older than you are. It will be there still when you have gone." Supposing, as it well may be, that barbarians one day burst over the civilization that we know; that the whole of it is brought down about our ears, as all other civilizations have been brought down, and that all our fine towers lie in ruins to be rediscovered centuries after. Yet we know surely that even though our civilisation passes the family will abide. It seems so weak, this little group of father and mother and child, huddling together against the storm outside them, tyrannized by politics, assaulted by unclean passion, denounced as dull by wretched scribblers who earn pay and publicity but no respect by their pens, and yet it is older than they, more venerable. They will soon be forgotten and for always. If it be forgotten it will return. It is the source of all our culture. Out of it came the State. Out of it grew the tribe, till the tribes settled and grew in the ways of culture, and built cities and made laws. But the family began this. The family will outlive it. It is older than they. If you go down among the pagans who have never been debased by an evil civilization, a civilization of an industrial age, if you go to the pagans you will find, perhaps, polygamy. You will find that a man may have many wives, but that he has no wife that another man can take. You will never find the sanctity of marriage in that sense lost even among the pagans, unless they have been degraded by a civilization that has failed.

Only a few months ago I was told away off in South Africa of the Basutos, a tribe with the grace of natural life; they have a language far richer than ours, with far more exquisite touches of expression, and far more delicate shades of meaning. You cannot get into English the beauty of some of the phrases they use. They are an old tribe. Among them the Catholic missionaries have been busy. Today the paramount chief of them is a fellow-worshipper with us—holding the same faith, the same Lord, the same God. When he was a young man, a prince in the tribe, he went to the Catholic missionary and asked to be instructed and received into the Church. The priest said to him, "No, I can't take you." "Why?" "You are drinking too heavily. You are not fit for the kingdom of God. You are just going the way of the beasts. Go your way. Don't come to me." "But I am a prince," he said. "Were you a king I would not have you. Not for you the kingdom of God." However he came back after a time and said to the priest, "I have finished with drink," and the priest said, "Very well, now I will instruct you. We will begin." When the young man came to the end of his instruction he said to the priest, "What am I to do? You know I have my wives. I can send away the rest of them but there are two I have above all the others whom I love. I think I love them both equally. Both are of noble lineage, both come of the houses of kings. I don't know which of them to choose. I can't choose now so I must wait. God, I know, will show me a way to settle my perplexity. It is not my fault that it has come on me. He will show me a way out." Now these two women realised somehow that the prince wanted something and that one or the other of them stood in the way of his obtaining it. They were pagans, mark you, but they had felt something of what Catholicism meant to the man they loved. So in their blind pagan way they went out of the kraal in the royal village and wandered on to the wide, rolling veldt, open, treeless, the sun overhead, the arching blue sky. There they prayed to the unknown God of the Christians that if they stood in the way of the man they loved, he would do what he willed with them. Let him take one or other of them in death. As they prayed out of the sky came the lightning. One of them was struck dead there and then. The other came back and told her tale. Her husband became a Catholic. He is now the paramount chief, one of the great Catholics of that colour which has a majesty of its own, and he is a Catholic by the grace of a woman who guessed, somehow, that here was a unique way to show love. Savage? Uncivilized? Compare that woman with the women whose lives you read of in your daily press. Do you think it was she who was the uncivilized? You say perhaps that she had strange old-fashioned ideas of love. Old-fashioned? Why, yes, eternal. She, though pagan, had some concept of love. To her it was something so great that under its impulse gladly you would die just to set a man in the way he should go. Oh, if the Christian women of our time, women of culture, of civilization, had half the delicacy of this woman, it would be a nobler world, less vulgar, less flaunting, less gross. Let them learn from this the tenderness and the strength of love.

For us, my brethren, the word of Christ matters. It is his law. Other reasons for what he orders there are, but none of them matter compared with that reason which is higher than reason, the glory of the faith. For us that matters most and must matter. We accept of marriage as an unbreakable bond. An unbreakable bond? We don't deny that to the people who chatter to us about freedom. We say, Yes, it is a bond, just as he said his teaching was a yoke and a burden. There was never any pretence in the preaching of Christ. He didn't pretend that things were easier than they really were. When he taught his doctrine of the indissolubility of marriage, the apostles were scared of it. When he laid down his doctrine that henceforth no divorce was to be allowed they said, "Why then, it is better for a man not to marry than to venture into such a hard way," and he said, "For them that are called, it is better, but not for all." Not for all. It is a bond. It is a burden. It is a yoke. It is something laid on a man, something that binds him. Yet a man can be bound and free. When you talk about a nation achieving its freedom, you mean that it now governs itself, you don't mean it has no government at all. You mean that it has broken away from tyranny, and tyranny means that someone is ruling it without the justification of law. You mean that whoever has possessed himself of power is lawless, using force but not using law. A man should be free, and that man is free only who is of himself obedient to law. No man is free that denies all obedience, just as no man is free who obeys because he must. A free man is a man who walks upright, upright in his soul and takes the law, justice and truth, all those fine things that all your fathers thought worth dying for, takes all those fine things and says, "I will obey them because I should obey them. I will obey them without force or tyranny. I will obey the law." Now that is freedom. A bondage, yes, but the bondage of free service. Thus too does God's authority bless the free choice of a woman, of a man. Marriage consists of their free choice, and God's blessing on them and holding them by the bond of love. For us the word of Christ suffices. When they question you about our doctrine, go back always to that. Let that be your answer. "Will the church ever change?" She cannot, for she cannot alter the teaching of Christ. She is here to explain it, and you and I are here to listen to it, and listening, to obey it. We know that his words are not the words of blind power but of wise power directing the society of men. We know that those that follow him though they be laughed at, jeered at, have created and continued the only society that will survive. We know we carry with us the healing of the nations. One day people will realise, centuries after, that in the heart of a civilization that was corrupt, we kept our part sacred and because of it some remnant of our civilization endured. The ways of the others will be forgotten, or described in far-off days as unbelievable. We alone who follow Christ in a world of madness are safe, on his assurance, who knows all.

SERMON FOR THE FIRST WEDNESDAY

The Vocation to Marriage

The one great result, my dear brethren, of believing in the unbreakable bond of marriage is, or I suppose should be, that people are more careful how they enter into that irrevocable life. Yet often a priest hears it said to him by one or other who wants to be married that the real reason that is impelling them to marriage is that by it they will escape from the bondage of the home. "I don't love; at least I can't exactly use that word to describe my feelings," they will say to the priest, "but honestly, I am very tired of home. I have had so much to do. I am so much interfered with that I will take this or any other opening that gives me my release." Or again, sometimes at least, cross-questioning those you know well enough to cross-question, you will find that they look on marriage as something which will give them a good time. Now all these reasons show complete misunderstanding not only of marriage but of life. For us, my dear brethren, under the faith, we have to look on the married life as a distinct vocation, as solemn, as personal a life, as life is in the cloister. The vocation to marriage is as definitely, divinely planned as that. It is not even a mere alternative to the cloister. "I haven't a religious vocation, or a priestly vocation, and therefore I

must go and marry." That is not a true argument. Life is not quite
150 like that. Sometimes in the books one reads, in the novels, people go off to the cloister because they have been crossed in love. That could not be a justifying reason for even attempting a vocation; but though the idea is silly to us, it is also tragic, as it shows us what an insipid view the author must have of every sort of life. It would be impossible for the soul to continue in religion under such a mere negative impulse. So, contrariwise, people will say, "I have no vocation for religion or priesthood, and therefore, I must marry." That is not a true argument; or at least that is not a real argument. There must be something far more solemn than that. Moreover, today the single life is being lived increasingly outside the cloister. As far as we can tell, more and more people have a vocation from God to a state neither of marriage nor cloister, but to a very different way of life. Sometimes perhaps the single life is sought out of selfishness, because men or women love too much the comforts of their world. To marry would be almost to halve their income, and at least to share it with someone else. They have been accustomed to a definite amount of material comfort so that they have not the necessary unselfishness to enter into the married state. Or as a further reason they defer marriage to a date beyond their endurance of chastity and because of selfishness they open the door to troubles, evils of the soul.

God has his own designs for each one of us. Each of us has his own way of life. The married life is as much a vocation as the life of the cloister and marriage should dominate the life of the married as the life of the cloister dominates the life of a nun. She has her religious vocation and so she has her religious life to live. Now that fact limits her life. She has probably to fit into her days somehow a great deal of external activity, but also a certain amount of religious activity has also to be fitted in. If she be a good religious, she will not allow the activity of life to interfere with her religious obligations. Her first obligation is to her own development, and she may have to diminish her external activity if she finds it to be hurting the religious obligations of her state. What is true of the religious, is true, or should be, of the married person, wife or husband. Marriage is a sacred vocation of God. Just as the nun, under her solemn obligations of the cloister, must not allow external activity to reach so high a point as to interfere with her spiritual obligations, so also a man or woman must not allow external activity to reach so high a point as to let it interfere with the obligations of the married state. Here too then, is a positive vocation, dominating, limiting the amount of activity to be given to other works, howsoever good. This most, this uttermost, is the solemn obligation of their lives.

We must suppose further that one who is called to a life of marriage, will not be safe outside the married life. Those who have been called to it and have not accepted it because of their selfishness, will live lives maimed to the end. Something in them that would have found expression through human love will never find its expression. God's work will be left undone. God is wise, which means that God acts for a definite purpose. A fool drifts. A wise man plans. God is wise. God made every soul for a separate purpose. Each was born for that. Every soul of us came here marked by God for a definite work in life. Moreover Providence of course guides the fashioning in the world, of the human lives that intermingle. God is over all. So God fashioned our soul deliberately for a work and gave an individual purpose to the individual soul. This purpose is not fulfilled in a single act of life. A nun doesn't fulfil her vocation by the mere act of entering the cloister. That is just one stage of her vocation. A vocation is something always opening, unfolding. It is the pageant of a life, the drama of a life, moving on. You watch a play, and you see a character unfolding itself in scene after scene. The dramatist who wrote that play shows you the character unfolding to its climax, and then achieving its fulfilment or failing under it; but in the theatre a life unfolds to those that sit and watch. Here it should unfold to the actor himself. Now God has planned each life of ours as a story, scene following upon scene. You can go back to your childhood, and you can see already how gradually all sorts of things that at the time you hardly noticed have led on to what you are today. Just a chance acquaintance ripening has moulded you. Not a chance acquaintance really, but one divinely planned. It seemed by accident. But this is God's world, and there are no accidents. It is only God's plan gradually fulfilled. God has a purpose for every soul. If you follow it, and as you follow it, your life opens and leads on. You don't notice the plan at the time. Indeed it seems probably as though life were almost at the mercy of anything and anyone. It is not really so. Thus a biographer dealing with his man shows you the gradual unfolding of his character: from his birth almost, the destiny seems to have marked him for its own. So has it been with us.

Moreover if we find our vocation, we find a place where our talents at least will have their opportunity, for there must be an opportunity always for the talents God gives to man, since we were given our talents for use. God made us for a purpose, and because he meant us to do something, or be something, he fitted us for the work that awaits us. Every soul has its work, and because that soul is destined for a work it is divinely endowed with the gifts necessary to do the work. Further, from the parable we know that we must use our talents else a severe judgment will await us at the end.

Now there are souls that can only develop the gifts within them through the married life. Their souls left solitary, would be maimed, never achieving their real richness. There are others whom he has designed for the way of the cloister—separate, untouched, alone. Each has to find the place to which God calls him and for which he was destined and endowed. His vocation is a positive way of life. The married life, if it is God's choice for you, will contain for you the highest thing you can ever do. One way of life may be higher than another way of life, one way of prayer higher than another, but this can be only in the abstract, for that is highest for me which

God has called me to—whatever it may be. To do God's will is the noblest thing; by this only are both cloister and the way of marriage justified. Now which is God's way for me? That is what I have to find out. That is what I have to discover. To do this is something evidently to be studied solemnly, something that I have to go into with careful thought. I should not drift into my life's work. I may, of course, but that were foolishness. I shall only achieve success if I find that way to which God has called me, for which he has fitted me, and where alone such talents as I have shall find their fitting result.

To come back then, we say that marriage should not be looked at as an escape from the home, not a place where one can have a good time in life. Not that. Not even a cure for some unnatural desire. Sometimes you hear this advice given to people who have a habit of unnatural sin: "There is something wrong with you. What you want is married life." But married life is a holy way, not a remedy for unnatural evil, nor a legitimate escape from trouble that is not born of natural desire. Lawful desires are achieved in matrimony, not unnatural desires. To remedy such a nature you must change the nature, or you must discover some way in which these desires can be sublimated and made whole. Matrimony is no cure for something which is contrary to the nature that God gave us. It is a positive vocation to which God has destined, I suppose, the vast majority of mankind. It is the opening of a vocation. It is not a cure in that sense; not a remedy in any sense like that.

Again it is not a romantic dream, though there may be romance in it. There is romance in every life for the soul that cares to seek it. But marriage is no romantic dream. It is real and earnest. Marriage is a solemn vocation, something for which a soul must prepare. A doctor has years of study to equip himself for the work he has one day to do. A lawyer has to undergo his own preparatory studies fitting him for his subsequent career. If he neglects his studies, whether he be doctor, lawyer, priest, or whatever else, and because of his neglect fails in some single instance in his profession, because he never studied in his schooling years, he is to blame for the mischief that follows his ill-done action. A soul that the priest hurts because he never studied properly in his seminary days is a soul of which God will one day demand from him, the priest, an account. A body mangled through the ill knowledge of a doctor or a case in the courts that goes awry due to neglect in preparatory studies—these men are answerable for the damage they have caused. These are ignorant, who should not have been ignorant, ignorant therefore with a culpable ignorance for which they must be blamed. Now do you think that marriage is not also a profession needing preparatory study or that people can just drift into marriage and expect, somehow to find their way through?

You know human nature. You know your own, its curious outlook, personal, unique. You know the strange self of yours, how it hides from you, how difficult it is really for you quite to analyze your own character. Can you with less difficulty understand the characters even of those you love? You, that perhaps enter so easily into partnership with another soul, do you realise it has its own life that is worth studying, reading about, that it is a soul as complicated as your own? The Catholic Church has had a great deal more to say about marriage than merely lay down her laws for it and leave it. She has provided her children with the results of her experience of the conduct and direction of human souls. Surely it is only fair to that other whom you have joined to yourself, only fair to yourself, that you should try and discover if there be not laws and principles, if there be not some way of conducting the married life as a positive vocation so as to get the best out of both your lives. The best of you will be called out only in married life. That, remember, is what we mean by a vocation. Your own heart, your own life, your own character need precisely these conditions of marriage if the best of you is to be brought out as it could and should. Marriage is a door into a life wherein your talents and capacities are tried to their uttermost, and you, all that is best in you, developed, and an opportunity offered you in which to achieve your best. That is the life God made you for. That is the life you will fit into, but carefully, foreseeing, watching, learning, above all praying, asking God to help you to deal with this other soul so that you may lead it always nearer to his ways. Actually you are hurting one another. Not for that were your lives mingled. Not for that did he link you once by love. Are you lifting one another Godwards? It says in Scripture, "He who is alone has no one to lift him." Eve was given to be a helpmate to Adam, not a burden, that she might help him nearer to God. She failed at first but in the end she triumphed. God has planned then his direction of the human soul, has endowed it with definite and personal gifts, and so intended that not drifting, not blundering, but deliberately and carefully it should build up its own life.

We say then that marriage is a positive life to which, perhaps God calls you. Remembering that, you must give to it the fulness of your capacity. To make it a success you must put all your heart and mind to it. Thus her married life is above all things the supreme business of the mother. Success in other lines will not compensate for failure here, so nothing must be allowed to interfere with that, with her obligations of motherhood and wifehood. These come first. Let women be emancipated by all means. Allow them to enter, if you will, into every business or profession that there is; but if they marry, their family obligations are their firsthand no piety, no parochial activity, no hobby of amusement must be allowed or encouraged that hurts the conduct of the home, for this life of marriage carries these obligations for her. This is justice. All other activities are but charity. Great as charity is, justice comes first. Before you give alms you must pay your lawful debts to those that are your creditors. The mother's creditor is always the home. Social life, kindness, religion, these are duties to God. Yes, but this also is a duty to God. That is the reason why the Church has spoken so nobly of motherhood. That is the reason why she sets as our leader the maiden Mother of God. To her the ideal of motherhood is most 156 noble, because it is most unselfish. A mother has the pains, but she has also the rewards of love. Even has the Church claimed it as a title. It is indeed the very name that we give her: our high praise of her is that she is "Mother Church." We think of her in her greatness as though she were almost a mother. Hence the same title seems to us the finest thing we can say of a human soul. The mother is the centre of the home; and if the home is hurt in our day, by whose fault do you think it is that such a thing should have come to pass? If the family has failed, whose is the cause of failure? Everybody, perhaps in part to blame, but she perhaps most blameworthy who with such little wisdom has dealt with human souls, most difficult and most delicate of instruments, linked to her by duty and love. She has her quiet time for thinking. Though all of her day is busy, she has many a time to think; and in such times she must study each soul committed to her and puzzle out by memory and her experience and instinct how to deal with each. She is the mother, even of the man that calls her wife. She is the great protector of the family. So we think of her. Always a mother is carved for us holding her child, or with outstretched arms. That is the mother's place in the world, in the home. Indeed she is the home. It is not a place really, this home of which men sing. It is her heart. She is the priestess of this intimate sanctuary. She is the mother. What more is there to be said?

There have been days when our people have been persecuted. She all that while was the inner shrine of the faith. There have been ages when the exercise of everything that is holy has been prohibited us. Then exactly the Catholic family, and in the family the mother, has been the centre of the Catholic shrine. There have been ages when the voice of pulpit was hushed, silenced by the persecutor. Then she was the only preacher in the only temple of God. Altars were levelled. Her knees became the only altars, where age by age the children learned their faith. No catechism class existed, no

Sunday school. She was their catechism class and Sunday school, she was the Church of God for them. She taught them their prayers; that they kept the faith was due to her. Oh, that age of valiant motherhood! Not mere love had she, but wisdom, too. Indeed love must include wisdom, for love is no mere passion or impulse, not even a mere instinct like that with which the hen gathers her chickens about her. Love is not that merely. Love includes wisdom also, for character comes in as part of love. A mother's love then is a vocation, a calling; so too is the love of father and child. Into that sanctuary God calls some human souls as he calls others to the cloister. A way for each; and to each of us a call of God to follow the way. And to all of us, whosoever we be, St. Paul speaks those solemn words, "Walk worthy of your vocation."

What is your vocation? What is your place in the home? Whatever it is, realise God called you to it, positively; gave you the gifts to manage it. If you have failed, not his has been the fault. One day he will ask of you what you have done with your talents, how you have dealt with these souls. He will question your patience, your wisdom, the care with which you searched for them and used them, whether you have studied to understand them as the teacher studies the children in her class. You have had individual souls in this group joined up with you. Love is not enough to help you to deal with them, nor is power enough. You need the blessed trinity of wisdom, power and love.

God will surely give us the grace to do whatever be our duty in the way to which he has called us. Pray we must that we may do our work, for it is not ours, but God's work, and that we be worthy of the vocation to which we are called, because it is God who has called us to it. It is a highway of life, this, high and noble, for there can be nothing petty or small in a world planned by God.

SERMON FOR THE FIRST FRIDAY

Courtship Days

Since, my dear brethren, marriage must be a distinct vocation for certain souls, a life, that is to say, for which the divine Wisdom destined them, and for which also the divine Wisdom definitely endowed them (provided them with the character and the gifts necessary for such a life—not spiritually only, but naturally), so also it must demand from those that would enter into it some sort of preparation. No man, no woman, should do the work of God negligently. It should be done, if it be the work of God, thoroughly, that is to say, with due preparation as well as afterwards with faithful care. And that means not merely that each boy or girl is apprenticed, as it were, to the trade of family life under their father and mother, watching to see how such a life can be well lived, learning wisely of such as have made a success of marriage, not merely that they are preparing in that way for the life itself, but that they are preparing themselves no less for that other soul who shall, under God's blessing, one day share their life with them. Each has not merely to study marriage as a life lived under the divine command, but to study also the other soul, to which it is to be joined, as we believe by a divine destiny. Thus we hold that lives are interwoven

by the Providence of God, and that marriages are made in heaven
160 by the foreseeing will of God.

All the more is it necessary that each should know the other well before the married life begins, since in these days each has a right to choose who the other is to be. There was a time, almost now forgotten, when the social structure of society left with the parents, the choice of a husband or wife for their child, when the parents of the girl or the boy settled the marriage beforehand. There are even now countries in Europe where that custom still prevails. If it be done by the parents, as once upon a time it was, then of course, the boy or girl have nothing to do but accept the one given them. This was not an obligation, but merely a custom—but so it went. But in a society differently organised, where the man and the woman have free choice, where nothing is settled by an outside influence, but only these two wills are joined, it is more than ever necessary that he and she choosing should know as clearly as they can whom it is they choose. In an age where immediately after childhood comes independence, where each one settles for himself whom his wife is to be, or at any rate can settle where he shall offer his heart, it is essential that each should know the other before they enter into partnership, that they should make experiment of each other's character, to discover whether there be community of taste and interest between them, for else the choice may be a mere matter of passion. After marriage the passionate choice of a pretty face will lift some time or other. There must be something more enduring than that if soul is to be held to soul. There must be something they can speak about to each other besides their own affections each for each. There must be some community of thought, of soul, else boredom will wear down love. While there is time, therefore, they should make experiment of each other, before the act is irrevocable, before the bond unbreakable is sealed. For this experiment and knowledge, the days of courtship are essential in the modern organisation of social life. There is no harm in courtship in itself—indeed it is necessary for the due and proper choosing of marriage at last. Nor is there any shame in it, though there is something in it which provokes to laughter those who make fun of the solemnities of life. It is a prevailing jest in comedy to create humour out of the jest of the lovers, out of the bankruptcy of love's language; its dull repetition, the childishness of lovers' speech. So at least it seems to those not in love's secret at the time. Is it comic? Only the solemn things are ever comic. Comedy is just something solemn and dignified, or it may be even tragic—pulled a little out of shape. The more dignified the situation, the more comic it can become. The solemn, pompous man who sits, thinking mistakenly that there is a chair for him to sit on where there is none—his extreme dignity makes his unexpected fall comic and laughable. The scene is only comic because it was meant to be solemn. So is it also with love. Because it is great or even tragic, you can make fun of it cheaply. Anyone can make fun of God.

There need be no shame in the courtship that leads up to marriage. There need be none; but no one who watches human nature, or reads of it, or listens to it when it wishes to unburden its soul to him, but must realize that such a time is, anyhow, a time of danger—not evil necessarily, but dangerous to those who are young and inflammable and passionate. Those that are in it or are entering it must walk warily, a little bit afraid, not of each other so much as of themselves. The tradition of the Church, the custom of the Church in all Catholic countries is, I suppose, for that reason, to urge early marriages on her children. It is a pity to drag out this courtship stage longer than need be. The danger met and dealt with increases the strain each time, and with it is increased also the difficulty to withhold the strain, support it, bear up against it; for you can only meet strain with restraint. Hence it is certainly a dangerous period, dangerous perhaps especially in our own age because of the extraordinary obsession that men and women and children have now, the obsession of sex. If you said today of anyone that he or she was a sinner, you know quite well what everybody would imagine you meant. There is only one sin that people talk about, only one failing implied usually by the words sinner or sin—just carnal sin. The Catholic Church, of course, has never denied that that is a sin, but has insisted always that there are other sins than it and sins a great deal worse. There are spiritual sins like the pride of intellect. There is the spiritual sin of discouragement or despair. There is loss of faith, which is far worse than carnal sin. But men have forgotten these and gloss them over. To the modern mind there seems to be but one sin. You know, an age that is simply steeped in that obsession is all the more in danger in such a time of life as courtship. This generation can't but be coarsened by this obsession. Almost every book you read is sodden with it. Almost every play. Almost everything is tainted by it. The posters, the advertisements, how they drag in the lure of this thing! As you pass a theatre or any place of entertainment, what gaudy pictures are set to attract the passer-by, and how they border on the unclean and go as near as they dare under the law, flaunting it. Once upon a time, of course, there was the theory that if you said nothing about sex, people forgot it. There was a time, the Victorian era, when men didn't mention even natural things. Then there came the reaction and they said, "That's all false and impossible. If you only talk about sex, the world will forget." Equally foolish, equally criminal! All the world talks of it; has all the world forgot? "If you are only frank and natural about sex matters, people will forget about them." Man's not at all like that, never has been like that. Man inherits a fallen nature. He has a tendency towards evil which is tangled with the very roots of his being. An age which is obsessed with sex, which talks of it, writes of it, paints it, describes it so that hardly ever, can you get away from it, must be morally a dangerous age. "Hardly," said a young man to me, "hardly can I have a decent friendship now. At once into my mind come trooping memories, thoughts, ideas. Everything I read comes sweeping back to me in my holiest moments even when I would be alone with God." A dangerous period this, the mind, the memory and above all, the imagination steeped with evil things. Take minds so prepared and so coarsened, and set them out side by side, one with another, in youth—a man and a girl. Give them the stir of love, love dawning, with its desire to express itself in the only language it knows. Then to embrace will be dangerous, though it be good in itself and not evil, for we are what God made us. We are after his design. Such natural ways of love are not evil in man, but a deadly danger runs all the way through. So tumultuously passion easily enters by all the doors of human sense—eyes, ears and speech, passion can spoil love. Everywhere passion can enter in, passion which is just selfishness. In passion it is not the other, it is just self that the man, or the girl, is thinking of. It is not love, it is self. To pander to their own passions, that is what they are seeking, cloaking it under love's disguise. They may dress passion up, they may give it fine clothes to wear. It is still passion. You know it is just themselves they seek. There is nothing noble, there is no unselfishness in that which is merely passionate, directly passionate, dress it out in whatever terms you will. A kiss—ah, yes—the passion of Christ knows its meaning. He knew it, knew it as a foe. There was one under the trees in the moonlight. "Friend, dost thou betray the Son of Man with a kiss?" Was he betrayed only by Judas? Has he never been betrayed since by a kiss?

Remember only that we assert it to be dangerous. The whole road is beset with danger. You must go down the road, but if you are honest you will be on the look out for danger, prepared for danger. You will remember there is a danger, though not be obsessed by it. You will walk warily, if not for your sake, at least for his. In courtship there is danger everywhere, danger in everything, danger in the dance. Dances, they tell us, began in the sanctuary. They seem earliest to be connected with religion. The dance has always, somehow, been part of religious ritual. It had religious origins, but it is dangerous none the less. "But other people get no hurt from it?" It doesn't matter about other people. Your conscience has got to deal with it honestly. You cannot hide behind such excuses as those. We are men and women. We are no longer children. This is an age that has grown up. This is an age that boasts its independence. Hence the only question is, what is the effect on you of the dances you attend? That is the only point. Is it a danger to you with this one or that one, under these circumstances, under those? Don't bother about other people. They may be able to do all sorts of things that you cannot. That is a matter for their conscience. You must be guided by yours. This is an age of emancipation, of independence, an age therefore when the conscience must stand alone except with the light of God and faith's teaching. Under these a man's conscience is his light. Now if you find dancing dangerous to you, if you find it full of evil, remember that. Be honest. Let there be no pretence. Don't dress out your experience with any wonderful words, but just realise the weakness of your own heart. Keep touch with that. Remember, and out of remembrance you can win strength.

There are other sorts of ways in courtship time by which men may fall, or women. Thus, at least in my own country, there has grown up a custom for those that are engaged to go away together for a holiday. Perfectly innocent this may be and without hurt, over and over again. There might have been hurt to an older generation with the introduction of this custom. People now can do all sorts of things apparently without ill results that once they couldn't do. Perhaps now these girls and boys are better able to take care of themselves than were their grandparents. The custom at any rate is in vogue, but it is dangerous, isn't it? Human nature is inflammable. Both passion and love ride dangerously near the earth. If people will only realise frankly, honestly, that such as this is dangerous for them, it would not be so bad. It is the lie and the pretence that disgusts us in the literature of our day. A soul may even have to say: "For me what another can do without hurt is impossible. I must not go by other people's consciences. I can only go by my own."

Of course, all these dangers are made much worse, more full of their fire when drink is introduced into them. There is nothing wrong in drink in itself. It is God's creature. He turned water to wine; He knew the joy of life; He knew men's hearts, what would gladden them, under the sun. But there are times when even moderate drinking of intoxicants is a danger for almost everyone. All the more so is it a danger for youth. Old age has its needs. Life is ebbing, life must be replenished. It is all very well for these to drink that need it. Does youth need this? It begins to drink, doesn't it, just out of bravado? It doesn't like it. It thinks, poor pitiful youth, that this is big and fine! "Oh, I must have my flask." It begins with bravado. It doesn't remain there. It becomes a need. That is the way of human nature. Its stimulants begun are at first taken out of a momentary weakness or out of fun or excitement, ending—but is there ever an end? Taken one by one the things in courtship are dangerous. Add to them the stimulant, the fire. It is making these things even harder to control. If you ever listened to the other side of the confessional screen, you would have heard terrible things, I assure you, telling of this period, the after anguish, the distress. Youth, that seems so radiant, so wonderful, so triumphant, youth has its tragic hours. "I took too much, father, and it happened." "What?" Oh, shame! Silence and darkness. Not a word more need be spoken. The priest knows what is meant. Danger? Human nature itself is always dangerously near the earth. Add this fire and the danger is greater. "Why don't you give it up?" "Oh, father, I am afraid. Everybody else is doing it." Oh, this blessed age of independence! This age that is so sure of itself, this age that has thoroughly grown up! Wonderful age, yet tyrannized by fashion. "I am afraid they would laugh at me. They would say I wasn't a man." Are you afraid of the others, afraid of their laughter? Child that you are, in an age that is in such a haste to grow out of childhood, are you still such children, afraid of fashion, what this one or that will say? Yet the faith can make men of you. It was meant to build up character, not break it down. This cringing to fashion pulverizes character, undoes it, weakens it, making it

afraid of fools like itself, timid of the outcry of the world. This age, that would have us believe it has out-grown fear, has its fears and superstitions no less than the ages that went before.

The fact, I suppose, that should be remembered through all these dangers is that old fact taught us by the faith. God has made us tangled, spirit and matter, body and soul. You can't separate them in life. Wherever the spirit goes, the body enfolds, embraces it. Spirit meeting with spirit tends to desire a meeting of flesh with flesh. Whatever you do with the spirit, the body follows after. You can't rid yourself of your body. You can't ignore that side of yourself. It is only wrong deliberately to provoke and intend fleshly things without thought of the soul within. That is what the Church says. Embraces, dancing, books, pleasures, holiday, what you will, enjoy them all, but what is your purpose in seeking them? Is it just affection, is it just the fun of the thing, or are you seeking the stimulant of passion? Do you love the danger? Are you thrilled by the possible chance of evil? What are you out for? Is it to give or to get? Is it really because love dominates you, or is it because of self-love, masquerading under some more wonderful disguise? There, face the facts! Deal with your life openly to yourself. Be frank. Don't intend passion! Honestly intend goodness. If the passion follows, perhaps it can't be helped, but it may not be sought for. When you know that what attracts you is passion, you know that what attracts you is wrong. Lay it aside as far as you can. It will follow after? Let it follow, but don't let it run before. Nothing is gained by giving way in those courtship days. Nothing is gained. The mysterious, is always attractive. People will always follow a veil. All the world is interested in it, fascinated by it, wants to peer behind it. Purity is attractive. Do you wonder that the Protestant young man seeks the Catholic girl? Do you wonder the Protestant girl seeks the Catholic youth about her? Do you wonder? The others are unveiled. To have seen all is to lose interest, to get sated. It is over and done with.

Familiarity breeds contempt. There is nothing but shame and scorn when that business is done with. Purity holds all men's hearts. Else, why is it that in an age obsessed with sex there is this love of childhood? Else, why do they follow Peter Pan? Why do they crowd your theatres to see this piece and escape from evil? Why do they go searching the little child? What is it but the last bulwark of virginity in a world that is coarsened with sex, in an age that is violent with passion? Exhausted violence caught by the innocence of a child.

My brethren, it is our business, surely, to hold by the way of God, along the way by which Christ came to lead mankind, he who bade all mankind be born again as a child; He who set among those eight stars of his beatitudes cleanness of heart and said that they possessed it should see God. Oh, see God hereafter? Yes, certainly hereafter. But, that is not the only blessing, for they see God here; where the unclean of heart find all the world smirched for them, the clean of heart find it lit with God. They see God in the human souls into which they look. They search for God and find him in the eyes of a friend. It is the cry of the New Testament that our bodies are but the shrines, the temples of the living Presence of God. He that defileth the temple, surely him shall God destroy. Every soul that you meet is but a spirit tangled with the divine, spirit. It dwells with that spirit in a shrine. The shrine is the body that enfolds it. Reverence, and respect; then, must be set about the body; they are the twin guardians of love. They stand with flaming swords at the great gate of this garden of Paradise. They preserve it undefiled. Such a message as this Christ Came to teach us. Do you remember the prayer of poor St. Augustine, agonized as he tells us in his Confessions, following beauty wherever beauty lived? "Give me purity, but not yet, oh Lord, not yet," that double cry of the human heart that sees purity as something wonderful, something set as a star might be, to lift men's gaze above the earth, but cries out "not yet"; that pull between man's higher and lower nature—"purity but not yet"; desire hitched to a star and drawn down by heavy

gravitation to earth; the star and the earth—the dream and the pas-
168 sion of man. Tonight, my brethren, remember all those the world over that are entering into the high places of this dream of their lives. Pray that God's spirit may go with them and that they may find him in each other's hearts; that they may so see him that they reverence one another in the darkness, or the firelight, or under the stars; that they may find him in all human hearts that beat in sympathy with their own heart, find him there, who is in all things and to be found. Can they find him? "You will surely find me," so he promised, "if you look for me with all your heart." Oh, look for him wheresoever your eyes turn, in all souls seek to find him, and make him a shield in your friendships throughout your lives. Bring those you love here to this sacrament of love, his own down-stooping, because he too loves them as he loves you and all human hearts. He will hold you both hand in hand; His hand holding each of you, he will lift you each to each. Remember he is by you in this age of your youth, this age of exquisite beauty, fragrant with the perfume of love. May he who fashioned men and women, drew all lovers to follow after his own blessed design, may he teach them the way that is serene and stable, the way of purity, the way of the clean of heart, that seeing God on earth they may be at last led to see him in heaven, that their love begun here may endure and be made even greater by his love divine.

SERMON FOR THE SECOND SUNDAY

What Is Love?

In all the teaching of the Catholic Church wherein she deals with the subject of marriage or the home, she takes for granted that it is built up on the foundation of human love. Hard as she may sometimes seem to those outside her borders, absolute, without apparently the wish or power to relax her laws, this is only because, first, she has no teaching except Christ's teaching and this she has no power to alter and, secondly, because she supposes the home, the married life, to be possible as Christ taught it, but on terms of love. It is precisely that love, i.e., the human element within it, may be preserved and protected, that all her rules and regulations are drawn up. They are to protect love. Thus she teaches that Christ gave a sacrament to keep love's fire unquenched despite the inconstancy of man.

As we speak of human love, we speak a word which in all our language is the strongest word we know. Scripture tells us that it is stronger than hate, and the power of hate is strong indeed; that it is more powerful than death even; stronger than hell; than an army set in battle array. Love is a strong word. It is not a strong word only but one of the strongest powers in human life and human history. What

an amount of evil it has done! What an amount of good! To turn
170 over the pages of history is to come on records of the ravages in history wrought through love. Passion—what fabled cities of antiquity were destroyed because of love that went astray! What giant figures in the pageant of mankind in history have been spoilt to us by the stories of their loves. What characters, emerging triumphant, have yet at the last been rotted, spoiled by love. Or, to move away from the great figures of history and come to the world we know—what hearts have broken by it, what homes ruined. If you walk down the alleyways of the hospitals, what, do you think, of all that total of suffering would represent in one fashion or another victims of love? Love has been hurting, degrading, leading men falsely. And yet, what a deal of good love has done! Man, at his noblest, most unselfish moment is so, precisely because of love, love of something or some one, of his country or of God. The greatness of man uplifted by its power; the littleness of man broken and hurt by it. Strange effect it has had on the lives of men! Again, how differently it affects people. Some made eloquent by it, who else were but dumb, halting in speech; and others who are by nature voluble find that love halts their tongues. They cannot say what they would care to say, for love has silenced them; whereas the others have been made to speak. The pleasures, the joys it brings, and yet what terrible agony! I suppose if ever we have seen anyone in agony because of it, the sight will linger in our memory as one of the most distressing of all human sights. Joy and sorrow, gladness, agony, good, evil, what strange power has it to evoke all these! Yet when we think of it and try to analyze it, disentangle it for ourselves, see exactly, or as nearly as we can, what it is in itself, I fancy that our first idea would be to class it as something emotional, an instinct in man. It is often so strangely sudden that we cannot look on it as rational or deliberate. Sometimes without warning, without preparation, without knowledge, it begins to move. "I loved at sight," men say. Suddenly (they will tell you) it swept over them—it woke an echo between soul

and soul. The external appearance or beauty will so seldom account for it. It is something invisible, disturbing, a wavelength that carries its message, irresistible, sure. So men tell us. It is an emotion, an instinct, something that moves them strangely. It stirs and thrills them beyond their power to forbid.

Now that is true, but not the whole truth. For man's instincts and man's emotions are not just as the instincts of the brute beast. Man is rational, we say; man has reason, and his very instincts must therefore be rational, that is to say, they can be controlled. The instincts of an animal are almost automatic. You show it something and it follows at once. It is stirred. It matters not who it is or what it is, whether it attracts or repels it, there comes at once the automatic reaction. Of course, man can train an animal not to respond to its instinct or emotion—can show it food and tell it not to approach it. An animal can be tamed from outside by another. Man only can be tamed from within. A beast can be taught all sorts of things, can be taught to control himself, taught by another. Man can be taught self-control by himself.

Love is an instinct then; it is an emotion; it is something that sweeps over man, something unaccountable, but not something beyond his control. Man can fight it down if he thinks it is hurtful. He can bring in arguments to make himself renounce it; he can reject his instincts, his emotions—certainly at first. I am sure many a priest has had some one come to him and say: "Father, I am in love. You know the man I love. Some speak ill of him. If you think—you that know him and know me—if you think I should not go on letting myself love him, I can break it now. Later on it will be too strong for me, too terrible. It will be terrible enough now, but I can do it." That is true. Man can at the start control all, or almost all of his emotions, some at once, and all at the beginning, before they have grown too strong.

Love is an emotion, but you have not finished with it when you have said that of it. You must remember also that it is something that can be controlled at the start. It can be controlled even later, when some of the fierceness and violence of it has lifted from it. At the beginning certainly it can be controlled. No man or woman really can ever honestly make the excuse and say: "But I was caught; I just fell in love." "Fell," as though it were something beneath them, as though it were something they slipped into, into which they fell. Yet it is always controllable at the start. It is an emotion, a rational emotion, and, like every other emotion, needing to be guided by art; for it is not only a passion, it is an art; not only a science, but an art. It can be dealt with, it can be managed, it can be supported, it can be killed.

People talk of love sometimes as though it were something immortal, but the dreadfulness of our passage through life is to see love so often die. Though those whom it holds do not break it, yet of itself it may fall apart. It can be managed; it can be dealt with. I suppose those that are acquainted with it could formulate for themselves or others rules for the management of love. They would tell you, I fancy, that it can be easily over-sentimentalised until it reaches boredom. Like food, it can be too sweet at first, but then later, because too sugared, tiring; it can lose its force because of the amount of emotion with which it is too heavily stored. You know love can't live upon sentiment. It can't possibly survive like that. Men and women, after all, have a sense of humour, and humour at last may kill sentiment. Love should be careful, tactful, managed wisely if it is to last. Especially perhaps, in an age like our age, which is extraordinarily sentimental, lovers need, if they would keep each other, to use sentiment delicately, to be ready (as the phrase runs in boxing), "to break." Partly this is a sentimental age because our newspapers are full of sensation. They have by now created a generation which lives on its sensations, which must, be stirred, before it can be interested. This means that we have to be worked on, pandered to. So we have become extraordinarily sentimental. We are swept by sentiment, not by reason, but by speech, by an appeal to our hearts. We are over-sentimentalised.

On the other hand, love can get broken if it has not some sentiment to allay the irritating little things of life. It is quite possible to find that those who once loved each other, now are almost tired of each other, bored, weighed down by the dreariness of life, of its material cares. Riches, they say, make men wordly, but so does poverty make folk worldly. It does more than merely distress them, it breaks in on them and hurts them. For just as wealth can make people too devoted to their comforts and too full of care lest they should lose what they have, so poverty too can load people with cares and anxieties and make life full of solicitude. There is no romance in poverty. The poor have little enough cause to see their lot in life coloured with glory. It is just a round of daily, dreary housekeeping, menaced with material cares. Those that are affected by it so as to allow their souls to be made grey by it, can never keep the flame of love alive. You must shelter love, protect it from being hurt by these outside worries. Nothing breaks love so easily as the constant irritation of the soul.

I suppose, too, that love always should be mutual, that it should be always active; that if it is to be kept alive both of them must practice. One sided love has little chance to survive. Both must go on loving, if love is to go on. You know life is more or less what we make it, what we bring to it. If you find life dull, it is because you are dull. It is your dullness that swamps you. If you are always waiting to be enlivened by others, you will always be oppressed by your own dead weight. And if life is adventurous for you, it is because you are adventurous, because you are always looking for some adventure beyond the dreary curtains of life. If life is full of laughter for you, it is the echo of your own laughter. If all men smile on you, it is because first you have smiled. Love is but the echo of your own voice. Do not wait to be amused. Don't wait for that other love to uphold you. You must reawaken your love if you would find it again in the other. Love is mutual. It is not something that one only can carry through, of which one alone can provide enough for a home; it needs the work of all. It is fire catching fire; it is active. Each must bring love and not wait for it; let no one say, "I am the one that is tired. I go out to work all day. Love should be waiting for me at the doorway when I return." Everyone in the home who does his business is working all day. There is no rest for anyone that is really interested in the home-life, really taking his proper share in the work, out of doors, within doors, dealing with things or people working at home or in a store. Both are always tired when the day is ending, both should be tired if they have done their work. Don't let each wait for the other to be the first to show welcome. Bring love if you would find it. It is but the echo of the cry of your own heart. I suppose, though it must come differently to each and the other, that love runs mainly on the same lines. The mother is always a mother, even to the man she has wed. The father is very seldom a father, even to his own children. He is much more of a companion or a friend to them, but the mother is always guarding them. That is her fashion, she must, she can't help being active like that. The father will play with his children, going on all fours on the floor. Though he is the father, he has no sense of his dignity in dealing with the child. But the mother always has. She is the mother. The child is begotten of her. The ways of love in father and mother run on different lines; love acts differently on them and employs on them different forces. But they must be active always if love is to be kept alive.

You can test love always in every age by one simple test—the attitude of man to women. That is the test in every age of the realities of love. If in any particular age, generally men despise women, there is no love in their hearts; men who follow after sex have no love in them. "The fallen woman acts the love she cannot have." He can never respect her and she knows that she is despised. This is not love. This is passion, or you can call it by a sadder name. It is not love. Reverence has gone from it, respect has gone. Where women are not honoured, men certainly are not in love. When then, our quack scientists talk to us about companionate marriages, we know that they have reached the bankruptcy of love. There is plenty of sex possessing them, but no love. Companions—that is all they want to be. What they want is friendliness coloured with sexual pleasure. No one can call that love. Love is unselfish; love lifts people. This just places them side by side. Love is not humiliating but it is humbling. It makes the man or woman go down on their knees. They don't see each other as companions but as raised above them. It is not so much that they build a pedestal and put on it the one whom they love. It is really that they kneel down low because they recognise their own unworthiness. The very Sacrament of Love puts this natural cry of man on our lips when we approach divine love. You would not come to the altar until you had first cried "*Domine non sum dignus*; Lord, I am not worthy" in your heart. So is it in the sacrament of human love. Marriage, says St. Paul, is the divine counterpart of that which happens in the love betwixt a woman and a man. It is something humbling, something that puts the lover on his knees before her that he loves. Companionate marriage is cheap and costless: it is the glorification of sex and dooming of love. Love cannot be a companion, love can only be a god. Love has flown out of the window for love has wings. So, when our blessed Lord came to bless this great power of mankind for good or evil, he fenced it round about with law; He made love something that should last a lifetime, something that only death could break, if aught at all. Christ exalted human nature, knowing it and knowing it to be inconstant, restless, knowing how hard it is ever to be permanently loyal to any ideal or to any soul. But he worked miracles to make the inconstant constant. He walked dry shod upon the raging sea. He hushed the winds and the waves and made them silent and grow quiet. He bade Peter come walking to him on the waters, unafraid. He knows human nature, knows how faulty it is, knows how restless, and so with his grace he blessed the home.

When men, in the early stages of society, drifted aimlessly over the wide plains, when men were nomads, wanderers like the Indians that were scattered over your land, who had here today their camping ground and tomorrow had left it, following their food, stalking the other tribes, with whom they were at war, when they were thus homeless their only home was the mother and the child. That was home. Home was not a place set in a single landscape; in it there was nothing permanent, but love. Love held them, though they were wanderers. Under God's blessing, though they were restless, they had rest. Man is always a wanderer. Man is always restless in the world. Only love tethers him, holds him only love makes him a home. Man is restless except for home. There he stays. Love holds him there because it is unselfish. Love holds him because it costs him all he has to give. If either of the two must be blamed in love then both must be blamed. If one be selfish, the other can't be wise. Neither need be at fault. God has taught us love's true ways. But remember that you cannot let it drift, go alone of itself. You can't expect a fire to go on burning, you must feed it, keep it alive. Man is fitful, changes like the wind, but God can make him constant. God can keep the fires alight in his heart. God will. "This is his will; your sanctification, to keep each his vessel in honour," says St. Paul. God is there to help us stay the restlessness of human hearts, and to find constancy where alone it must abide, in the heart of the eternal, for God is love. Through the grace of the sacrament, we can see even human love abide. Through grace human love can become constant, immortal even. Through the miracle of grace, the restless heart can find in another heart its home.

SERMON FOR THE SECOND WEDNESDAY

Love's Choice

We have been trying to see, my dear brethren, in the unfolding of human life, nothing less than the gradual fulfilment of the individual vocation in life; that every soul whom God has created has its own purpose and destiny here; that its vocation is the fulfilment of that destiny; that not merely those souls that are called to the cloister—not those only—have a vocation, but every soul that God has made; and that this vocation is not determined or not fulfilled by any single action, but by every action of a man's or woman's life. The entrance into a cloister does not finish for the religious the business of their vocation; it is but one important step in its unfolding. So, too, we have tried to see (as the Catholic Church teaches us, following the way taught by Christ Himself), that in the taking of this step of marriage, those who are called to it have fulfilled but a part of the unfolding of their life. A vocation is not completed by marriage. Marriage is merely an important step in the unfolding of the vocation. Again in the old phrase, "Marriages are made in heaven," we see a public profession of the belief that a divine Providence watches over all, that God chooses, indeed, that God creates, souls for souls, that all life is lived under the divine Power. That is the teaching of the New Testament, the teaching of the Sermon on the Mount. Every hair of your head is numbered; every moment of your life known to the Infinite God. Hence we account for that strange, sudden recognition of soul by soul. "Love," they sometimes call it, "at first sight." We in the faith of God's power and love and wisdom, see in this but the recognition by man of a divine providing will who has destined each for each. So love, as we see it, is no mere instinct. It is not even instinct governed by human reason, not even something which can be managed, directed, fought down. It is not something that just moves and sweeps over a heart beyond its governance, but something which, if a man cares and wishes wisely, he can manage and control. Rather, then, we hold that love, this instinct and more than instinct, is a high following and fulfilment of a divine law. Love, because it is divinely planned, enables him that loves to find in the beloved one things that are hidden from other eyes. You hear men and women talking of some marriage that they know of—"What could he have seen in her?" "How on earth could she have chosen him?" Strange! Unaccountable! You know in the old ways of art they showed you love as blind. And men, in their cynical outlook, explain these unexpected marriages shrugging their shoulders, saying, "Love is blind." Love is not blind. All the world else is blindfolded. Love alone can see! Hate closes the eyes, closes the vision. Hate balks knowledge. You cannot know anyone you hate. Once you have the flaring up of any hatred—racial, national or individual—for that time men and women and children are blind. Hate blinds people. That is the folly of it. When the hate dies down, they see what fools—blind fools—they have been. Love opens the eyes. "What did he see in her?" He saw what God first had seen! Love means confidence, means that someone has believed in you. Blessed you, in whom some one has believed! They have believed in you because God first believed in you. God made you. He made you only because there was something he wished from you and gave you power to achieve. And love sees that, sees capacity and greatness as divinely intentioned; love loves the soul because of the treasure hidden in the soul by God.

For us, then, love has a sacred purpose. It is to develop the power of another soul. Marriage is to lead people Godwards; that is its purpose. In it love is the instrument of God's design. These two joined here at the altar, the ring that holds them, God's blessing solemnly given as they start out in their new life, what has marriage to show for this? What does it mean? What does it do? How should marriage always be remembered but as the sacrament by which souls are to help souls? Marriage is to lead men by God's power, through God's will, to God Himself. To the souls for whom God has destined marriage, there is no other way by which they may properly reach their home. But men question us: How can there be heaven made marriages when after all you do find sometimes incompatibility of temper? Sometimes they cannot really agree. Perhaps this merely means one soul of the two is blind. God gave each to the other. If you don't see how the other can help you, if you don't see how you can help him or her, yours is the fault. The divine purpose is evident and clear. You and I believe the word of Christ. We believe that this is God's world, that God created it, that God wisely governs it. We believe this is God's world, and now, knowing it to be so, we say to those in difficulty, "Go on with your life. It is God who has brought your souls together that they may help each other." "Oh, but this one hurts me, makes me irritable, makes me impatient, leads me astray. This one is no help to me. This one is a daily temptation to me. To separate for the day is to gain a little peace; to come back is irksome. It begins all that difficulty again." That is just blindness. This other was meant to help you. God knows your weakness. God knew you had something to gain. Here's your chance; here's your opportunity. "I see no chance." You will, when death takes the other away; then you will realise what you could have done. You will wake up to it. You will see almost

year by year the hurtful things you said or did, or the things you left
180 undone—to help that other soul of yours nearer to God's throne. This is no pagan world to please you. This is no place where men and women wander free of their will. Here it is God's world, and God's great will is over all. A man, if he wishes, can find the way of God, and finding it, be big enough to live it, if he has love in his heart. Love will let him see.

But if there be no love between them, what then? Sometimes a girl will come and say: "Do you know I am going to marry him?" "Do you love him?" "No, I can't honestly say I do, but he has asked me, and I am tired of home and the interference of these elders. Here is an escape. I am going to take it." "But you should not marry without love. It is not fair to him, even though he asked you. It is not fair to yourself. One day there may come a time when love will cross your path, and you will suddenly see it and know the torment of the difference as it goes." Love we believe to be God's gift to us of divining a soul that was meant for our soul. We call it love. It is only just the will of God, drawing one nearer to the other. That is what God meant. They fit in as the notes of a harmony fit in, twin souls—that is, fashioned each for each by God.

Of course, the world over, and growingly, there are souls whom God never leads that way. There are souls the world over that God has never meant should lift another soul in that fashion to Himself. The way of love is a great way. But, you know, there is a strange paradox about love. Though it be so wonderful, it is wonderful because it has made its choice or chosen its beloved. Love has made its choice, and because it chooses one, that means to say it rejects the others. Though love is wonderful, love of its very nature is narrow in its choice. Love seeks, primarily, a single soul. Motherhood—that stands always as the great example of unselfishness—is yet in no ignoble way selfish. For at least it holds by the home. Here is the centre of love for it. Sacrifice it will make willingly, yes, but for these who form its home. Here are its gods. Here does it find God

Himself gleaming in the heart of the husband, in the eyes of the child. So is this true also of the father. Even under stress of great emotion etiquette denies to the father the right to express what he feels. Mothers may weep, but the fathers must hold back their tears. Yet fatherhood has, in its way, all the feelings of a mother, without any right apparently to express them. Its sorrows have such little relief. Yet with all the greatness of the father's love, it is busy only with the wife and the children. It is a narrow garden that love tills.

There are other souls in the world for whom God has chosen neither the way of marriage nor of the cloister. Both in their way are narrow—the cloister and the home. In a way this narrowness has power, and again, it has weakness. But there are souls whom God calls to an almost wider life. Their scope is not merely some other fellow-being, wife or husband or child, but a wider world lies before them. It is said that sometimes selfishness keeps people unmarried. Sometimes a man, when the years are at their youth and fulness, grudges that he should halve his pay, knowing that life will be more austere for him, more poverty-stricken, if he carries another on his slender means. It may be that she, herself, refuses the burden of motherhood. She wants yet to have her fun in life. It is sometimes selfishness that makes them wait till the best years have gone by them, and then selfishness hardens and narrows them till they would not alter even if they could. Such a soul as finds its lonely path deliberately and selfishly will never find another who will wish to share it. As it has chosen so it will remain. But it is not always selfishness that dictates this narrow choice. Sometimes it is because something has happened to them, within, without—nobody quite knows what. Why haven't they married—folk ask? So likely they seemed for marriage, so eminently desirable, yet nothing has happened to them, and the years have gone by. Later in life they seem to have mean, pinched souls, till people almost despise them. They have missed romance. Ah, this is not always the true verdict! Sometimes they are the only ones that have kept unsullied their dreams. Oh, the others have married, have had their romance and their dreams and visions, and have talked of the laughter of children and the patter of the little feet on the stairs; but all this romance and these joys have been killed for them by domestic worries, rent and prices, and having to ask always more money of their man. But these others, some of them, have a romance to live by—though it be only memories or things they hoped might happen and never did. They waited, were lonely, and somehow were forgotten. Romance, dreams, possess these dreamers, and the others, practical people found their way to life. Sometimes it is due to neither one nor the other. There is no cause other than a deliberate will. It just happened to be God's call, for there is a place for them also in God's wide kingdom. God's kingdom is as beautiful as a great show of flowers—colours and scents, shape, height, all beset with difference, such a glorious show to your vision, beautiful because of the variety that you see—massed blossom on blossom, massed glories of shrub and bush, the little flowers nestling, the big ones spreading over them, and high above them, the flowering trees. God's world is as varied. This Blessed Gardener chooses his plants as his wisdom directs him, placing them where he will. There are these souls that are called to neither marriage nor cloister—but to a vocation of their own, wider in a sense than the other, more unselfish, carrying perhaps never a reward this side of death. The others have a reward in the love the home engenders for them. These are the fairy godmothers of their surroundings, sharing their limited time and money with the younger folk who turn to them when they despair of their own homes. And some share not time nor money only, but what is more blessed, a silent sympathy. They are God's silent, eloquent ones, who listen to the grumbles of those who have none to whom they dare tell them at home. To unburden your troubles to others and to be met with, "Oh, I know that. I have been through it myself," is irritating—to find someone who claims his sorrow is as keen as yours. But these others are silent, they just listen, and they become almost the confessors of the community where they live. People will go to them, but don't always remember to return with gratitude. These, these unmarried, they listen and share, but they have no claim for any return. "Thou shalt honour thy father and mother." This is one of the commandments. This is in his preaching. A child remembers this even when it displeases its parents. A divine command will thus sometimes bring souls back to pay their thanks. Gratitude! What a stunted growth of soul those have who demand it! If it is not given, it should not be asked. But these souls listen and share with those who confide in them time and all they have to give, knowing that many will never come back to thank them! When they opened the window in the Ark the bird only came back when there was nowhere else for it to perch. When the waters covered the earth it came back. It wanted somewhere to stay. Once the waters had gone down and the land appeared again, the bird had found its shelter. It was a bird, no one expects gratitude from the dumb creatures of God. And there are hearts like that in the world, my brethren, to whom men, women and children came back only when they need comfort; when that need is over they pass them by almost with disdain. These grow at last lonely. Oh, they have lonely lives. Romance? No romance or dreams about it. Their last years are lonely. There is no one to care. God's ways are wonderful, and every soul, as God calls it, is destined to a way of its own. Some have the course of human companionship, are not single, living nobly in the ways of love. Others have the cloister. The cloister is not lonely. There are in it always other human lives that meet and pass. But there is no life lonelier than the soul's that has had to live through the world in single blessedness, unlimited by walls of cloister or of home, touching wider margins, yet on that account more alone.

But no soul need be lonely, no soul that believes in God. Said the Master, as he went out to the garden, down the valley, up the hill, to the garden of his doom, "I go alone," He said, "but not alone, for the Father is with me." To us of the faith there need be no lonely lives. Carrying the Sacrament of God once to a poor woman in a high attic in a London slum, I heard her crying as I mounted the bottom of that stairway,: "My God, but I am lonely, lonely in my fallen years." As I entered, I put the Blessed Sacrament down on her poor dresser. "I overheard you," I said, "saying that you were lonely. Are you really lonely?" "God forgive me," she said, "God forgive me. Lonely? I am always with God."

Souls, all souls, are divinely fashioned. God has cut their pathway through the valley, over the hills. God knows what he is about. God has created souls, destined them for their pathway in life, and he knows that some souls need human love to develop them. Were they to give it up, their lives would be maimed and stunted. Virginity would hurt them. They were not made for that. There are souls that God calls into the cloister. They have a life that must there be lived. Their talents there will find ample opportunity. There they will find a family that never dies. Others God calls to the way he went Himself on earth—lonely, save for the younger friends, the friends to whom he was the Master and Father. He who cared for the growing world at his feet, flowers and little children and the sparrows, gave up all the life he loved when he went to his doom. Always God chooses noble ways. Let no man point a finger of scorn at any way of God. God knows what he is about. God gives to every soul a capacity, brings them souls that they can manage, whose lives they can refashion and send back remade. Fairy godmothers are these—the unselfish aunts and uncles of a younger world.

God calls us then. Our business is to listen uncomplaining, and to obey. One of your poets has said, "Life is only a small house, but love is an open door!" Life so narrow, so small, so petty—birth and death and the little narrow years between. Life, even greatness in life as men count it, is itself so narrow, imprisoned between this year and that. Birth, death, what narrow boundaries! "Life is but a small house, but love is an open door!" Greatness?—love is all man's greatness. He has none other than that. Love has elevated man. Love is the flame that has inspired him. To the apostles of Christ, love was an open door. If your life is narrow, you can yet find in it a greatness wider than the horizons that your eye may see; though it seems to you petty and small and unworthy, do not believe merely this judgment of it. If it is petty and small, the fault lies with you. Love is an open door! Go out through that door and find the souls that wait on you, husband or wife or child, or a wider world. God gave you that world to deal with, to touch, to help, to inspire, to listen to, to hear its cries and help, not only by advice, more often by sympathy. Eyes searching and a heart that finds! An open door! "I am the door," He said, and truly for God is love!

SERMON FOR THE SECOND FRIDAY

Mutual Love

One of the things, my dear brethren, that it is sometimes most difficult for a priest to do, is to give advice. People come and speak to him because, I suppose, in every Catholic family there is some priest who is a friend; who knew the children when they were little children; who has watched them grow from age to age; who knows perhaps better than any one other can know the strength of their character, and its weakness; knows what they can stand, and where they are most likely to fail. And they will come to him, first with their childish troubles—to them as great and as overpowering as are the grown-up troubles to grown-up souls. They will come to him again when they have grown out of childhood, and when they are beginning to realise the difficulties of grown-up life. As children, it seemed to them almost as though only children were naughty, as though grown-up people were always right. Then they reach a period in life in which at last they learn that children are never really naughty; that sin is something which exists almost all together among grown-up folk. Youth has to re-construct its world. When it comes perhaps to the threshold of manhood or womanhood or that "space of life between," again it is troubled. Everything

is more complicated, more difficult to deal with because at that
188 period of life the soul is for the first time seriously grappling with itself, fascinated by itself, studying itself, almost necessarily growing morbid in consequence at this most difficult period of all; for its problems are the problems of love, human or divine; or the problem of the life to be settled, realising that this step is the great step. They will go back to the priest who knows them, that priest whom they have known all their lives, and ask his advice. Indeed, all he can give is advice. They have their individual responsibility to God. The priest cannot order them, he cannot decide for them. It is they who must decide. Moreover, the advice that he gives them must depend largely on what they tell him; and not all they tell him is necessarily always true. It is as true as they can see if, but they have got to the age that does not see clearly, that cannot unravel the tangled skein of its own character. So they go to their friend, telling the trouble to him as they see it. So much escapes them, yet he gives advice and judges also on other knowledge of them that he has. He can remember so many earlier scenes, fits of temper when he alone could be called in to settle matters, the child with a terrible will of its own. Remembering all, he can give his advice.

And then will come one of those questions that sound at first so ridiculous. "Do you think I am really in love?" Some find it perfectly easy to settle it for themselves. They know. Others hardly know at all. After all, there are people who are incapable of vehemence or of any real vehement desires. Love? Even love cannot sweep them off their feet. It does not seem in them to have that overwhelming feeling; their nature is more calculating, colder; it does not catch fire. Then there are others again. As you watch them, as you read them as you reason with them, you realise that they have another type of character which is slow of growth; which needs marriage to stimulate its powers of affection; which is only able to love when it is drawn into neighbourly contact and familiarity. Out of marriage only will spring the fire of love for them.

In dealing, as the priest must, with all sorts of types and characters, using what he can of the knowledge of the life that waits before him, of such books as he reads, obviously knowing absolutely nothing of the married life, he must advise with second-hand materials, not personal experience. He may make mistakes. He can only say what he sees.

In the choice of love then there must be some fitness between the two. I suppose one would call it compatibility of temper. There must be at least, of course, a liking, and a liking which is exclusive of others. That at least is necessary for a start. There must be respect and reverence. Otherwise it would be foolishness to embark even momentarily on the perilous waters of life. Respect, then, and reverence must be there. Otherwise, there will be many long years of suffering, unless there is reverence each for the other kept always. Unless love lift soul to soul to a level of equality, of esteem and respect, love cannot last.

And confidence of course. Each soul must have confidence in the other. Otherwise it is not worth while starting out together on any joint adventure, either in business or in love. No partnership is possible without mutual confidence.

But out of all this material will come a subtle sympathy which is for some the dawn of love. As Elias put on the altar the dry wood, and then called the fire down from heaven, and the fire came down on the altar and set the dry wood ablaze, so with these materials for the divine Fire invoked in the Sacrament of Matrimony in the prayers of the Church, these souls will be set ablaze.

Love for each other, therefore, though mutual need not be equal. To be equal in love is not always possible. Some souls are bigger, greater than others. Love, then, should be mutual, not necessarily equal or in all alike.

And this mutual love between soul and soul, even though mutual, will be vastly different in each. Men and women are different. God made them so. They are equal, of course, they stand equal

in God's creation, but two souls cannot be wholly alike. Each has
190 its character. Each calls for something like, yet unlike itself. Man seems to love because he needs love, and a woman because she sees she is needed. Each has a different point of view. Man gives because he must give, and she takes the love that is given because it seems to her only so can she also give what she has to give. His generous, yet almost touched with selfishness, and hers seeming selfish, is generosity itself. Don't you see? Mutual then love is, fitting in each with the other; not equal, or at least not quite the same. Each is frail, each is a frail human character. Each has to realise that he or she is frail. There is no use pointing scornfully at frailty or failure. All are failures, if not in action, at least in thought. The Master, when he taught his disciples the gospel of marriage, with its rights and duties, said that when a man looked upon a woman with evil in his heart, that man had already committed adultery. So again when the woman who was in sin was brought before him, he wrote in the dust, "Let him who is without sin, cast the first stone," and there was not one to accuse her. Outwardly each was respectable, within, each a sinner; each desperately frail. Seven times seven must I forgive my brethren. There is no end to forgiveness. God forgives us anything when we are sorry. God has shown no end of his forgiveness of us. We must have no other mercy than the unlimited mercy of an infinite God: mercy—no end to forgiveness. You need mercy. Give the mercy that you will some day need in return, not from man, but the mercy you will need as you stand before God's throne.

Mutual, different, will be the love of men and women, and all their ways different. How different are the pleasures of both! And the woman must realise that the man is a boy always, and will take his pleasures always as a boy. He must have his own circle of fellow men. That is his way of pleasure. That is how he escapes. Sports, games, recreation—he is a boy again; living a boy's memories even to old age. But her pleasures are friendships and visiting those she loves; and that is why when her children are little she has little pleasure away from them or her home. When her children are grown-up—she looks for and lives again her motherhood with their children. That was one of the tragedies of the war, shattering the hopes of so many mothers, knowing that they would never have grandchildren, knowing it with the tolling of the bell.

Duties rather than rights, you see, have to be considered in marriage. You will have sorrow, that is the badge of all humanity, but never show that sorrow even for a moment. Sorrows are linked with human nature, so that each one should bear his sorrows, not talking of them or telling them to others, for sorrows bring with them gifts that joy cannot bring. There are sorrows in life—in the home: "I am weak and exhausted; I am still expected in the evening to keep my spirits up." The woman tired. She is a good housewife, tired with her long day's labour. Each day should bring a day's labour for a woman, and the mother too. And the man coming back tired in the evening and perhaps finding no one at home, his money quickly spent, and then his friends forgetting him, comes home white and tired. Each must give; not waiting for the other to give—giving first. Give because you should give—considering not your rights, but your debts. Rights have a way of taking care of themselves. "I owe it to myself?" The debt you owe to yourself you need never pay at all. Go without paying it, and pay the debts you owe to others. You will find yourself happier so.

You expect to be interested? Don't wait to be interested but interest others. Don't wait to tell your sorrows but listen to those of others. Be always comforting. Give all to the one you love—that is how God has loved.

When the Church blesses a marriage ring, she reminds those to be married of what is marriage by this symbol of bondage—"B-less O Lord this ring which we hallow in thy Name; may she who wears it hold her loyalty and fidelity always to him whom she has now taken, and may they grow together in mutual love." That means mutual giving and mutual forgiving, the mutual love, that

God blesses, that Christ taught, that the Church repeats again all

through the ages to men and women alike. Each in some sense obeys the other; each is the master or mistress in his or her own way; each rules; each guides; each settles difficulties. Love is the same. Purity, therefore, is asked of each equally, though perhaps harder for the man; but each is asked for purity because love needs it, for love is a consuming fire. Moreover, God meant that man out of human love should find a way to Himself. "Unless," says St. John, the beloved disciple, "unless you love the man whom you see, how shall you love God whom you shall never see till one day in heaven?" Human love is in itself something that should teach souls the way to God. Will you love right? Listen to love's language. Would you know what love of God means? How it entrances men? Then know the language of human love first. It will teach you also the doctrine of spiritual life. "A great Sacrament," says St. Paul. The Sacrament of Christian marriage is magnificent, really divinely great. You feel God's own splendour shining through it. That is the way it should be seen. What a pity it is not always so! Love means it to be unselfish. Love is unselfishness. Marriage is based on love.

SERMON FOR THE THIRD SUNDAY

Love's Expression

In one of those long quarrels that have been drawn out between the Catholic Church and some of those outside her borders, one of the points in dispute has been the origin of the world. There are all sorts of scientific theses, suggestions, suppositions, as to how the world began. Of the theories themselves a scientist only, I suppose, is competent to speak, but there is one condition that the Catholic Church insists upon in all such explanations of the origin of the world. However it began, it was God that began it. We give the origin of the world to a divine creative act. God made the world; and we say that the Catholic Church insists upon this truth not merely, from the point of view of abstract reasoning nor because it is something Catholic philosophers have considered proven or learned people debated in their books, but because apart from this it has a very practical bearing upon human life. To her, in the government, direction, and inspiration of human souls, she considers the remembrance of it a matter of grave importance. God created the world, and therefore (the Catholic Church argues) the world in itself, since it is divinely created and divinely planned, is good.

Behind the origins of all things is God working, and what
194 follows naturally and of its own momentum follows the action of God, and therefore is in a line of goodness. Man, however he began, was created by God and man in himself was made good by God. In the Sacred Scriptures we are told that God looked out on the world which he had created and saw it was good. “God made us,” said the psalmist, “and not we ourselves,” and that saying is meant not simply to put us in our right place as a portion of a larger world or to see ourselves as creatures of the great creator, but also to show us that our human nature is in its own mechanism a divine thing.

God made us, and as God looked out on the world (so we are taught by Sacred Scriptures), he saw that man was good; looking also at man, he saw that it was not good for man to be alone, and so he created for him a helpmate. Man was created after all the world was done. In the Scriptures, you must not look indeed, for scientific but dogmatic teaching. Morality is taught us there by divine inspiration, the truths of faith and the laws by which we are to live. Now Scripture tells us that it is God’s judgment on man, that it is not good for him to be alone. Because of this judgment God provided him with a helpmate; and as on every other living thing, wheresoever it is placed in the scale of creation, so on man God laid the command to increase and multiply. God created the world; the world in itself therefore is good, having a divine origin, fulfilling a divine purpose, working out a divine plan. God not only created man and gave him a law, whereby normally he is enriched in the development of his own character by the way of marriage, but he also inserted love to enable man the better to achieve his command, to lead men to the fulfilment of what he wished from them. It was then with the purpose of providing them with what should unite them one to another, that he gave them love. Just as in the ever Blessed Trinity the Holy Ghost proceeds from the Father and the Son, is the love between Father and Son, is the spirit of love, just as the oneness of the Trinity is achieved by the love which is the Spirit of God, so in a lesser fashion, through love it is that God has gathered into one the units of mankind. To love is a divine command, and it has a divine motive governing it.

God laid then on man a command to express externally the love that he had inserted in man's heart. This expression of love has a divine origin, is something that we must judge with reverence; with the same spirit with which you gather into your museums the handiwork of great artists of the past. You house in palaces of marble the shattered carving of some Greek artist of long ago, though it be defaced, broken, hardly more than the outline of humanity, headless, limbless, still it is something precious to you; for it came from a great artist's hand. "You," says St. Paul, "you are God's workmanship." We have been fashioned by the hands of God. So the Catholic Church as she looks out on humanity, insists upon that belief in the divine origin of man, namely that he is divinely created, because she wishes ever to keep alive in human hearts man's reverence for man. Moreover she also wishes us to remember that whatever follows directly from a divine action must be good and blessed in itself. Not only was this teaching given in the Old Testament, bringing to a people that had been degraded a revelation of high notions with which to inspire their lives, but when Christ our Lord came, God made Man, wearing the vesture of human flesh and blood, he came with his Incarnational teaching, to show man how it was possible to see matter in the light of the spirit; how it was possible by our ideas, by our wisdom, by our true understanding to rob matter of its grossness and its evil, to lift it up somehow and to give it wings. The gospels, the story of the gospels, the whole teaching of the New Testament is to bring that home to man. Good men naturally tend to be puritans. They tend always to denounce everything dangerous as wrong. Our Lord would not have us accept that spirit. Things may bring evil. That does not say they are evil. It is for man to see them truly, sanely, with the eyes of purity, with the eyes of a child. So he laid down his great doctrine that it is open to the spirit to lift matter heavenwards, and that this elevation of mind is the purpose of the law of increase and growth. This is its purpose. This is why he inserted in man's heart love, to justify what else might seem repulsive, to lead men to what else, I suppose, they would never, or but seldom, have been induced to do. God has his own way of persuasion; God has his own way of leading man where he would have him go. To spiritualise this desire and hunger our blessed Lord came and taught to mankind his doctrine of the sacrament of marriage, pledging, giving, joining these "two into one flesh," He said. Utterly fearless in the words he uses, this strong teacher, knowing the needs, knowing the passions of man, says this (it is the teaching that we inherit), that these human actions are the expression of human love; that they are not, or they need not be, the mere emotions of the animal nature of man. They can be justified to the spirit by human love.

There are laws and limits to this sacramental teaching, but they are wide enough to satisfy man. There are words and actions divinely planned, divinely purposed, sacred and to be looked on with reverence, to be realised as an ideal. Not of mere animal origin are they. The Church will have none of that. They are not the mere growth or development of nature, as though nature stood outside the governance of God. He made it, and he gave it its own laws and character, otherwise it could not achieve what he wanted the world to do. God deals with man in his wisdom and then reveals to man his action and his motive and then teaches man to look at these from his own point of view. Man is still able to spoil this, as he can spoil everything. Man is endowed with his free will; man is able therefore to take her whom God gave him as a helpmate, and use her as an inspiration to complete and enrich the character with which he is started out in life; but man is also able always to degrade his use of her, able to exploit her, for evil purposes of his own. You have only to walk down a modern city and look one by one at the flaming advertisements, at the flaunting billboards to see how man can exploit every evil that may lurk and linger in the hearts of men—a kiss, a caress, something of God's own purposing, something God fashioned for high destinies of his own, degraded, exploited, to appeal not to man's highest nature, but deliberately to appeal to what the designers of these know is lowest in man. Books and plays, everything has been made use of to appeal to our instincts which can be degraded, as everything else can be degraded, even our faith. Man can barter sacred things for wealth and power, can buy and sell them. Man can degrade the high purposes of God. But these need not be degraded. They should not be degraded. They should be looked at with clean eyes. They should be looked at with eyes that remember that from God's hands men come and to God's hands they go. The expression of love is no mere movement of material instinct. It is an action which should be justified by love. It is matter which can be relieved of grossness by the spirit, as you can see a solid block of stone relieved of its heaviness by an artist and fashioned to express some noble hope or dream. So too for us man must always remember the divine origin of mankind. It must be remembered that this expression of human love is the command of God, for usual humanity, the normal fulfilment of a nature with its own clamorous desires. God knew, God gave, those desires to man from the beginning and God has his own means of answering man's clamorous desires. God gave him someone to help him towards the heights for which he made him. God gave man, not merely love, but love's expression, to achieve a purpose, fruitful of what he wished done in the world. And God did all this that he might lead men nearer to Himself. A noble purpose! God would have each man and wife see it so. A purpose of his own, this same expression of human love, though it is in a sense only a secondary purpose. Even when the time comes in life that there can be no living result from it, still even then love justifies it, so noble is love in the creating eyes of God. Thus it is part of the Christian teaching that each should give and receive with unselfishness, whatsoever may seem the hardship to one or the other. Husband and wife must be unselfish here, as unselfish everywhere. They are gathered, they are placed together, their union made blessed, in order that each may help each. Man or wife must think not merely of themselves but rather how each could help the other, namely by unselfish giving of all each has to give. Thus is it at times an unselfish achievement of a divine purpose, where each is thoughtful of what will hold the other nearer to God. Man and woman have their own natures, their own natural likings or dislikings, for human nature is as varied as men are themselves. Each must in this act be conscious of the other soul made one with it, and each must remember that his business is to bring the other nearer to God. How shall I help him or her? How shall I keep him from evil? How shall I help him nearer to God? I know him. I know his strength and his weakness. What must I do? Remember this act has a divine origin and a divine purpose; remembering that, you can be left to judge adequately what you should do.

One of our poets has sung in his praise of good women, "What prayer, what priest, can stay, the fury of the beast?" What can tame the animal character of man? Apart from faith, which after all works on man through human instruments, there is no other means to rest on for him than this very flame itself of the human heart lit by God, which men call love. The beast in man can be held down captive by it. There are moments, indeed, when a poor agonized soul, beleagured with its enemies, feeling almost on the very edge of a moral breakdown, yet led by the memory of the human love which it plighted at the altar, still can find its ultimate escape. A woman's courage and love, her undaunted laughter, ringing like a clarion in the great warfare of a man's soul, when the hosts of God seem almost routed in him, at times will drive back the beast within him and give him peace and relief.

It is a divine command, then, this expression of human love. Men of divine workmanship, have reverence for your own human hearts, remember that you have been fashioned by divine fingers. Remember that as you are God made you, and you have a purpose to fulfil. There are still the untenanted thrones of the angels in heaven, who were driven out of it. These thrones were made empty. These are the places still to be filled by faithful souls. You men and women, have your own apostolic work to be fulfilled by you to raise children to these places on these empty thrones. This work of divine destiny has been committed by God to you, has been revealed as a belief to you and is made possible to you by the spirit of reverence when you see that men and women are greater than they seem. We are not the mere result of blind forces of nature; not something that is a little higher than the beasts, but something only a little lower than the angels, as high pitched as that. The Catholic Church alone in the world now, fearless and remembering, teaches this sacredness of man. These others that appeal to man would appeal to that which is lowest in him, that of which he soon grows tired. She appeals to that which is highest in him, noblest, that which can never die. The rest passes, age may quench it; this is never quenched, even by age. This is a flame lit by God's hands—God who is immortal. He will shelter the undying fire.

SERMON FOR THE THIRD WEDNESDAY

Love's Restraint

We have insisted already, my dear brethren, that for us, love like every other human emotion, is a rational emotion, that man is man wholly, and that his natural instincts are not merely like the instincts of an animal, but that they partake of man's own nature and are in some degree rational themselves. We must now remind you that it is part of our Christian faith, that we inherit a fallen nature, by which we mean that we are born heirs to a human nature which is in a state or condition of disorder. We are heirs to it, for original sin is no act of our own wall. As children we were taught to distinguish between actual sin, the sin of our own doing, and original sin, which is a sin we inherit. We must not think of it as an action, but rather as a state or condition in which we find ourselves born. It is not an act we do ourselves. Here then we receive a nature which is in some sense wounded in some sense set in disorder, and of that we are painfully aware. You can see it for yourself in the various faculties that go to make up your own human nature. You can think of your reason, that which argues, discusses, understands; of your will, which chooses and decides; and then of the series of emotions—love, desire, hatred, anger, joy, and the rest. In perfectly ordered humanity those various powers of man would be in perfect order or control. At the summit; would be reason; then will obedient to reason, choosing what reason urges it to choose; then the emotions obeying in their turn the will—thus; a man would be angry because the will commanded the emotion of anger and the will commanded anger because the reason had shown the will that it was right. That is man perfect. That is not you or I. We inherit a fallen nature, which means that for us all our emotions have broken loose from the will. The will itself has broken loose from reason, and reason no longer reflects perfectly the divine reason—that is to say, the law of God. Perfect man reaches such a height of tranquil blessedness. Even philosophers have sometimes grown near it. The nearest perfection are the saints. They are saints because at weary last they reached some measure of perfection in that control. Beyond the saints is another. You see why we have such honour for God's blessed Mother. She began where the saints leave off. She was from the first moment of her conception free from that disorder of original sin, her intelligence was unclouded, reflecting calmly the divine intelligence, not infinitely, but adequately, in her human nature. Her will chose rightly and well. Her will dictated to her emotions. For us emotions outrun the will. We are angry because we are moved by emotion to anger. Before the reason has had time to think we hate out of prejudice or ignorance or irritation. Our anger is often unreasonable. When we have had time to think it over, we realise we have not done right. Emotions, then, are those lower powers half spirit and half matter, joy and desire and love and hatred, all those passing moods of man. We inherit a nature in which they have broken loose from the will that should dominate them, according to the dictates, as we call them, of right reason. Perfect man has all that in security. You and I are aiming to achieve, by God's grace, something of perfection. That is our ideal.

It has been fulfilled in our Master, Jesus Christ, whose unsullied humanity is the model at which all should aim. These emotions, these powers, these faculties, these passing moods come and go untrammelled with us. They should be obedient. But even when they are disobedient, they are still human. Our business, then, is to control them, because they are emotions of a fallen nature which has not wholly been remedied by baptism. Baptism gives us the power, through grace, to control them. We are thus not left an impossible problem to solve.

These emotions of ours may also err by excess. Good in themselves, they may be excessive. Anger, for instance, is sometimes good. The world needs anger. The world often continues to allow evil because it isn't angry enough. Our Lord, with his knotted scourges driving people from the temple, was angry and rightly angry. Emotions we need, but not to excess. It is possible to be not angry enough or to be over-angry. We can fail also in excess of desire. We can fail, my dear brethren, because of excess in love. Not that you can love too much, if love be lawful to you, but there can yet be excess not in love so much as in love's expression. Speech may be wrong, even though the mind speaking meant aright. In love, too, there may be excess—not in love, but in love's expression. You can be intemperate in your expression of love, as you can be intemperate in other ways. If after hunger and thirst you eat to satisfy hunger or drink to satisfy thirst, these acts are good because rightly proportioned; but men can eat too much or drink too much.

Excess not in hunger or thirst, but in the way in which they are satisfied is a sin, because it is intemperate. What is intemperance? Pleasure beyond the purpose: eating merely because you like eating and eating beyond all measure of your need. That we say is intemperance. We are also taught in the household of the faith, that it is possible to be intemperate in the expression of love. Beyond all imaginable limit of need to human nature, to go beyond that in things even good and natural is to sin by excess. Or again, not merely in the expression of human love, but in the times of it; when for instance the violent expression of it might be hurtful to one or other of those involved in it. There are seasons in life when it would be wrong to allow it. There are times like sickness, again, when it would be wrong. Sometimes, unhappily, it would be wrong because there would be danger of dread disease from it. Prudence, in other words, must govern this as it must govern all other good actions. It must preside like a controlling mistress over the actions of man's moral self. Love should be prudent.

Here then we have to urge, as part of the teaching of the Church, that it is possible to do wrong in love; though love be lawful, love can still be ill-used. Though there be in itself no limit to love, there may be a limit, indeed there must be, to its expression. Times, seasons, and other conditions must control it. Nature otherwise may very well have her revenge. I don't mean that whenever we do wrong we suffer physically for it. That is not true. Nor, my brethren, in this sacred place would I urge on you any such argument of fear. We follow Christ, our Master. We go his way because we love. You may with success for a while frighten people with the threats of nature's punishments for evil. But hardly in the time of youth can you frighten with success. Danger does not drive youth off from action. Danger adds one more attraction to human command. These men that seek speed are attracted by the very danger of it. There is a thrill and a stir in danger, especially, I fancy, there was in the days of one's youth. Old age is cautious. You expect it to be moved by threats of danger. But what would you find attractive in a boy or girl who was moved by threats?

For us the Catholic Church lays down the doctrine of Christ. Christ urges the restraint of love by the human will; Christ teaches that there is a remedy against excess, and that this remedy is the restraint of human will. The Catholic Church believes that men are men. She cannot be persuaded that they are just blind animals; that they are simply at the mercy of desire. The Church judges men, however faulty, to have this rule, this governance, this empire, a reason over them. She believes men have will and reason and the grace of God over them, and so she bids men when they must restrain, when they should restrain, to do so by human reason, by an act of their human character under the power and influence of divine grace. She does not allow that anyone should, when performing the full act of the external expression of human love, directly prevent its natural fulfilment. She does not consider it a humanly justifiable action, to seek pleasure and escape the responsibility which the pleasure brings. The purpose justifies pleasure, take the pleasure and prevent the purpose is to frustrate that which justifies what is done. The Church looks on love as something higher than uncontrollable passion. She urges on her children her fine ideal, that love is something which teaches men of God. She considers marriage to be a sacrament and declares that it brings to men and women the graces that they need, not just merely the graces of patience and sympathy, of understanding, but the grace also of self-restraint. People should have no fear or no expectation that one day the Church may change her mind on this matter of child-birth of child-prevention. She has faced this problem before in the past. It is no modern problem merely. It always emerges when society reaches a pitch of physical comfort. It has always been the attempted escape of a cowardly age. I do not mean cowardly in the sense of faltering. I mean cowardly only in this way, that it is too accustomed to comfort to forego it for a moral principle and that it is losing something of its austerity and its strength. Her teaching is clear. Her teaching cannot be altered. It is based upon the nature of things. It must always be wrong to frustrate the powers of nature in the sense of taking the pleasure and denying the purpose justifying the pleasure. Such an act becomes gravely wrong when the matter with which it is concerned is grave matter. Impurity must always be grave matter to man, who lives so close in his heart, so neighbourly, to a dreadful beast within.

Of course, it is true that you will find medical opinion divided on this question. Some will say that it is hurtful to the woman, that it is always the woman who pays; that if the man is satisfied by the act even when its complete result is prevented she is never; that her nerves are strained and obviously get no relief. It hardly matters whether medicine says it or says it not. We take our morals not from medicine, nor from law, nor from government. You and I take our morals from Christ. We are grateful, as all Catholic people must be grateful, to that inheritance of fine Catholic doctors, whose influence in this matter is more than a priest can ever hope to have. We would urge on all Catholic families that they should have as their doctor one whose faith they know to be not only Catholic but an enlightened, instructed faith. We realise, we whose business lies not only with the sanctuary, but with the confessional, how a doctor has a far wider opportunity to give sane advice in this matter than a priest. He can help where he sees nature shrinking from its duty. He can exhort, out of his knowledge, out of the experience that he meets with day after day. Fine, skilful, experienced, kindly, sympathetic, he can speak with wife or husband on matters which they hardly dare broach each to each. He can take, he does take, often, husband aside and wife aside, and tells them what it is wise for each to do. He can lift their thoughts to the high Christian ideal of human nature. He can deny that man must always seek and have gratification. He can deny that a man may not be continent and well. Even our philosophers deny it. Bernard Shaw here at least strikes a blow for continence, when he denies that a man must go wrong, denies that a youth cannot keep his youth unsullied. The Church believes that youth can go by unscathed the ambush of young days. For us Christ's teaching stands, reaching us through the faith. We believe in man's power not just as human power, but in man's power re-enforced with divine power to live up to Christ's teaching. Under this all things are possible to man. Certain things are forbidden men, ruled out by the faith. Man is capable of still holding on to the ways of Christ if he will patiently begin by learning what is right, what is wrong. Your nature will not necessarily teach you what is right or wrong, or will only teach you too late.

You must go for instruction, if you are uncertain, and ask a priest or a Catholic doctor. You will get the right answer to what you ask.

"But," men will say to you, "but we can tell you of hard cases." Oh, you can tell no harder cases to the priest than the cases he already knows very well. "What does he know of family life?" men sometimes ask, almost sneering, "What does he know who has never tasted what it brings, its joys or hurts?" It is true that he has renounced these and yet, after all, he listens week by week to the open anguish of souls. He knows better than anyone the secrets of human hearts. He knows tales of anguish that are known only to those that feel them. They do not speak to others. They feel too deeply. They speak only to him. Hard cases? Why, surely. Over and over again a priest knows and realises that some Catholic souls that come to the confessional and have followed the way of the Gospel are not just ordinary folk. They are heroes and heroines walking erect on the hills of God. There is nothing that better teaches a priest humility than the stories of anguish that he hears from human lips. Hard cases? "Why should we suffer? We? But are we not followers of Christ? Why should we suffer?" Suffering, surely suffering is the badge of our profession. What is our symbol but the cross? Hard cases? Why, yes, these things must be, to anyone who anywhere, at any time, in any line of life, follows the way of Christ. Would you have it otherwise? Would you go through life with perfect ease, with never an inch of suffering? If you did you would go dwarfed, maimed. You cannot get the full fragrance of sweet herbs until you have rubbed them. Then only the fragrance will exhale. You must burn your incense if you would notice the sweetness of its fragrance. You must pay for what you value dear. Everything that is worth anything is to be paid for, and the highest are paid for with the highest price. Hard? Yes, of course it is hard, but it is the way set by our blessed Lord, and he will help you to follow where he leads.

"I love too much to restrain myself." Love can always restrain itself, for love is strong. Passion, passion is weak and lacking restraint. Passion may be something that escapes you. That is the way of passion. Know it for what it is. It is something untamed, is passion, while love is strong enough to obey. But untamed things are no longer serviceable because they are untamed; because they are wild. Love is not wild. Love is something that holds, something that restrains or inspires, something that will lead men to death; love of a human being or love of country or love of God. Men will die for that. Men have died for some fine hope like that. When your leaders spoke to your sons or brothers or lovers of democracy and liberty and justice, measured against those things did they think death great? "We dare look death in the face," said the youth of your nation, because they loved the country whence they came. That is love. That is love. Love is not this untamed, wild passion, that can't be bridled and can't be put to love's service. Love in itself does no wrong. Christ for us is the supreme Lover. Love led him to death.

One of the poets of our time, praising the ordinary woman, speaks of her in those very simple terms:

> *I stood by, in unflinching ignorance of man's duty,*
> *To do in darkness God's obscure command,*
> *And thrusting by intelligible beauty,*
> *I followed what I could not understand,*
> *Because I knew that that alone that passes* [*understanding*]
> *Must be true.*

To you it is given to know the mysteries of the Kingdom of God. Never deny they were mysteries. Don't dread knowledge, but remember that here we do not and cannot know all. To you it is given, God's gift, to know you are the saviours of your people. You can be. Men will look back to you if you carry the great tradition of fatherhood or motherhood to the generation about your knees. What you receive, are you handing on? You are the children of a great ancestry. What will your children's children say of you? That you were cowardly? That you let passion ride roughly over you? That you had forgotten the beauty, the high beauty of love? No one knows. Men here keep their secrets, sometimes in the confessional they are silent when they know silence to be a base thing. Some tell us this, that our people do not confess this wrong they do. Hardly can a priest believe so evilly of them across whose lips have passed the flesh and blood of God. Love is the texture of our faith. Love brought it to us. We ourselves must bring it to love at last. Love divine, of course, is what we worship, but love human is only a mirrored image of the infinite love of God. If you will not love those that you see, but merely seek your own passion in them, you shall know nothing of the infinite love which is of God.

SERMON FOR THE THIRD FRIDAY

The Unborn Child

After considering, my dear brethren, the joys that human love should bring, and again the way in which under the creative command and guidance of God that love is to find its expression, we come inevitably to that which is its normal consequence, the gift or grace of motherhood and fatherhood, in our minds holding it to be something sacred in itself, the response of man to divine command, something which in its consequence links every mother to her whom we call the divine Mother, not that she is divine, but that he that was born of her was God. So every mother has to say her prayer, she who wondered and was bewildered by the angel's message, and yet answered, "May it be done unto me according to thy word." A divine command commissions motherhood, a divine creative act. The birth of a new human soul, and the mother rejoicing in it, its secrecy, its mystery; her first great secret that must rather be hinted at at first than told, the experience of a life within her life.

And then there begin for her those months of mystery, something happening in which she bears so wonderful a part, and yet over which she has so strangely such very little control. What will the child be like? How will his body be fashioned? What his character? What the sex? So many uncertainties, things of which at any rate at present we know so very little, or it may be just nothing at all. Yet with all those uncertainties there are, so those have told us who have watched the thing happening over and over again, there are certain things of which we can be almost absolutely certain, things in which mother and father both fashion to some extent the character of their child. We know, at any rate it seems to come to us on the word of those that have studied the matter, whose honourable function it is to help mankind in the dawn of life, that something, at any rate, depends upon the way of the mind, the condition of those who express in human action the love God kindled in their hearts. We know that something of the character of the act itself, in its particular circumstances, in the motives and conditions that surround it, something in the act itself passes into the character or temperament of the child. How sacred then are fatherhood or motherhood! How vitally and nobly should be performed the supreme expression of the love that holds them each to each! Love must be its dominant motive, if the child is to start free in life with the happier chance of a life lived under a pleasing sky. We know that between them, they may mould, to some extent, not merely the character, but the history of the child of their love.

Boy and girl preparing for the sacrament of love must needs then recognize the responsibility of their life, not to be taken lightly as though they two alone would suffer. Not they alone, but that which comes of them will suffer or will gain.

Our Lord, speaking of the little children growing up among older folk, speaks in words of terror when he says that they have angels who see the face of God; and that if these older folk lead the children astray, teaching them what else they had not learned of evil, "It were better," (said he, the kindest, most sympathetic of mankind)—"it were better that a millstone had been tied around their neck." What think you of the mother and father who, in their moods, who in their impatience and their quarreling, start their child ill along life's road?

The father, who would be a father, must choose not someone merely to be a wife to him, but a mother to his child. He can't think merely of himself, nor of her as though she were only his companion. She is that and more. She is the mother, under God's blessing, of the child he hopes to have. And she, if she chooses, must choose not only a husband, but a father for her child. No selfish choice it is, or should be; no mere personal choosing, as of a dance partner. There is responsibility in parenthood, responsibility towards the child to be born.

Every artist shows his character in his art: Fra Angelico, with his exquisite gentleness showing it in the charming pictures that he draws in lovely colours; Michelangelo showing in the strength and straining of his fingers, that fierce, impetuous character of his. The mother is also an artist. She fashions, moulds her child. She should remember that her state of mind will fashion it. The father should also remember that not the mother only is responsible for the serene state of her mind. We are told, we watch and see, how it happens that all through the time of carrying there is a tendency in the mother to become depressed. Over her broods the weight of uncertainty. In her heart stirs a hope that sets all the world ringing for her, and yet there will follow after it a feeling of oppression, of a desperate doubt. The joy lessens as the time passes, and correspondingly the doubt grows more heavy. The clouds come up, turn grey, darken to black. Now is the father's day; now is the time for his unselfishness; now he can lift from her shoulders something of that greying depression and melancholy, that is marking her for its own. By his sympathy, by his comfort, by the interest he shows in her, by his devotion and especially by his presence with her, he can help her to hold that serenity of mind which he will see one day, please God, reflected in the child. Much depends on him now. This is his day. She carries the pain and the anguish. Surely he won't deny her the comfort of his love? She holds within herself not merely the secret of their common joy, but she carries the burden of their responsibility; she alone must bear its pain. When the time comes for her travail he too may have his agony of anguish, but now at least let him give that companionship, sympathy and attention that it is his alone to give. Her state, dulls her, drearies her, depresses her spirit. When he comes back in the evening she is no longer able to entertain him. Now it is his turn to entertain. As the months pass she grows more and more the hermit. He grows larger and larger in her world. Always he was the centre; now he is the circumference as well. Always it was on him that she leant; now he must uphold her lest she fall.

Marriage, we said from the beginning, is a sacrament of God, by which each must lead the other nearer to God's throne. It is no selfish sacrament. It carries a joint responsibility of each to the other, and so here they must find between them how best they may carry this common load. But the Church deals not only with father and mother, their responsibilities of health, of mind, the unselfishness that she calls from each of them. She is solicitous also for the child. If needs be she asks of the mother that act of heroism which a mother is always willing to give, which must pain the father more than the mother. If there be a choice of life and death, let the choice lie with the child. He was not asked whether he was willing to face life. He was brought into existence. Not for his sake, for their sake he came. Nothing therefore directly or deliberately may be done to the child to destroy it. Killing is murder always, under whatever conditions, if it be unjust. Once upon a time public writers and speakers denounced the Catholic Church for her attitude in such cases. Yet it was the attitude of the Church that developed this department of the science of medicine. Until the Church had insisted on their devising some other way of dealing with it, the doctors went crudely about their business, crushing the poor child's life. Under the Church's inspiration, they have found many other ways of dealing with the problem and have saved both mother and child. The Church gave them the incentive, to discover new methods. She forced their hands. And now medicine proclaims her blessed. She urged them along a road where at last they found their way. She is not hostile to medicine. She has developed it precisely because of what she forbade it. Of course there are still clumsy, skill-less doctors, little touched by that idealism that runs through their most unselfish profession. Here and there some lag behind out of sheer laziness, but the leaders of the profession have gone finely on.

Just as the Church is careful for the child's life, so is she careful for the child's baptism. Howsoever small, it is a soul which must in every way be helped to God. Yet it sometimes happens that, whatever precaution be taken, the yet unbaptized child must die. It is God's creation. God fashioned it. It has committed no fault of its own will. It has done no hurt. It has done no sin of its own. It has inherited a state of sin, but by no act of its own deliberate will. Does God punish it? How should God punish it? God is just always. His mercy out-tops his justice. It cannot be thought that he would be unmerciful to a child. Is he not the God of Justice? Oh, yes, he is justice. It is just that where there is no supernatural life, there can be no supernatural vision. If all that has happened has been natural life, then there can only be a natural vision at the end. It shall see God somehow, not as those see him, I suppose, on whom has come the grace of God. Shall it then be separate hereafter from its mother? Who has ever said so? It can be side by side with its mother and father, and yet not see what they see. Mother and child go down to the pantomime, go down and watch some child's play acted. They both see the same things, and yet the things they see are different to each. Side by side they watch the story of Peter Pan unfolding. Side by side they hear the question put, "Do you believe in fairies?" And both of them answer by cheering and clapping their hands. Both hear, both see, both answer, and yet what they see, hear, and answer is different to each. Each may stand side by side before the unveiled infinite beauty of the Godhead. Side by side, hearing, seeing, and

yet what is seen and heard will vary, must vary, with the capacity of
216 each. Justice, yes, justice must be done to the state of original sin in which the child was at death. Yet mercy, but infinite mercy, shall be done to the mother and the child, for God is love.

For you who are blest with fatherhood or motherhood, you have that which is nearest to the creative power of God. He called light out of darkness. Out of chaos at his voice came order. Out of the slime of earth he fashioned a man. You who are fathers and mothers repeat again the story of creation. At your will comes light out of darkness, order out of disorder, birth out of anguish, love out of pain.

Plato and the Greek philosophers urged that father and mother should place in the chamber where they dwelt together beautiful statues of the gods, so that when the mother lay in her months of waiting she should gaze on their carven loveliness. Let her gaze on beauty, they thought, and she will fashion to beauty that which she carries in her heart. In the Catholic home we would set up again statues of beauty, the Foster Father, the Mother, the Son. She in her waiting, sharing the life that is to double her love and halve her burden, she waiting may carry some of the beauty that her heart dwells on to that which lies beneath her heart. Looking at the saints, she may be the mother of a saint herself.

It is foolish, isn't it, for the mother and father, when it does wrong, always to scold their child? Better would it be perhaps to excuse it. The child is of their own making. If they would look carefully enough, what they have blamed has come from themselves. That passionate temper, where is it got but by imitation? That greediness of desire, who gave it to the child? Who out of passion begot passion; out of some vile act begot something vile? At least because of their parenthood they should learn sympathy with the child, and an understanding of the child. The child is but themselves in little. Of right it claims sympathy and understanding and love. Their responsibility for it should provoke a power to help it to be a monument to their love seen in their own lifetime, a comforting blessing of God.

There are others to whom God denies that blessing. God has his own strange ways. But they that are denied children often find for that very reason they are each nearer to the other. There is no one to halve or distract their loves and lives; but when death takes either, the cup of sorrow is bitter beyond all other bitterness. They were everything each to the other; when one goes, to the other there is nothing left.

Oh, but death is really no ending. Love, we say, is undying. Be it for husband or wife, be it for the child itself, death is no ending. Rather death is the beginning of life on the further side of death. Death is but a road we all must traverse; a river we all must cross. That those we love are on the other side of it is no loss, but a blessing. We here may be lost, not they. They are lodged in the tents of life. It is we who are pilgrims, we who are wanderers; it is we that are dying. We die daily. These, they shall live for ever more. Death for us, we who hold the faith and live by it, death is but a curtain they have passed beyond. For you, said your own poet, Longfellow, addressing in his poem the Catholic girl on the lips of her lover, the prince, death for you is different to what it is for us who are not of the faith. For us it is an awful chasm. "For you naught but the lifting of a latch; naught but a step into the outer air."

For the child, alive or dead, gathered or living, for the husband, the mother, the lover, death is really the beginning of life. Love here is fitful, fading. Love here is so easily set aside or crossed, but love there is in its home. Here is just its lodging place. It was not born here. It was born there. There God began it, for God is love; so love there shall never end.

SERMON FOR THE FOURTH SUNDAY

The Child Newborn

You will remember, my dear brethren, that when our blessed Lord would comfort his apostles by saying that he would leave them but that he would come again, when he wished to give us the most perfect example of those whose sorrow had turned to joy, the comparison that he made use of was the comparison of the mother with her child, sorrowful because her hour had come in labour, and then after remembering no more her anguish for joy that a man was born into the world. Our Blessed Lord, as he thought of the souls that would look for him, and of the souls that as they went through life would seem to themselves for a while to have lost him, promised that he would come again to them, and he gave as his best comparison to their joy in finding him, their perfect master, friend and lover, the joy of the mother of the newborn child. He was thinking of those previous months of her uncertainty, of her fears, of the depression of her soul. He was thinking of all those months that inevitably made her lonely as she grew a prisoner to her home, and then of the freedom and the joy of that freedom, when a man was born into the world. He that knew men's hearts singled out that joy above all others as nearest to the spiritual joy that overflows the hearts of those that have found the Christ they thought had been lost to them. Thus in his eyes the mother stands at a spiritual height by her sheer unselfishness under what has happened to her. She was a parable of the pain with which the finding of Christ was to be bought.

This time, then, is the beginning of her real motherhood. Her first thought now must be of the child's new birth (not merely external but spiritual). She must with the father fix the day of baptism, the great day in the child's life. We keep our birthdays. The birthday is a family festival recurring year by year. Yet though baptism is a great sacrament for us, and the memory of it should be a great memory in our lives, which of you here does remember the day of your baptism, remembers, I mean, the date, the day of the year on which its anniversary falls? A great day, the day when we were born again to Christ, our Lord, we should make the anniversary a day of thanksgiving for the day itself is a great day for the child.

But then the mother has to think not merely of its spiritual birth, but of its growth, its living. It was fashioned of her, and she must still give it the food that it needs. To give it this food should be her work, her duty. A mother should have counted beforehand the cost of the child. The child came because of these two that loved each other. Love brought it. Love must guard and cherish it. Only the motive of love can bring her through the sacrifices that have yet to be made for the child. Her pain, her hour, indeed, is over for joy that a man is born. But that joy too (unless she loves greatly) will be quickly over under the pressure, the steady pressure of the demands the child will make on her energy and her time. Yet the child is hers, so she must surrender everything to fulfil the needs of the child. She will need other help in her care of it. Yet it is always sad to go into a home and find that the child cries not for its mother, but for its nurse. It is sad to see the mother uncrowning herself in her home, handing the child entirely over to another, however good. She is the mother. This is her child. Years after, her power is going to depend upon a subtle sympathy between them. This is the hour of its birth. The child was born of her, but she can break that which holds her to her child. Subtle...delicate...a strange intermingling of life with life, of spirit with spirit, flesh of her flesh, fed from her breast. If the child be near her always, if the child be her chief care, then early and late the child will call for her, she will be always first and foremost to the child.

It would seem that always just at this time there is a danger lest the father should feel that in some way the child has pushed him out of his first place in the mother's love. The months of her waiting were the chance that he had to show his interest and his sympathy, to share his presence with her and lift her a little from the depression that went with her state. Now it is her turn to give back to him what he lavished on her in the days of her need. He must grow accustomed to the stranger that is no stranger, to this link which yet can somehow break the union between them. Man is jealous. He will have no god but love. Sometimes, as we watch a young family, we see this to be almost the most dangerous time of all. She is still a prisoner and all her heart seems now centred on the frail visitor, and the father somehow at last may seem to find no place for himself in the home. He seeks distractions for his hurt feelings...it is so tiresome to be forgotten. Of course there is no excuse for such conduct, yet it sometimes happens so. Wisdom, a woman's wisdom, can surely go side by side with love. Husband and babe are both children to her. Love, with eyes open, looking, watching, will be subtly aware of what is happening in the home. The child is a work, a labour, a burden for both of them, though essentially it is a joy.

Broken nights of sleep will follow for both of them—broken nights. Sometimes, being awakened by the distress of a baby, both will experience a sense of weariness. Then they must look out into the dim future, for at some future date, the roles will be reversed. The night's sleep will be broken again, not of father or mother. Now it will be the child's turn to watch. There will be darkened rooms again, and a dim light, showing. Someone asleep...not now the child. There will be wings beating in the air, not of a life coming, but of life ebbing. The mother's care now to be answered by the care of the child. What she does to the little one, the little one grown will one day do to her, watching in a sick room, waiting, ready to be of assistance as far as one can be on the edge of that strange country, ruled, on its shores by death. What she gives, she gives not indeed because of what is one day to be the reward given to her, and yet as she wakes in the night time, with the cry of the child, she must remember the child one day will be wakened perhaps in the night time, or suddenly, to come to her side when she at last needs care. Always her motherhood is the great work of the mother; it is indeed her sole work. Nothing else really matters. Out of nothing else really can she gather what will give joy all her years.

There will be always excitements, unhealthy excitements beckoning her away from her duty. The thought will come, why shut yourself up all day with the child? Why not come out and share your life again with others? Why not just mingle with the stream? But no, her motherhood is her work. She is, before all things, wife and mother. Nothing else is finer. If that be lost what matters any gain? It is in her motherhood, it is in his fatherhood, that is really achieved the purpose of the love betwixt him and her. God planted that and has nourished it, and the child is the purpose of it. Here is the child. So with her as with that other mother and foster-father—all the fine things we think of them came from their relation to the Child. She is great because hers was the womb that bore him. hers were the breasts that gave him life. Here is an old man (so we think him, though nobody knows really whether he was old or not; we know so little about him), who would have been forgotten were it not for the Child. We are told of his dreams, we are told of his name, but he is to us only the foster-father. That is enough for us. He took the place of a human father in the child's life. That Child was God. Thus came their great work, to them from their Child.

So is it with the work of fathers and mothers the world over. This is the work that is noblest and best. It is the work that is the best rewarded of any work, from horizon to horizon of the daylight or the darkness. There is no love that earns so blessed a reward as that of the parents who have lavished wise love. So will come sweeping back to them the echoes of gratitude. Not love merely but wise love, will earn its perfect reward.

To us who watch life's pageant, there is nothing so beautiful as the young mother playing with her child. That she has foresworn the other attractions of lifetime, insipid at best, seems to others a marvel, but to us only a thing of exquisite beauty. How the artists love her, the mother with her little child! In her you see the tenderness, the grace of her love; in her eyes the sacrifice of her time and sleep and attention. Then the little child growing up under her care, watched at every instant, every new stage almost an epoch to her as she tends and nourishes it; the first signs of its recognition of an outer world, its character faintly showing itself, its early speech, and the mother watching, pondering, seeing what none others see, the opening of that human intelligence as exquisite, as fragrant as the opening of the spring flowers. Such nurseries, I suppose, we all have known, where the mother plays with the children and the children play with their mother. She with her happy stories training their fancy. They will abhor evil. She will have trained them true. As the mind opens to the beautiful things, she will tell them stories of beauty, fanciful, full of imagination, or holding the deep truths of faith—telling them of a Child also, of rugged beasts and shepherds, and the glorious colour and magic of kings, the star overhead and the beauty and the wonder of all God's world gathered to the feet of Christ. In their childhood she can make their lives. She can help them to choose well ever after. She can set, if she will, the rhythm of their marching feet to the harmonies of their days. She can train them, oh, from the very little years of babyhood. All our science now echoes that. The Church has ordered it, and science has suddenly woke to it and said, "Why, the Church is right. It is in those early years that the thing matters." Then most of all is she thoroughly a mother. Then is the father the strong centre of home, playing with the children as their fellow, this man whose reputation is beginning to lift among his neighbours. He has his dreams, but this is the reality of his love. I have been into one such nursery, where every child was bidden give to every comer some present from the few things it had; trained to give to whoever came something, however foolish, something the child held dear; taught sacrifice from childhood. Now I watch these children who are almost all grown up and see still in them the exquisite unselfishness of manners and morals they had been taught from babyhood; and with this has come a corresponding depth of life.

Only here in your city not many days ago, someone grown to motherhood, told me that in her own hour of solitary pain and anguish, while her man went out daily to his work, her own mother who lived but a few streets away, never came to see her; even when the child was born, she, the mother's mother still showed no care. "Won't you preach," she said to me, "just some word to tell mothers that they are mothers always, even when their children are grown up?" She, this mother of this poor young mother now crying because her child has died, this mother of a mother, oh, yes, is busy with good works, so busy with her committees, so busy with all these wonderful things that she is doing for others, that she hears never the cry of this mother that is still her child. Surely motherhood should be a blessing that is always with them—their care, their deepest care of all. Other things? Why yes, there is room for other things in life. The human heart is wide enough to hold many interests, to staunch many wounds, to wipe the tears from many eyes. But this is its real vocation. To this it promised itself here at the altar rails: love, and the hoped for gift and blessing of childbirth that the priest prays for in the exquisite liturgy of the nuptial mass. Children, aye, and children's children, and she a mother again even though the years of her bearing have passed.

The exquisite beauty of the family is a beauty that can be dulled in these swift moving days. The family is broken. Do you wonder, then, that your plays are so full of unpleasant things? Do you wonder that the books they write for you to stimulate your jaded taste must be books that bring in subjects that, before men could not bring themselves to mention or when they spoke of them spoke only in half words? Now they talk of them openly. Why not? The family seems to have fallen, "And though a mother forget her child," He said, "I shall never forget." You see how exquisitely he talked of motherhood and childhood! To him motherhood was the most unselfish love of all. When he would tell us that he would go beyond what even man could do, if it were within his human power—He speaks of the love of friendship, a greater love than this no man hath, that he will go to the greatest limit of what a man shall do. But when he would speak of the memory of love, this eternal God, undying, chooses to match Himself against the memory of a mother for her child. To him in this was exquisite beauty, love and wonderful strength. To the mother he returns for the comparison he would choose for the passage from sorrow to joy, for faith dwindling and faith reborn; for the missing of emotion in piety, and the finding of it serene in the latter years: motherhood, and the joy of a man born again, and the soul in anguish finding again its God. But for strength of memory, outstanding memory, God, with all the world to choose from pits Himself only against a mother's love.

SERMON FOR THE FOURTH WEDNESDAY

Many Children

It is the teaching of the Catholic Church, my dear brethren, that the purpose, or one of the principal purposes, of that sacrament of marriage which our blessed Lord Himself instituted, is the continuance of the human race; and consequently, the Catholic Church, feeling it to be her whole purpose to continue and to foster what Christ our Lord came to teach, urges that doctrine of his on those who are called by God to such a life. Of course for very grave reasons, it is permissible she says, where circumstances are compelling enough, for parents to restrain themselves through self-control from the carrying out of that purpose. But she insists that it is not permissible to perform the act and then directly and deliberately prevent its natural effect. Nothing, that is to say, is permitted, which allows the pleasure and at the same time deliberately prevents the responsibility which justifies the pleasure. On the other hand, we repeat that the Catholic Church does not lay down as an obligation that those who marry should necessarily have very large families. We must insist on this because so very often in the books and pamphlets and articles and speeches that are directed in our own time against this sacrament instituted by our blessed Lord, whether by deliberate malice or simply from ignorance, that accusation, as they intend it to be, is levelled against the Catholic Church. Now whether it be from malice or out of ignorance that the statement is made, in either case it is utterly untrue. It is true that the Catholic Church does look on children as a blessing in a home. You have only to read her liturgical prayers in the nuptial mass, you have only to read that liturgical blessing that follows the mass or may be given outside the mass, you have only to read these to realise that it is not only the mind of the Church today, but is her historical mind as well as the mind of the Scriptures that children are a blessing to the home. That service of the nuptial mass and the marriage ceremony and the nuptial blessing are amongst the most ancient fragments of her liturgy. Varying ever so little, this ideal is widespread through the Catholic Church, not only now, but in the past ages. It is the traditional mind of Christendom. No one has a right to speak for primitive Christianity except that Church whose memories go back to the dawn of the Apostolic Age. She who has continued without interruption has certainly the first claim to represent what is the traditional view of the faith. Children, so understood, so seen, are looked upon as a blessing of God in the home to which they come. But again, though the Church looks upon them as a blessing, the Church does not look upon them as an absolute obligation. That is, there may be all sorts of grave reasons which justify to the conscience of the father and mother (who know the circumstances as no one else properly can) their withholding themselves from the marriage-act. The Catholic Church does not insist against what is gravely reasonable to the consciences of the people most concerned.

Further, it is not necessary to accuse the present generation of evil habits when there may be other reasons to explain a deplored result. It is sometimes said that a particular evil practice must be widespread (a practice that is openly spoken about and easy means to effect it so openly advertised) it is said sometimes that that custom or practice must be widespread because everywhere in almost every nation under heaven there is a falling birth-rate. That it is this which is the cause of the actual fall in the birth-rate need not be true. This may not be the cause of it, though it may be. No one ever can tell. It is, for instance, perfectly sure that the more progress a people makes in material comfort, normally the more the birth-rate of that nation declines. Whatever may be the cause of that strange connection (and no one yet has discovered or ventured to decide what is the reason for it), the fact seems normally to be accepted by those who have studied the matter with such accuracy as is possible under the circumstances. It does seem from the amount of evidence that has been collected, that those nations or peoples or cities that live under conditions of hardship do, on the whole—you cannot lay down any absolute law about it—have a far larger number of children in each family than the nations which live in what is called the upward grade of civilization, by which is meant in material luxuries and with a more comfortable living; amongst these inevitably the proportion of children gradually declines. Hence merely because there seems to be a falling birth-rate in any particular country at any particular time, it is not fair, not just, not charitable immediately to suppose that there must be something desperately evil in the moral conditions of that particular nation. There may be, there need not be. Nor, again, is it fair or right for people within the circle of their own acquaintances to come to hasty conclusions of their own, merely because they happen to see that in this or that family there are hardly any children or none at all. It is very easy, in a world in which the judgment so quickly (unless restrained) runs to evil, it is very easy to make entirely false judgments about those whom we happen to know. One must rule out absolutely, as beyond our competence of knowledge and beyond any real power of careful analysis, one must rule out altogether the justice of any judgment that lays an evil character upon any race or generation or family unless there are sufficient proofs to justify the point which the accusation makes.

Of course, in our own time, under the conditions in which most of those we know live, it undoubtedly does require a very great deal of courage on the part of the father, and a very great deal of unselfishness on the part of the mother, to bring into the world a large family, if God so has blest them. Yet the Catholic Church has instinctively from the beginning looked upon such a condition as a happy condition—happy for the family which God so blesses. There is something in the very conditions of hardship resulting from a large family that produces a sense of happiness which may else easily be wanting. People sometimes urge it as a reason that were they to have a family, or a larger family, the conditions of their life would cease to be as comfortable as they are. We must remember that comfort and happiness are not necessarily the same; that if anyone is to choose between happiness and comfort, happiness is not only the higher, but the more abiding gift of the two. Comfort, after all, undermines or tends to hurt character. Because we are accustomed to comfort, once we are severed from it and find ourselves in conditions where the comforts which are normal to us are denied us, we whine and complain and lose our human dignity. It means that we have become simply the slaves of this or that comfort, and that we cannot get on without it. We denounce conditions which we say are not so high as our own, and mean by that that we ourselves have become so weakened that unless we have this or that comfort, life is unhappy for us. Our happiness has been built upon a foundation of pure accidental comfort, and we have grown up to be the slaves of more things than our fathers were. We lose just so much of our natural dignity in proportion to our dependence on the material comforts of our normal life. A family, a large family, must entail a great deal of thrift on the whole family, a great deal of self-denial. But don't imagine that necessarily breeds unhappiness. It may, and again it need not.

I am sure that it is our experience, that amongst the families that we personally know, those where there are many children are certainly not the least happy of them. There is, for instance, an education in itself which comes simply from living in a family, a large family. There is an education in sheer character; and it is, or has so often happened that those who stand out strongest in the history of mankind have been moulded not merely by some fine type of mother or father that sheltered and inspired their beginnings, but also not a little by the family that surrounded them as they grew up. The very conditions of hardship, the conditions of thrift, establish a fineness of character that else is more difficult to acquire. Again, you will hear it said of an only son or an only daughter that it is time they went to school, time, that is to say, they mixed with other children. Thus it is implied that they have missed some broadening influence in the narrowness of their home. They have been spoiled. Everything has been done for them. They are precious because they are unique. And it is precisely that character which over and over again, I am sure, in our personal experience produces the less attractive child. Larger families not only stimulate character, but produce a distinct variety of type. Where there are one or two children the family opinions on politics or art are repeated by the younger generation almost as though the turning of a gramophone had created the records of the speech. In a large family there is always variety. There are endless discussions. There are so many separate characteristics distributed amongst them, each child with an individuality of its own, that such a family is large enough to allow a rebel. So that as well as strength tolerance is the gift of such a home. The child of a large family growing from its smallest years has had so many other points of view thumped into it that it grows even more tolerant by the sheer experience of having to put up with the expressions of the views of others older and younger than itself. On the other hand, often narrowness lies like a curse on the small family. Breadth and tolerance are more usually found in the wider circle. So, too, out of it comes the echo of laughter. To laugh alone is to laugh but a short laugh. You laugh longer in company with a large family.

The laughter is louder and longer, and seems to ring more true. There are jollity and joyousness and a happy home. Not always, I know. But sometimes, when you are tired of life's responsibilities as you find them, when you have had things pressing on you, when you wish perhaps for a little while to forget it is to the large, jolly family that you go for your comfort, to this scrambling mass of childhood, with their laughter and their games; amongst them you feel as though you had broken out from your world, larger indeed and yet somehow narrower, obsessed with its own sorrows and its own fears; as though you had come to a new world where an infectious joyousness enabled you to put aside, indeed, forced you to put aside, all those things that had weighed on you, and cut a way out for you, an escape from the torment of the drudgery of life.

Sometimes, indeed, of course children are a sorrow to mother or father. They see these children grow up, watch them grow out of the charming age of childhood, watch them pretending a manhood that they do not as yet possess, claiming maturity and showing how little they possess it by their claiming of it, stretching themselves to a height beyond their true height. Sorrow sometimes comes to the parents in their grey hairs, sorrow for children who have wandered beyond the fold, despite the Catholic education that was given them; for children who have shamed their parents by what they have publicly done. Children sometimes may be a sorrow. It may be that a priest has to comfort parents about their children and try as best he can to assure them that maybe all will be well with them in spite not of what he fears, but of what he knows.

There may be a sorrow in children, but, the world over, the greatest sorrow now is of those to whom God has not given the blessing of children. God's ways are strange ways. God's ways are higher and deeper because they are wiser than the ways or the wisdom of men. How often it puzzles us that those who seem, as far as human judgment can go, to be unfitted for the gathering and the bringing up of children are blessed with children, and to those who would seem to us to make such models of Catholic parenthood, this great blessing is denied. In our day, at any rate, those are the hearts that are most sorrowing. Perhaps for us this denial of children to them is the hardest thing to understand, and yet, again, we know that some blessed purpose is this way achieved. Here and there some whom one would have thought deserved, if any could, so high a blessing, are clearly called by God to inherit a wider family, to gather beneath their generosity souls that will never carry their name; as though God asked of them a width of heart and denied them the very reward that is so intimate, the most intimate reward he has this side of death. But God in his wisdom, knows and judges what is right for human souls. There is always sorrow in the world. There is inevitable sorrow. Men and women have what God brings on them. We must not judge any soul alive. We must simply accept God's wisdom as infinite. We must respect and admire what is his way. God blesses and God withholds his blessing here. But here life passes. More truly this is not life. This is simply a preparation for life. This is simply a getting ready, a noviciate, an apprenticeship for the life that is to be.

Father and mother have the wide paternity of earth. There are fathers and mothers in heaven that call those as children who never claimed their name. There are great saints in heaven, names famous and illustrious, who denied themselves marriage and have found themselves fathers and mothers of many children, carrying perhaps their name, following their rule, and holding a habit that once was theirs. Just then as in God's courts there are founders of religious orders who denied themselves the narrowed limits of home and who gathered a wide horizon of following hearts, so we must remember that they are not the only founders of famous families, though it may be theirs are the only names we know. There are others who also gathered children not of their name, not of their knowing, yet children who no less than other children owe to these parents who were never parents all they have, who owe to them

under God the grace of being fostered in the faith and out of that
234 faith have received all the blessings that came their way. Love, in the family, because of children, has a reward that its eyes see. There are those who have no reward that their eyes see, who never meet with the intimate affectionate gratitude of children they have helped and trained and yet who also in God's time will have their blessed reward. Thus there are teachers in schools who have the honourable task of training, who never know whether what they have done has been well done or ill, who never see the ultimate ending of what they have fashioned, who live and work in the future and who walk by faith. A veil, and beyond it the future, and into that future no eye seeing: such is the vision of the ante-chamber of life which is all the teachers see of the fruit of their labours on human souls.

You must work, whatever your work is, under the power of infinite wisdom of God. You must take life for no other reason than that it is he who gives it to you. Not because life attracts you to it but because the hands that give it to you are the hands of love. You must take your life, you must know that God has chosen it wisely because he is God, who is infinite wisdom, not only wisely but tenderly. His wisdom is touched with love. And what God gives he gives wisely, and what he withholds is wisely withheld. What he gives he gives because he loves us. What he denies he denies for no other reason except his love. You come on broken hearts sometimes to whom something has been given and then taken away again—something they have learned to love and now must miss for all their time; and others to whom God never gave anything from the start. God knows us and God knows our courage. God knows our generosity and he never tempts us beyond our courage, but up to its uttermost limits we are tested. That is God's way. If God deals hardly with you it is because God knows he can trust you to bear hardship. If God makes all your life easy, what can the reason be except that he knows you could bear so little in your life? If he scourges you it is because he knows you are strong enough to bear his scourging; have courage enough, faith enough, hope enough, love enough to bear with it all. God lays on us the cross that we can carry. If our cross be heavy, we should thank him with our heavy hearts. It is his way of rewarding love to lean ever so heavily on it. The Son he most loved he most anguished. To the Mother whom he loved he denied even Himself. From her at Nazareth he took Himself away. Ever since that day he has taken other children from fathers and mothers. But usually he has given other children in exchange for the children he took. So he dealt with the mother of St. John the Baptist and the mother of the sons of Zebedee, who, standing behind the Cross saw her own St. John taken from her and given to the Mother of the Lord. She stood under the Cross and she watched John taken from her, and never again, this side of death was she to be his mother. He had another mother. No longer was he hers. We think of the happiness of John. Do you ever think of the empty heart of his mother, robbed of her child? Not robbed really for what you have had, you can only lose because you choose to lose it. What you have had once you have had forever, if you really love it. Love is continuous. Love is eternal, and death cannot touch it. By its side there is no death. There is only a life beyond this life which is no life but only an interlude. Death is no undoing. Death is robbed of horrors for you. In death you shall meet them again. Even then if the blessing of children has been denied you, praise the infinite wisdom of God. Take him as your portion. You shall have none other. You need no other. Let him be your child. He set a child in our midst and he was the Child that was set. He gave Himself to all the world to be their child, to fill all the width of their horizon: "Thou shalt love the Lord thy God with thy whole heart, whole soul, whole mind."

SERMON FOR THE FOURTH FRIDAY

Mixed Marriages

In speaking, my dear brethren, on the subject of mixed marriages, I would ask you, in order to understand the point of view of the Catholic Church on this matter, which is in many ways important in our countries and in our own time, I would ask you to remember what, in the eyes of the Catholic Church, is the purpose of marriage as regards the individual human souls. I would remind you that marriage, as the Catholic Church understands it from the teaching of her Master, has for its great purpose, to help souls that are joined in marriage; to help them not merely materially, but spiritually—that each should help the other nearer to God. In the Old Testament, in the story of creation, God created woman because, looking at our first father, he said it was not good for man to be alone. Her purpose was to help him with affection towards the fuller love of God. God gave her to man as a helpmate. And he too, because she was to be his helpmate, was to lead her also nearer to God—the journey individually possible, but difficult; with another, made more easy. Such was the purpose of God in instituting the Sacrament of marriage; and marriage, as the Catholic Church confers it, is a divine Institution of which one great purpose is the spiritualizing of each by each. Again the Catholic Church deals in her laws with human nature as a whole, with what is probable, with what she has realised from long experience. Therefore, in some of her legislation she does not consider the possibilities of individual cases, but deals merely with the subject as a whole. So in starting, it is possible to sum up the attitude of the Catholic Church to mixed marriages by saying that she tolerates them, but deprecates them; that when necessary she allows them; that in themselves they seem to her not good. They are not things necessarily evil, but her experience suggests to her that more often than not they turn out ill.

Human souls are joined by marriage to help each other to a more spiritual view of life. They have moments of crisis, of severe temptation. Each can help each, each should. This purpose, whether they are of the same faith or whether they are not, this purpose remains intact. They were intended each to help the other. Inevitably, it is more likely in the general run of things that they will find help in each other if the Faith of each is the same.

Husband and wife must have their troubles, arising from their characters or temperaments, or some particular circumstance in which they suddenly find themselves. Wherever we are, we are bound to meet difficulties. We are in danger of being made bitter by some of them, in danger of becoming downhearted, depressed. To the view of the Catholic Church (granting as one must grant the existence of human love, joining each to each) human love can be more easily sustained by the common reception of the Sacraments, by going to Confession, by mutual prayer. The married man with his faults, whatever they be, that are making the married life difficult for the wife, the man who is conscious of them asks her to help him. She, frankly desirous of his own good, will suggest a novena of Communions, or Communion on Sunday mornings. Thus in the old days, when two armies made peace or signed treaties, it was not uncommon for them to kneel side by side before the altar; for the priest to break one single Host and give a particle to each of the generals, as a symbol of their reunion, symbolised by the broken Host shared by each.

Again, as father and mother, they clearly may have difficulties, for human nature has its weaknesses, and men and women can go astray. Of course, there are temptations by which each can be assailed. The temptation to that which robs a man or woman of self mastery, by which they lose consciousness, intoxicated by what they have taken, perhaps because they are overwhelmed by the sad circumstances of their unhappy lot. Individually hard to fight the temptation may be easier if they both join in fighting it, fighting it by common prayer; thus to them come help, comfort, inspiration, arising out of their common Faith. And the Church, knowing men and women, having had experience for two thousand years of married life under her care, records her judgment, her pure judgment, that it is better always that these two should share a common faith. So she urges it, and says this thing is better in itself, in the abstract, because the purpose of marriage is for each to lead the other nearer to God.

Again, looking at it from the opposite angle, one can see all sorts of difficulties that can arise. It does not do merely to look on love as something romantic. There is romance at least in its birth, at its dawn. But married life is practical, dealing with difficult things, with common life and common conversation and interests. There must be subjects for conversation morning and night, weekday and Sunday. Supposing there be one subject that must always be barred, not necessarily because of active hostility, but because of lack of interest. Thus conversation amongst parishioners, gossip in a parish is of local interest, but one not in the parish will not understand, and will be bored. What could it mean to someone outside the Faith? Thus there is a subject, religion, which is barred, not only in its higher state, but also in the ordinary give-and-take of conversation. There is something interesting to one and not to the other, an interest of friends, of this one seen again, of the sorrow that has stricken the other. "I don't know her." "She was in church. No, you did not see her." Even these quiet subjects ruled out. Not very interesting, perhaps, any way, but men and women must interest the other somehow. Subjects are not easy to find that will always interest. The woman often finds it hard to interest her tired husband anyhow. It is harder when some subjects are ruled out. To some it may seem only a little thing, but in life it is the little things that count. Big things anyone can bear. The little things most hurt. A thorn's prick festers. Big wounds can be cut open. It is the little things that can and do irritate.

Or again, the children with their prayers. They are shocked at the father or mother, scandalised in the gospel sense of the word. They see, as it so often happens, that to one or the other, these things are not sacred. They are interested in their children, but the prayers hardly interest them at all. The mother, when not a Catholic mother, does her level best with loyalty; she says the words, in some sense, but not in the same sense that a Catholic mother would say them. Or the father listens to the children saying their prayers; these are not quite the phrases that he would use; he is a little afraid of saying them with them, for these are not quite the expressions to which he is accustomed.

Or again, there is of course the difficulty of those conditions which the Catholic Church imposes. Quite reasonable to her, they are reasonable because the Catholic Church takes it for granted that the non-catholic who marries a Catholic is tolerant of Catholic things. Otherwise the marriage must be disastrous. It is only because the non-catholic is somewhat tolerant that the marriage is possible at all. And therefore it is reasonable for the Church to impose these conditions on the non-catholics. It is hard, but reasonable.

Can't any of the little family go with her or with him to their own church? No, they are forbidden, they cannot go. They must go to the Catholic Church, they should go to the Catholic school. "Can't they go to the school where I was?" "No, I should not let them go." Hard, yet reasonable; but hard none the less. People feel it. When they feel things bitterly and love, barriers may arise to shut love off a little. Love must have all.

The Catholic Church says, "Know what you are doing. Be prudent." Love is wonderful, but it may break down. This is human nature. It is not persistently smooth. We are creatures of moods.

Or again, there are certain things in married life that the Catholic Church insists on, and the Catholic accepts these things even when he does not understand them. A Catholic may see that the Church is hard on a point: "I do not understand why she orders it, but she is my Church. I obey. I cannot call myself a Catholic and not do what I am told." He doesn't see, but he obeys. But the non-Catholic, you cannot say that to him. You, the Catholic, cannot say, "My Church teaches me, I will obey," and expect the other to do else than say: " I do not understand, and so I will not obey." This is likely to be difficult. It is likely to prove a difficulty where the Catholic says: "My Church preaches it," and the other says, "I see no harm in it. Why should I suffer?"

It is possible, but difficult to fit these two in without hurt. We see that, and should count the cost. Years may bring, some other storm-centre, something more difficult even for them to face, something that may tend to divide them, the fault or failure of a child. Christ gave us religion to unite people, and it has broken up many homes. Faith and love of a common Father Christ our Lord gave us to unite all hearts in one, not to separate them. So, too, he gave this Sacrament of marriage, that each might help the other nearer to divine Love. A difficulty at least even where the same religion holds them, more of a difficulty where there is no such support.

There have been, of course, numerous cases where mixed marriages have turned out wonderfully well. The conversion of my own country came about in this way. St. Augustine brought the faith to England, and at the invitation of the Queen of Kent the monks were able to found their first monastery there. From her

Christianity and the zeal of the Papacy, the faith came to us. There are other cases where whole peoples turned Catholic because of a mixed marriage. It gave them a chance to hear what the Church taught. Sometimes, however, a partner in love becomes Catholic, not because he believes, but because he wants to marry one who insists on this. That is no real conversion. He is trying to please not God, but man. But a mixed marriage may be a way of learning of the truth. It often happens that men are led that way into the Faith, into the way of God. But it is a dangerous apostolate. Go into it with your eyes wide open. Do not say that the Church is unreasonable. Realise that she has had experience. She speaks of what she knows. Recognise, when applying it to your own case, that under similar circumstances, others have gone astray. And remember the enormous difficulties that may beset it—go into it with your eyes wide open. Troubles that are not apparent now may come later. You have had the sad experience in your own country of realising suddenly that all sorts of people that you met and treated as just ordinary acquaintances were desperately hostile to your faith. Opposition some call it; others call it bigotry. By its right name it means opposition to the fundamental truths of your religion, to the Catholic Church. Things men never dreamed of hearing again said seriously were said seriously to them. You were suddenly awakened to this opposition to your Faith, to the Catholic Church, to the Pope of Rome. So too with those you love who are not of our Faith. You may suddenly awaken to their opposition and realise, that you have been wounding them over and over again, and never known it, must have said things that hurt them, when speaking of hopes and dreams dear to your heart. You may wound those you love without knowing and after long years realise what harm you have done. Men and women may have distressed each other beyond measure. Catholic and non-Catholic, each to each, may have said things that hurt desperately and were never meant. Wounds abide. Forgotten, forgotten are the hurts that the wounds gave, and yet the effects abide. Little things overheard as a child, then forgotten in childhood, but remembered later on. Secret things, forgotten, but later on held in the memory of a wounded heart. All sorts of difficulties arise; and faith that was meant to gather all together in common prayer and make of home a house of love, may prove something that sets souls lonely and apart. There is not the harmony in the home that there should be—with its comforts, its hopes, its inspiration, its open thoughts and lives.

Strength and tenderness are what we should feel from our faith, and there are cases to which these wonderful blessings have come; but there is a desperate list of cases whence has come sorrow, not only in the present generation, but in the generation that follows. Out of discord or hardship, loss of faith or loss of love. Desperate for any heart to have to choose—between love of God and love of man—between love and the faith! Hard to choose, to witness the anguish of a separation, to know that that which is highest is breaking love in two! To witness courage and know that it causes a broken heart; to know that God, who suffered so to save mankind should really have come to make lonely the human home: "The rise and fall of many." "The rise," we all know that, and "the fall" too, perhaps we know of many, who have fallen through religion and its dividing lines.

Just a misunderstanding? But more mischief has been done by misunderstanding than any other thing. Not quite seeing, lack of faith, lack of sight and insight, these inevitable divergences may grow to a separation of hearts. Love or faith chilled; they grow apathetic. Faith and love both chilled—because they belittled the experience of two thousand years.

SERMON FOR PASSION SUNDAY

The Tact of Love

In thinking or speaking of that foundation of the human marriage and the human family, namely human love, one must suppose at the very least that it is sensitive or sympathetic to those whom it loves. You cannot love, so we are told, until you know, and that is true; but also this is true, that you cannot know unless you love. For on the one hand, you must have some knowledge before you can love; otherwise there will be no real, rational, abiding love. On the other the opposite is also equally true, that you do not know properly anyone whom you do not love. You hear sometimes comments made of one or another—what does he see in her, or what does she see in him? Blind, the rest of the world are. These see. They have that sympathy that is almost an echo. They at least understand one another. They at least know. The story is told of one of the writers of my city who lived about a hundred years ago, that he said of a certain family that he hated them, and his friends said to him, "How can you hate them; you do not know them." "Of course I do not know them. How could I hate them if I did?" You do not know anyone unless you start by loving. Or again someone has said (it was Cardinal Newman) "sympathy may not see clearly, but antipathy does not see at all." You may see too romantically, you may magnify the greatness of those with whom you are in sympathy, you may think you understand them and yet not really know them, you may see them greater than they really are. It is easy to make such mistakes. But to hate is to close the eyes, or to close the mind to knowledge.

"Love is an open door." This necessarily means that it is the business of each person who is joined to another, who is called by the will of God to this estate, out of the love each bears the other, to study and to understand. You cannot blunder into happiness; it is something you must foster, understandingly. Is not love infallible? Love is sometimes incredibly foolish. Love should start people out on the road to knowledge. It should help them to understand. A man must study his business if it is to be a success. He must study more than the business. He must study his clients. He must study those about him, and those below him in the firm. It is not just mere knowledge of things that matters to anyone. Men in executive positions must also know men if they are to make a success of their dealings with other human beings, must study them, must know how to take them and treat them—what to say and what not to say. All this is true, far more true, then of this intimate relationship, established by God to draw souls nearer to him. So that if it is really to be the success which each of them desires at the altar, when they pledge themselves each to each, if it is to be a success, it can only be so with study. Love is the cause, love is the purpose. Love may also be the reward. Love can be held only by patient sympathetic understanding.

But love needs something more. Love has its ritual. Love's court has its rules of honour like any other court; and that ritual and these rules of honour require certain courtesies and politeness. These must be the constant order of intimate life. Love, we have seen, must be founded on respect and reverence. These must not be separated. The absence of them marks the difference between love and lust, the whole difference between generous passion and degrading passion. If love be real, it is reverent. By it you are ennobled. This nobility is one of the fruits of the Sacrament of Love. Men and women and children go on their knees and receive the Sacrament of Love, and, with the priest, have said before they receive it, "Lord, I am not worthy." This is true, of course truest, in this relationship of the soul with its divine Lover, but it is true also in a human way of this other love.

So there must be respect and reverence always, politeness always. These are the courtesies of cultured life. These must exist always, whether other people are there, whether or not any stranger or acquaintances be present, always whether alone or in company, courtesy and good manners must preside. How hateful it is to go and visit people who are always (one must suppose from what one sees) fighting with each other, quarrelling all the time, who seem always to be saying the wrong things to each other. Unaccountable to us who have to listen, these things should not exist; not only should not exist in company out of respect for the guests, but should never exist either even when he and she are alone. Love is something which should elevate people; and the fact that they are always together is no reason why they should destroy the beauty of the intercourse of life with life. Yet it does happen; or so we hear over and over again. It happens on his side, sometimes on hers. It does happen that courtesy and politeness are set aside in personal relationship. This will not last. This is not real love. Here can be no sympathy, no understanding, no sensitiveness of one for the other. To each other each is blind and deaf and dead perhaps.

Or again jealousy comes in to hurt—another of these littlenesses and meanesses, so many straws in the wind which show you whether it is just selfish passion you have or whether it is the uplifting generous passion men call love.

And if we were to pause and separate each from the other, I think, we should say to the man that, what was asked of him was the tact of love. Especially he has to be affectionate. That is his contribution to the life. A man tends to harden. He is unaccustomed to show what he feels. He thinks it is enough to take love for granted and be silent. It may be enough and yet more may be needed. For her sake he needs to show what he feels. Not for himself, perhaps, but he must think of her, as needing an affection in its results practical. She must have a home. She lives in it; it is hers. There she reigns. He has his own interests, naturally. But in the home she is in charge. That is her place, where her work is, and her work needs to be done well. Now whatever work we have to do will be best done in our own way. Other people can give us advice. We can learn from this advice, but our own way is the only way in which we can do what has to be done well. People can tell you how to do it their way, but you will never be quite so successful if you follow it. Congenial work is the work that suits our own gift. True in whatever walk of life it may be—truest in this intimate organisation. The home must be left to her to organise in her way. Moreover, love never really ends except with the rhythm of the beat of the wings of death. Affection must then be shown her always and in a practical expression too.

And to the woman we would say "Obey." Of course, people say nowadays you must not use the word obedience to a wife. St. Paul, who knew human nature in its every aspect, who played on the chords of human souls, minds, hearts, destinies, says in his epistle to the Ephesians, "Husbands, love your wife" (v. 25), and to wives, "Be subject to your husbands" (v. 22). That is true, that is their need. Love is his command, and hers is obedience. She will always give love. That is of her nature. It is implanted with the roots of her motherhood. She always gives love. Hence the command laid on her is that always she must give this obedience of hers for the peace and for the needs of the home. She is not asked of course, for just, ordinary obedience. You know a child must be obedient, but you know the obedience of a child is different from the obedience of a slave. There is servile obedience and also filial obedience. Her obedience is higher than filial obedience. More that of an equal. Each of these two is an equal. Yet you can be obedient to your equals in other phases of life. Friendship claims obedience, must claim obedience. So they who are equal, because they are equal, can easily obey. To obey someone who is placed over you, higher than you, is galling to human nature. To obey such a one is hard naturally. Because of antipathy it is hard. But to obey those you love only demands un-selfishness. All Christian life demands unselfishness. You cannot escape that demand on you. You can never escape the call to unselfishness if you want to follow the way of the Cross. That way is an obligation: "If any man will come after me...."

So we would ask of each what each had to bring: a man rules and forgets to love, a woman loves and forgets to obey. It is what you would ask of each as they watch the daily Sacrifice of the Mass, what they should ask for each other, as kneeling side by side they gather from the Sacrifice an inspiration for their own sacrifice. "Go down those steps," we would say to them, "and climb those others, and carry that message to your home. Home is possible by unselfishness and by no other way. Shoulder the yoke that is sweet and light." That is what Christ our Lord would tell them both, that is the teaching of the New Testament, something that comes to them on the Word of the divineTruth. To us this teaching is sacred, and through faith in God we are made great enough to live it to the full.

In such homes the children themselves gather something of the beauty and the charm of love. What is so pleasing as a child with good manners, and what is so hateful as a child without them? These have nothing to do with family or wealth or a fine place to live in. For exquisite manners are truly the charity and spirit of Christ. They are not godliness in truth, but like unto godliness. "So let your light shine," said the Master, "so let your light shine before men that they may glorify the Father." So let your light shine! Not merely let it shine. Some lights that shine are hard lights, glaring, unattractive, nothing soft or warm, golden or mellow, but cold, freezing, repellent. So let your light shine that you will lead people to glorify the Father, that because they have known your affection and hope and love, they will love the Father and desire themselves to have the goodness they see in you. So let it shine! Thus you will show courtesy and reverence, and the whole family will be drenched in the dew of them, fragrant with their beauty and culture, with their refinement, with their peace.

We can have a personal respect for goodness without love carrying us in its train. We watch it go by and, unmoved by it, we turn about our other work. It is fine, but it awakens no echo in response. There is another goodness that carries you with it, the goodness that Christ must have had when he drew all hearts to His. When the man on the seashore said, "Master, tell me where you live," who he was did not at that moment matter. Where was his home? He wanted to meet Christ again. Just one sight of him and his heart held captive until death—and, of course, beyond death.

So children, and friends, and friends made by children are all influenced by this beauty of home-life, wise and tactful, full of love. If youth but knew, if children realised their power, what a revolution they could work in a country! This was the way, once upon a time, that a great city of Italy was won back to God. Licentious, wild with the wildness of its artistic tradition was that city; and a great friar taught them, as a city full of children, the way of the love of God. They brought their homes Christward: "A little child shall lead them." A child can teach them, train them. Children also can be apostles of beauty and wisdom and the goodness that leads souls back to God. Goodness and wisdom! These are indeed the windows of the Faith in the married home. Seeing through these gifts men can see true. These can re-unite hearts that were once in love, can make them see and remember and be faithful and affectionate, can keep him loving, her obeying. These make home possible. Neither should be an exile daily in his own home. Faith and sacrifice and the spirit of our Master are needed; to have not just goodness, nor love without its ritual, its courtesies and politeness, without its manners. Love without these is something clumsy and coarse, and not spiritualising—not of Christ. The spirit of wisdom and counsel mean these. The beatitude of purity in love mean these. The clean of heart that shall see God, they have these blessed gifts.

Love is beautiful, woven in a pattern round two lives. So we pray for the two as we see them at the altar, youth starting out on life's way. We pray God to bless them, not with love only, but with a wise love, touched with courtesy and a sensitiveness each to the other's way; that he should remain unsullied in his affections, and she by her obedience merit his confidence, his perfect confidence, knowing that in her sphere she is best, supreme. So we are taught by the teaching we believe Divine. This is what we wish them—pray for them. That is what the Sacrament of matrimony will give them; this is theirs if they remember to go for comfort and inspiration and light to his other Sacrament which is Love indeed.

SERMON FOR THE FIFTH WEDNESDAY

The Child's Education

Tonight, our subject is the responsibility of the parents in dealing with the child's education, and I suppose that the first point to be made is to get fathers and mothers to realise that that education starts from the very beginning of childhood and that when we insist upon the great value of Catholic education, primarily and essentially, we mean that education which is given them at home. When we talk about Catholic education, we are not merely considering the school to which the child is sent afterwards, but we are including in that the home as the child's essential school. There the real training is begun, or should begin. There it is continued, as long as the child stands in any relationship to its home. Catholic education, in the sense of a Catholic school, can be easily destroyed, the value of it, by the lack of Catholic influence in the home. Education begins with our earliest ideas—even before that, with our earliest impressions, and it would seem from the more recent study that has been made of human nature that it is almost impossible to suppose a child is ever too young to be impressed by what goes on about it. Impressions bite deep into the unconscious memory of babyhood.

And then the second point, idea, or thought that would come
254 to us if we tried to turn over in our minds what was the education required in childhood, would be that essential education in boyhood or girlhood is done by character on character. Education is not carried through by a series of commands. To educate a child, what is required is not merely that someone should say what is the right thing, but that whoever takes on himself the responsibility of educating should realise, above all things, that he must himself always be careful to do the right thing; for the particular genius of a child is to imitate. It is on its power of imitation that its early education must be built up. Moreover, it imitates not what it is told, but what it sees. Parents, father and mother, have laid upon them the responsibility of education, and that means first and foremost they should realise the effect of their own character on the character of their child. Education is not the effect of words, or speech, or fear. It is the effect of a person on a person. We are alive, and what moves us most are living things—more in childhood perhaps than ever after, but always true. As children, we are most affected by the human beings we meet with, and especially with those with whom we came into closest contact when we were very young children. We can go back in this to the memories of our own childhood. We can realise the effect on us of other children; what we learned from them. Education is the effect of character on character. Education is not a mere series of commands.

This work of education, this influence of a personality on a personality, requires for its perfection, love. No teacher has ever inspired a child unless in some degree sympathy had been established between them. No father or mother can really influence a child without somehow moving them by human affection. They may admire someone whom they don't love, but there must be, even if love in its ordinary sense is absent, there must be some sympathy between them, between character and character, if this admiration is to bear fruit. The child must, unconsciously perhaps, say to itself of its teacher, "That is a type that attracts me. Along that way I would like to go." Children are hero worshippers. They love the story of character—another child in a fairy story, some historic hero of romance. They are worshippers of human nature from childhood. That is what makes the Blessed Sacrament so natural to a child. That is one of the exquisite beauties of the story of the Incarnation, that it captures the romantic fancy of children. The shepherds, the kings, the stable, the mother, the Child. The influence of this story of Bethlehem carries an essential note of beauty and an inspiration to them. Children are affected by the perfect character of this other Child. This personal form of education runs through their whole outlook on life. They are intensely at the mercy of their imaginations; and a living man, woman, or child, may inspire them sometimes with a curious fascination. Father or mother, an older sister, brother, these can be of the great influences on a growing child.

The love that leads them is not a love of fondling, or the use of pretty names. That is a mere instinct. Love can go with it. Love can express itself in the foolish language with which the elders speak down to the level of a child. But that isn't love. Love can get along without that. Love undoubtedly does at times get on more nobly without it. Love isn't merely petting and fondling. Indeed some children hate petting and fondling. Love is made of sterner stuff than that. Love requires sometimes that the parents must steel their heart against the demands of their child, just as earlier they have to steel their heart against its crying in babyhood. A child that has found that when it cries someone always comes and talks to it, such a child realises that all it has to do, all it needs to do, when it wants anything, is to cry. Sooner than hear the continual crying, its parents give it whatever it desires. That can't be good for a child. It must be extraordinarily difficult to deal with the incipient character apparent even in babyhood, and for that the wisdom of motherhood is required. But wisdom in child's guidance must be asked

for from God. It can't be guessed of itself. To be always giving in
256 to a child can't be good for it. The balance, the difficult balance, of when to surrender and when to hold out must be discovered. It is a responsible business, this beginning of fatherhood, motherhood, because of the lifelong effect on a child of its early years. It is better to start hardy when the child is young, better to teach the child early to be unselfish. One day you will be hurt by it if now you fear to hurt it by enforcing unselfishness on it. You must begin quite young with that. You must start the child with the idea of generosity, and of course the finest way to do this is to teach it the example of the story of the life of Christ. Religion is something to which most children go naturally, especially the Christian religion, because it is woven round a human character, and deals with this God-made-Man. The baby Christ in the manger establishes some secret sympathy with all other children: "A little child shall lead them." The unselfishness of the Child of Bethlehem, the unselfishness of Calvary, is something a child can absorb; it is as beautiful as any of its fairy stories, as exquisitely beautiful, and children are sensitive to beauty of all sorts and kinds.

I remember a family of children whom I knew well when they were quite little. Their mother was a valiant woman. She was herself utterly unselfish, and she would have the children go her way. So she insisted that when anyone visited the children, these should make a present to their guest. It didn't matter what it was, something of their own, some toy, some trinket, given to whoever came. One day, after I had come into the nursery and played with the children and was going away, one of the little boys gave me an uncouth lump of wood that was lying there. His mother said to him, "Do you want it?" and he said, "No." "Don't give it then," she answered. "Never give as a present something you don't want. What do you love best in your nursery?" And he looked slowly around at all his treasures. "I think," he said, "I love the elephant best." A beautiful elephant it was; its trunk and legs all moved. She said, "Give that," and he gave it to me. As I went out of the house I left it behind the door. It seemed cruel to take it. But it was sent round to me next morning to give to any poor child. That mother was a most perfect example of unselfishness. The children are now grown up and are wonderfully generous. The whole family has been inspired by what their mother taught them when, they were quite young. She gave willingly to all her children. There was nothing too good for them, nothing too much to give them, but she asked from them also as much as she gave. On their part there was nothing too much for them to give to their mother. They gave her whatever they had. Out of their pocket money they would give extravagantly to the mother, or to anyone. That was the character inspired in them by the guidance of a generous soul. That is Catholic education, fundamental, stretching right down into the tangled memories of childhood. From those memories they shall never after be exempt. All through life they will be haunted by the early lessons of their childhood. They will be joyous because generous. They will be happy because they will always give. The mark that she made on their characters they will carry surely to the end.

Especially, I suppose, as the children grow up the positive beauty of the teaching of Christ must be given them. All teaching should be given them with sympathy. Even though they have grown beyond childhood, there should never be lack of sympathy with them, wherever they are, whatever they do. Stern? ... Love is stern. It is right to teach them the value of the divine way Christ taught us, but this will be coloured by the character which father and mother possess. If there be a curse on those that would lead little children astray, if he said it were better that a millstone were tied around their necks and they drowned rather than a child should be hurt; if that is true of everyone, most true is it of the father and mother of the child. It is they who most influence it for good or evil. It is they who affect the character of the child, and they affect it best by the positive goodness in themselves, the fine character they possess. That will really influence their children. It is the most they can ever give. A Catholic school has its power over those that enter it, but a parent best of all can prepare the child for life. Indeed all that can be done is to prepare them for it. Once they go into life they must go their own way. They must learn by experience themselves. You never can suffer for them. You never can learn for them. They must learn ultimately for themselves. They may listen to advice, to argument, but it won't come home to them, not really, till in some measure they have tasted it themselves. There no one can help. The only responsibility is to see that as far as is possible father and mother have given them through themselves, through a school, the best education that they can of character on character.

In education cleverness is not of very much account. It is those who are clever, who if they are merely clever, often become criminal. Criminals are nearly always clever people without character. Character is what holds to the last. Cleverness may secure an opening; only character will hold it. Cleverness is a mere entrance; with character is your ultimate appeal. Prepare, then, your children for life. Give the best preparation you can, and then you must leave them to face life. They are human, but God is over all. They are God's children. God will care for them. He made them, he died for them. He has given them their sacraments and the grace of the sacraments, one by one. You can but train them in the familiar ways of Catholic childhood by prayer, and, above all, by the character of Christ, by the sacrament of his love in the Holy Eucharist—when you have done that, all is done. Touching, you must touch the child's soul with the soul of Another, you must affect their personality through a Person. That is the only way."

And you must remember, if you are a parent, that you can never abdicate your powers. The Catholic school is necessary, but the teacher, secular or religious, a priest even—the teacher—is a mere representative of the parents. You parents cannot shelve your responsibilities by saying, "But I sent them to a good school." You are always responsible for what happens in the schoolroom. That is to say, you must never feel, "I have sent them to a good school. Now I needn't trouble about them. The school authorities have the responsibility of them now." No, the school can never usurp your place. You are the real responsible people, not the teachers. The true centre of responsibility is not the convent, but the home; your responsibility then can never be abdicated. It remains always to the end of their childhood. You hear parents say, "But I make it a rule never to interfere with the school management; never to interfere with what is done." That is normally right and proper, of course, but it doesn't shelve responsibility. You know your child. You can see what is happening to the child. It is wiser, of course, not to interfere, unless you must interfere. But remember that the responsibilities remain ultimately with you. You must study the children and see how they are developing; you may have to defend or restrain the masters. Always you must help.

And so we come back, as we must come back, to Christ our Lord, as the greatest influence in education. In education you can only give to the child what you have yourself. We all have responsibility to serve God and love God, and those responsibilities are all the greater in a father or a mother because of their children. They have now a new obligation. They are fathers and mothers. They have responsibilities for the child. Yet they can only give what they have got. You can't inspire unless you are inspired. You cannot move people unless you are moved. You cannot teach them beauty if you don't see beauty. You can only establish it because it is first in your own heart. You cannot give light without light. You cannot give fire without fire. So, with your children about you remember that you can only give what you have got and that you yourself must first be moved by his character before you can move others by telling them of it.

You must be patient. They will only mimic your impatience if you are impatient with them. They are sensitive. They can tell the difference between anger, righteous anger and impatience. They

watch. They do what you do. Your language is their language. Your judgments are their judgments. What you have, they see and copy for themselves. It is this awful responsibility which men and women need to remember sometimes, and above all, at the altar of God; to realise that they themselves must be rightly fashioned if they are to fashion others aright. You can only make the child what you are yourself.

Again the parent is expected to do his duty better than the child can be expected to do its duty. The child is only a child. You expect more from grown-up people, God will expect more from them too. We are always scolding the children for not being good children. Shall we scold the parents for not being good parents? Oh, no, they must scold themselves. The confessional is for that, and the altar of God is for that, and the Mass is for it, too. For them, then, most, because they have children, they must come to the feet of a Child. They must ask him who went with wisdom through the little pathways of childhood that he would lead their children the way that they should go, and because they love that Child they will be wise enough to lead their own child wisely, for the wisdom of their love for their children will grow out of the wisdom that is begotten from their love of this other Child. He came as a child to hold men's hearts and lead them. Other children are to be led by you, and to be led his way because you love him. If you will train your child you must first love Christ. It is this we mean by Catholic education, at the home or the school. It is not a mere matter of text books. It is no use saying, "They are so tolerant where my child goes to school. Their history books would hurt no Catholic." You don't send children not to be hurt. You send them to be inspired by the greatest of all inspirers, by the character of Christ. It is the right of the child. If you deny it, one day he who made you and the child will ask what you have done with its soul, how you have trained it, how you have led it, to Christ. It is not merely the duty of the parent that should be considered; it is a right bought for the child by the death of God. He died that we might live. What cruelty to strangle the spiritual life of a child! Cruelty even to chill the warmth of its love for God.

SERMON FOR THE FIFTH FRIDAY

What A Child Should Know

In speaking this evening, my dear brethren, on the subject of the sort or amount of knowledge that a Catholic child in a Catholic home should be taught, we come to a point that I think has and does perplex, bewilder and even shock the consciences of many of those who are older among us in Catholic life and Catholic tradition. It seems to some of them, perhaps almost all of them, that the traditions of Catholic people during these last years have changed; that once upon a time in the days, that is to say, of their own childhood, there was a great deal more reticence in speaking of the origins of human life—or as they would say, a great deal more modesty—than at present prevails; that once upon a time it would have been thought almost criminal to instruct young children in the knowledge of how they came into the world. These are shocked and bewildered by the new ways and can't realise or understand the reason for the change. It seems undoubted that there is a change among Catholic people, at least in the lands we know. Very simply, what we should feel inclined to answer to them is to suggest that the purpose of education is to fit growing youth, boyhood, girlhood, to fit growing youth to meet the life it will be obliged to meet; that

Catholic education is not a matter primarily of the school, but of 264 the home.

Catholic education is not purely a school matter. It should be older, earlier than school days. It must begin in the very centre of the home life, and should be an education of all the powers and faculties of the growing child. This education is intended to have, as its primary purpose, to teach the children to live, to meet life; that is, to live that form of life that Christ would have lived had he walked their way. And since the conditions of life, social life, and social organization alter, to some extent education must alter. It must alter to prepare the child for what that child inevitably must meet in an altered world.

We would ask those older among us whether there be not a change also in what children now must see? We cannot protect them always at every turn from that which is blazoned in public places for all the world to gaze at, though surely the children see but little of what they see. The world is obsessed by sex in a way that it was not fifty, forty, or perhaps thirty years ago. Everywhere you turn, people are obsessed by it. When you talk about sin the vast majority of the people listening will jump to the conclusion that there is but one type of sin. If you were to say So-and-so is a public sinner, they would only interpret it, ordinarily, in one sense. Sins are manifold, and that is not the worst sin. Somehow it has taken on itself the label that is wider than itself, applicable to all sorts of evil. This alone men talk of as sin. If you were to talk of emancipation, of freedom, people connect these also with sex. Again the words, science, psychology, philosophy often seem, by the way you hear people speak of them, limited to this one sort of thing.

In such a world, changed, altered, new, what are you going to do for the children? This is the world into which they must enter, into which they have entered. It is round them, about them. How can they escape it? There was a time when those things were hidden. Well then, at such a time you could afford to be much more reticent. The point is, can you afford to be reticent now?

Of course there are people at the other extremity of theory or practice who will say to you, "But there is no harm in knowledge!" That is not true, not true in its implications. It is true in itself. Merely to know is no harm, but this particular sort of knowledge does affect human nature. It would be foolish to suppose that the knowledge of things of this sort is parallel with the knowledge of the forms or habits of crystals, or the motions of the stars. This is human. This is fire, and we are inflammable. We don't, then, accept the point of view that knowledge in this case does no hurt. Ask any medical student whether or not the mere knowledge which it is an obligation for him to learn, ask him whether this knowledge, mere knowledge, this science, these diagrams, whether they do no hurt of themselves—anguish, torture for the soul struggling from the temptations that arise from this and yet knowing that this knowledge is knowledge which it must acquire. We are human. All this talk of mere knowledge doing no harm is either ignorance or pretence. Certainly it is not true.

Our whole point is, how about the children? What is the likelihood of their coming in contact with things inevitably set before their eyes? As we read the books that are given us, books that are open to the world, what a relief it is to us to find a book in which this subject is not blazoned in front of us, that does not hurt our conscience a little while we read! The thing is everywhere, gathering in its force, not losing. Everywhere! Children are going to meet it. There is no likelihood of their escaping it. It is all about them. Nor is it merely outside of them. They have it within their own human nature. They have the growth and development of their human life within them. It isn't a mere external knowledge forced on them from outside of them. It is something that grows from within. It is something native to that ruined nature that we inherit which tends, so were taught, towards evil, that has a twist, a turn, a bias towards wrong. Innocent childhood? Why, yes, childhood is innocent compared to the later years. It is not innocent if by that is meant that a child does no evil, or can do no evil. The child has a conscience. The child knows the sting of remorse. Moreover, childhood is at everyone's mercy. Parents may suppose that their child knows nothing at all of evil, it has been so cared or, so protected. They have been so careful of the friends that the child should meet. Over and over again, fancy, a priest has heard a mother boasting, or a father, "Thank God, my child knows nothing of evil." The priest knows quite well that that is a false judgment. The parents may know nothing of the child's difficulties. Often its parents are the last people the child will speak to. But the priest knows. You can't say of any child, however young, you can't say for sure that it knows nothing. It is at the mercy of the world. Anyone can harm it. There are men set with malice, cruel beyond all cruelty, who will deliberately teach them evil. These men walk our earth. There are older children. There are also others who should be their care and protection, who have been set by the parents over their child, who right in babyhood have already, not for any immoral purpose, but through some trick or violence or to quiet its crying, have taught the child what a little child of itself would never know.

The point, the only point in the world today is, can you afford to let a child you love run the risk of these terrible dangers? Say, if you like, that it is only a chance, a possibility. Won't you protect your child even against this? For yourself. Don't perhaps your memories, your experience teach you that evil mostly grows out of ignorance; and when it has fastened on you as a habit, all of a sudden you wake to the fact, and say, "Why, this thing is wrong?" You were too shy to ask. It seemed, something difficult to speak about but one wasn't quite sure whether that fact proved it to be wrong, for after all, there was a great deal one doesn't speak of, things about which we are shy, which are not wrong at all but only coarse. You didn't realise it was wrong. You just began the habit in ignorance. Well, that is always possible, isn't it, also to any child? Won't you help it to escape this that you have suffered? Who should help it? The parents obviously. That is their obligation. A child is entrusted to them. They must do their best for it. They must nourish it, protect it, physically, morally, from every sort of danger. Amongst other dangers is the world outside the door. There are all those books on the book shelves. There are your magazines coming in by mail. There are stories and pictures, and the advertisements! These may have nothing to do with the thing advertised, but the men who design them know that a naked figure will catch the eye. The picture has nothing to do with the actual goods spoken of in the printed advertisement, but at a naked figure everybody will stop and look, and they will read the caption. That is all they do it for. They are exploiting the sediments, the dregs of human imagination and memory. They are appealing to our wounded eye.

It is the business of parents, father, and mother, it is their business to train the child. But a father or mother will say, "But I hate talking of these things to my children. I should hate to have to do it." You are all the more the right person to do it because you hate. Are those better qualified who would be glad to talk like that to a child? Because you hate it you are far better able to deal with the matter. You yourself are sensitive. Teach the child to be sensitive too. These others who gladly talk about those things, keep them away from your children. Not their touch on the conscience of a child. They might so clumsily spoil the delicate bloom of innocence on the soul of a child. You, because you hate doing it, you are the one who can do it. But the fact that you hate it is never a reason for not doing your duty. In any other line would that be a valid excuse for not doing one's duty? What other duty are you excused from because you can so glibly say, "But I dislike it"? So many of us dislike our duty. It remains our duty. It carries an obligation still. So here, the father or mother should do this thing. It is their business. It is their obligation. They are the people set by God to train the child. It has happened, I suppose, to every priest in a confessional, that a girl has come on the eve of her marriage and said to the priest, "Will you explain to me what marriage means?" And the priest will say to her, "Go and ask your mother." "Oh, my mother sent me to you." And there, shame-faced in the darkness, he has to do a work that some timid unworthy mother out of what, if you please, she calls her modesty, is ashamed to tell her child. That is not right. It is her business. She should not shift on to other shoulders what she was meant by God to teach. Openly answer their questions. You should never lie to a child. Of course you shouldn't tell it more than it can know without hurt, but if you love your child you should know how far you can safely tell. If you have got love and sympathy, you can measure as no one else ever can the capacity of the heart of your child. You may be mistaken in your judgment as to their ignorance or their knowledge, but you are in the best position to know if you watch and listen, not inquisitively, not with any sense of interference, but with the eyes of love. Watch their development and, in so far as you can, explain what they want to know. Be always ready to discuss things with them. Sometimes, you see, the children come to us priests and ask us to explain things to them and we say, "Go and talk to your father. Go and talk to your mother." "Oh, I shouldn't dare. I shouldn't dare talk to them about that," the child will say. "You know they are much too good. I should only hurt them." It is not goodness that prevents them from explaining these things. It is an austerity of mind that should not exist between a parent and a child. Is not the whole question just simply, "From whom is the child to learn these things first?" Shall they learn them from lips that will speak of these things with honour, or shall they hear them as some vulgar jest? Do you prefer to see the little heads put together and one telling the other what someone older has told them as a jest, clumsy, awkward, unclean; or to speak to them yourself and have them well prepared?

You, can't you speak to them, you to whom married life is a living thing? For you, surely, it is touched with beauty, since it is lifted on the wings of love. You who have seen the beauty in it, are you not most fitted to speak of it to them? There are some, of course, who will say, "Well, you know, I teach them by letting them have their pets; the animals that they take care of will show them all they need to know." Teach them not with the lowest, but by the highest. Show it to them not as an animal thing, but a thing beautiful, that is guarded by a sacrament of God. Teach it to them as your Master would have taught it to the little children that he would not allow to be put aside from him. He would have spoken to them, aren't you sure? of God's kingdom, of God's creation, of themselves fashioned in the way of God. Oh, I know that though he was human, he was not tempted from within. But he could have been tempted from outside. He carried our nature, but not a nature hurt from within as is ours. He was freed from that, but he came the way of humanity. He was born of a virgin. He came, and through that fashion, into the world. Show them at least not the lowest, but the highest. Does not he or she, the little child, say in the Hail Mary, "Blessed is the fruit of thy womb"? Is this something indecent that you have taught your child? If it is not indecent, won't you explain it? Won't you explain somehow to the growing child, as it grows, what it means? Without it shall they understand the exquisite humility of Christ, or the very gospel of the Incarnation? It is part of the child's belief. Oh, not to be taught all at once but gradually; not the lowest, but the highest; not the animal, but man and God.

Don't hope either to keep them straight by the way of fear. It doesn't do with a child to say, "But you know these sins of impurity bring with them the heavy chastisement of God"; or to attempt to frighten them with statistics. Fear has a place in God's world, else he never would have revealed to us the awful punishment of hell, but fear is not a constant way. Our way is love. "Thou shalt love the Lord thy God with thy whole heart and spirit and mind and strength." Thou shalt love. His command is not the way of fear. Teach them fear if you will, but remember that you do not frighten

youth for long. Death seems too far off. They can hardly realise that
270 it means something personal to them. Old people die, they think, youth does not; and they think of themselves always as youth eternal. They cannot imagine themselves decrepit, knocking at the door of death. Don't teach them that way—not by fear, but love.

Moreover this isn't an isolated piece of knowledge. It should be brought into your whole scheme of their education, their training. You are training the child through knowledge of the world about him, God's world. You are explaining how God made us, how God made the world about us in his fashion and not in ours. We didn't choose it. It is not faulty. It is blessed; it came from his hands. He looked when it came fresh from creation and said it was good. This particular bit of knowledge we are speaking of this evening is just one department of knowledge. Be open and natural in your talk to them. Don't falter. You must go straight through, teaching mind and strengthening will. To them it should be part of that discipline of self-denial that you teach them at every turn. Their contact with the knowledge of the origins of human life should be thought of by them as one department of self-denial. You must not isolate this knowledge, hold it apart as something extraordinary, mysterious, veiled. That will make it morbidly interesting. The child has a curious mind. Don't pander to that. But just as you train their will in other ways, here train their will as well as their mind. This is a thing the imaginations of which they have got to control. This is something to which all humanity is subject. This is fallen nature. We fell from a great height. As a flying man might fall and limp all the rest of his days, so have we fallen, wounded, hurt. We must limp and stumble. We can't any longer fly. And as you train them in every other way, train them so in this. This training is partly of the will and partly of the affections; these too have to be trained, as our Lord trained the affections of those who came to him in sin. He took the Magdalene and he said of her that love would save her. Not the same love that had rotted her, for he now took Himself the place of love. He lifted her. All evil slipped from her eyes. She had always had affection. It would have been foolish to say to her, "Cut that out of your life." "Thou shalt love the Lord, thy God," He said. He lifted her by love. He brought her to love Himself and not love astray. Augustine, the great lover, who loved beauty whence ever it came to him, couldn't cut the love of beauty out of his heart. That was part of Augustine. God had made him like that. We bless the Augustine that God made, whose eyes he lifted to another type of beauty. There was a beauty higher than the beauty he had hitherto known, and, now converted, he salutes God with that unforgettable sentence that still rings down the ages, "Oh beauty, ever ancient, ever new! Beauty immortal, beauty undying!" Beauty carried now unerringly his love. These that falter have just a nature set alive with affection. Give them a centre. Give them a friend to love. Show them here on the altar the one unbroken Friend to whom they can speak of everything; who will treasure their secrets; who will teach them the way they should go. Bind up all friendship with the story of Communion. He came to give life, lifting us from the dirt in which we all began, lifting us out of it by the strength, the inspiration of his friendship, by the power of love.

Tell them the story of the Mother who knew before marriage what marriage meant. The angel, bright, pure, stoops to her. "You," this little maiden, "you shall be mother of God." "I?" she replies, innocent, not ignorant. "I? How can it happen? I? I know not man." She knew what she was saying. Yet she was pure, "all pure" we say. She knew what she was saying. Innocent, but not ignorant in thought, word, speech. She said, "How can this thing be?" The maiden and the angel speak unfalteringly of this divine thing; and because she knew why the promise of motherhood seemed impossible and yet was innocent in spite of that knowledge, we make her the mother of ourselves and all we love; we ask that she should gather her mantle about all of us, not hiding our eyes, but holding back the fierce passion of our will. We ask her that she would give us that which saved her, the love of her Son. "Blessed are the clean of heart, for they shall see God." Clean of heart. You see? That is what matters. The heart detached from evil and coarse ways. Teach them how they should guard their eyes. Teach them to set aside of their own will the book that hurts them. We want no laws forbidding ill literature. We want finer teaching in the homes. We want no eternal blockade of evil. We want a heart that rejects it, despises it as something that is abhorrent to a well-taught mind.

Here is our Lord on the altar of God. Our lips receive him. Our eyes that watch him, we hope one day shall see him again. Our hands we trust one day shall handle him. He is our lover, he is our hope and our ultimate reward. Because we love him, nothing lower, cheaper than he will do to hold our love. Because we love him, we would hold ourselves free from the rest of the world. We would help all the world towards that true freedom which sees God because its heart is clean. To hold God neighbourly, to love God is to be saved from the world's evil, to be in it but not of it, as he said. Teach them to know, teach them above all to love this Friend of theirs. Let them grow in knowledge and purity. God will help you to do this for it is the work he Himself has laid on you to perform.

SERMON FOR PALM SUNDAY

Through Christ to God

During these evenings of Lent, my dear brethren, we have tried to look at the sanctity of our Catholic world as centreing around the home, and, indeed, to remember that that home is for us not merely that which shelters our spiritual life, but that which gives it its energy and its vigour. We want to realise that the world as God made it has centred around the home, and that again, as God made it, the unity of the home comes, humanly speaking, from love, and even divinely speaking, from human love lifted to a higher plane than it could itself achieve.

It is through the family, bound up with family life; and creating one by one the family feasts, that our blessed Lord gave us the sacraments. The family begins with the sacraments, and all the various stages of family life are marked by sacraments. It is the way in which our blessed Lord has deigned to build up the home. In all those relations which must exist between the various parts of the family, our blessed Lord has given us his own tender teaching, clear and strong. The relationship of husband and wife, a relationship that is founded on a spirit of unselfishness, of loyalty, of exclusive love. He has laid down for us the rule that governs it. Again, the relationship

of father and mother to their children he taught us, a relationship
274 which demands from the parents a sense of their responsibility for the child, bodily, intellectually, morally, spiritually, an obligation of guidance, of care, of correction, and from the child the realisation of the duty of obedience and honour; they seeing to it that, as far as is possible the child shall be fitly prepared for life, the child striving to avail itself of what is done for it. Again he repeated the old commandment that fixed the relationship of children to parents, whom they should love, honour and obey. So too he dealt with the relationship of the family to that circle of acquaintances that works for the family: that there shall be side by side with the work that is lawfully demanded, an adequate return for labour and that a sense of brotherhood should never be forgotten, which bridges and includes, howsoever divergent and different may be the type, every character and class. If you would understand something, at least, of the new spirit that our Lord came to bring into the world, take the Epistle of St. Paul to Philemon, the shortest of the books of the New Testament, and read the injunctions that St. Paul there lays down for Philemon to guide his dealings with his newly baptised slave. The slave had run away from his master and come to St. Paul. St. Paul had received him into Christianity, and was sending him back to his Christian master. "You are now," he says, "still master and servant, but you are also a brother, and that sense of brotherhood must run through the whole of your relationship, each to each": one commanding, one serving, and yet both common brothers of the Father of us all. They were brethren not only between themselves, but fellow-brethren of Christ. Lastly, of course, our Lord has left us the teaching that should govern the mutual relationship of the children between each other.

It stands to reason, my dear brethren, that all these high ideals are difficult to human nature. They demand from human nature two things which human nature itself finds hardest to give. They ask, first, unselfishness, and we are all naturally selfish. Naturally we seek our own convenience and comfort, and especially, naturally, we look at life from our own personal point of view. We see everything as it affects us. We are full of self-pity. We are continually measuring the actions or the character of others by the effect these actions or characters have on us. We are naturally selfish. And again, we are inconstant. We are creatures of moods. We take up work, and then after a while, when enthusiasm has in some way or other been quenched, we get tired of it and lay it aside. We think of something else. We invent numberless excuses for giving it up, by dressing up our self-fancy or pride lest we should see ourselves as we really are. We have innumerable reasons to suggest to ourselves why we should put it aside in order to take up something new, something even more valuable. We are naturally inconstant. Whatever work we take up, we are bound, after a while, to meet drudgery in it. There is inevitably at last a sameness in it, a certain amount of monotony in it, and our tendency when we come to such a period in our work is to give it up. It is true of all duties. It is no less true of the duties of the home. So this is the second thing that is asked of us, first unselfishness, and secondly a constant loyalty, a persistent constancy doing what we have to do continuously and without complaint. Life, outside has its interruptions. Life within the family must normally continue along the same line. That is the dreariness of it, for we need change. We feel that we must break out from the home life. It is so easy to be full of conversation, of amusement, when you are dealing with people whom you far more seldom meet; but at home, to be alive, to be amusing, to be full of new subjects of conversation—that it is a demand upon human nature to which human nature with growing feebleness responds. Perhaps it is difficult always to be interesting and interested, yet it is much more difficult when we are continuously meeting the same people as we must at home; when there is steady monotony in life; when the same persistent stories have to be endlessly listened to; where you know almost inevitably what will follow next. You know inevitably this story leads on to another story, and you must sit and listen to the same things over and over again. You need desperately both unselfishness and a persistent constancy—the two things hardest of all to the human nature which we share.

But in this our Lord has taught us, as he has taught us in everything, the way we should look at human life. The Mother when he was to be taken out of her life, he bade see Himself, Christ our Lord in John, the beloved disciple. "Behold thy son." She was a mother. She was to take all the world under her mantle. She was to be a mother to every human soul. She, with her marvellous greatness and majesty, with the width of her heart and character, its firmness, its fire, how shall she take humanity, dull, dreary, simple, so petty, so small, so mean, how shall this greathearted mother gather to herself all human kind? One way alone would make it possible: in each one to find her Son. We were each to be for her another Christ. She was to find him in us. She could easily be a mother if she could find Christ in every soul. What he gave to her, he gave to us as our vision. To find him in each with whom we live. How are these things possible? They are difficult to human nature. How are they possible? He has told us. By grace we can find him in every soul.

The way of Christ is a hard way, because a high way. He lifts us up to incredible ideals. He teaches us patience, to which our human spirit is hostile. He bids us be meek and gentle, we that by nature are proud. He bids us serve, we who by nature want to set everyone in order. He bids us be pure, we whose passions run riot of themselves. He bids us hold together through human love when naturally men tend after a while to drift asunder. He asked of us everything which seems contrary to our nature, and yet he promised a power, a gift, an insight so that what seems impossible could yet be done. His remedy is always the same remedy. Why should we love our neighbour? Because of the good we see in him? Oh, no. It may easily happen that we see no good in some of our neighbours, that we cannot honestly discover anything in their character that can really appeal to us or attract us. Why should we love people? Have we got somehow to invent or fasten on to them some goodness that we cannot honestly find? Am I to take up the records of all criminals and say, "Oh well, there must be something good in them." We are not obliged to love one another, for the sake of the other; only to love them for God's, sake. We are not asked to see good in them or to pretend that there is a good in them that we cannot honestly see. It is not that. He has set us an unfailing remedy, something which depends not upon what we can discover, but upon something that we know by faith. He has built the family on this basis, on his word that we find in every soul we meet another Christ! "Because you did it to the least of my brethren, you did it to me." He has told us that he takes whatever we do to all the world as done personally to Himself. Whatever we do he takes as done to Himself. And just as he lays down that law, or if you like, that vision, by which we can regulate and sustain all those wonderful Christian ideals of charity and patience and meekness and gentleness in our ordinary external life, so even more he would gather us around Himself in the family, not for each other's sake, but for His. Children must honour their parents. It sometimes might happen that they find in their parents little to honour and nothing to inspire. You are not asked to honour your parents for their own sakes. You are asked to honour them for His. "Why should I? They are always interfering." It is not at them you are to look. It is at Christ. You have got to look for him in them. Somehow you must pierce that outward veil that hides all human flesh; you must pierce that veil that hides all the world from us, or that shows the world and hides the hidden God. We are taught, therefore, to deal so with all our fellows because we find in them God. True as this is of all the world, it must be truer of the family, those that God out of his own destiny and fate has brought into such intimate relation with ourselves. We find God only by looking for Christ. Someone once when he was preaching bore him the tidings that his mother and his brethren were without, and he said, pointing to his disciples, "This

is my mother. These are my brethren." Christ took all his disciples into the family circle of his own home. The pasch was a family fest, and he shared it with his family, the disciples, in that upper room. We are the family of Christ, and contrariwise, we must find Christ in our family if we would hold steadily to the observance of these high duties to which we are called. He is the centre. He is that which supports the whole family. Withdraw Christ and the family will fall apart. Will fall apart? Has fallen apart. It has lost its unity, its centre, lost everything since men have forgotten God. They have forgotten divine things and divine teaching, and of course they have drifted to the evils that we see in our time besetting family life. They have denied religion, and inevitably one by one the links are broken that hold the home together. One by one the members of the family have drifted apart. The children have drifted from their parents. The parents have drifted from each other. The whole family circle is separating because the centre on which the whole family is held together is gone.

God is our family. God is our home. God alone can gather again together the children of men. The sacraments, the feasts of the family, hold the family together, each sacrament in turn. Marriage gathers, is the beginning of the family, blesses it. By it the two, now one, go out to their life and their work. Baptism blesses the fruit of the family, that which promises a continuance of it, the fulfilment of the command of God. The sacraments, one by one, do their good in this way of Christ. Confirmation strengthens the child when it first becomes aware of life's difficulties, the temptations without and temptations growing within, needing grace to meet them and finding it here. The child realises the difficulties of childhood, learns at least that it has got a will of its own, that its parents have been set over it, and that the Spirit of God is coming within it to make it strong enough to obey. Weakness disobeys, of course. To disobey is the sign of weakness. The weak cannot control their will. They break away. For us to obey, in our age, in the midst of a generation that knows not how to obey, for us to obey and be docile can only come through the grace of God in confirmation. Moreover to hold the family together, to carry them through life, we have the banquet of the family, beginning with first Communion of each child, with the whole family assembled. This is one of the great family feasts. On that day each gives a present to the child. The child is a centre. Oh, no. Christ is the centre of that home. He has come for the first time to the child. It is now more than ever an intimately united family. "All ye are one," says St. Paul to us, "that partake of one bread." Here is the Bread that has gathered them all into one. Confession, too, has its place. For here is healing of the family. There must be, I suppose, with poor human nature, there must be at times quarrels, failures of justice, failures of charity, of peace. By the power of his blood in the words of absolution, these evils are blotted out, washed clean.

How shall you establish unity? Not one with another, but each of you with God. That is the concept. How shall the family hold together? How shall they hold hands all through life? Not by holding to each other, but by holding to Christ. Let him be the centre, so always shall the family be held in one. Distance cannot scatter it, if it is held together in Christ our Lord, remembered in the sacrament of his Body and Blood, remembered in Mass, remembered in prayer. Parents there in Christ can gather daily a scattered family, holding all of their children by the hands of God. Not holding each other, not resting on each other, but all of us resting on God. Unselfishness we need for this holding hands with God, but he will teach us unselfishness. We need constancy, loyalty? Where else shall we receive them but from the eternal unchanging God? He will give them us. Through Christ our Lord we shall find them. It is with this blessing that husband and wife go out of the church when they have been wed. "Through Christ our Lord." Loyalty, unselfishness till death, all the years ahead of them! Is it possible? Not to man, but to God.

280 He came Himself out of a holy family. He, too, found Himself in that narrow home of a mother's heart. He was the centre of that family. He is to be the centre of all families. Parents, children, and those that work and serve for them, shall find in him a constant home. He will gather them; He will hold them; He will establish them and keep the fire ever burning on the hearth which is the centre of the home, on which in older days the family fire was lit. They gathered around the fire in the winter time. In the summer they scattered. In the winter they sat gathered around the fire. Here it is always winter, in the bleak wastes of man's duty, in the wind-swept heath of human life. We need a centre, somewhere where we can gather. We need a hearth, a home, a fire to keep even human love warm. "I am the light," He said. "I am the fire. I am the door" that keeps out the cold, the outside world. He is the centre. He should be. He can be. He is our home.

BOOK TWO

Part III: *Holy Week*

SERMON FOR WEDNESDAY

The Blessed Sacrament

Although tonight, my dear brethren, we begin in a more solemn way to contemplate the Passion of our blessed Lord, yet tonight and tomorrow it is not only the Passion, for there enters into our contemplation of it the memory of the institution of the Blessed Sacrament, which despite all the sombre solemnity of Holy Week we still celebrate as a great feast. We think of it, as it must have been to our blessed Lord—something which lightened a little the sorrows of the Passion, and added an element of beauty to all that tragic doom. To him, as to us, it evidently brought comfort, that he and those about him whom he loved should, because of what they were receiving, be made one with him at that hour: "With desire I have desired to eat this pasch with you before I suffer." Suffering was near its ending. This was when the last solemn message of Christ, as on his deathbed someone you loved might give you his last message before his lips were made silent in death. This last communion was a comfort for him because he was a lover of mankind. For us also it will be a comfort in proportion to our desire to be lovers ourselves of God.

A comfort! He gave it to man as something that should be not only a comfort, but the very centre of his spiritual life. Indeed so it has been. In it you can almost see in front of you the pageant of Christendom in history and trace always the Blessed Sacrament as the centre of that pageant as it goes. Go back to our earliest knowledge of the Christian faith. Go down to the catacombs and see, in those mysterious passages under the Eternal City, those places where still the old altars stand solid, and where you can notice the spikes meant to impale the flickering candles for the Mass; and as you stand in the gloom you can almost hear primitive chant sighing down the galleries, the chant taken over from the synagogue and the temple, echoing in the half-lit darkness, echoing the Christian mysteries, "the death of the Lord until he come." Wherever our faith has suffered persecution (it has suffered, it must suffer somewhere to the world's ending), it has gathered itself for its strength and comfort around that blessed altar. Go back to the old countries of persecution and they will still show you perhaps on the hillside under a cliff, perhaps in some cave in the rocks, perhaps in the rafters of the beams of the roof, some secret hidden chapel; the little chalices no larger than an eggcup, the scanty vestments, the altar stone a small piece of slate marked with the five crosses—sacred to them these insignificant-seeming parts of the liturgy because, perhaps but once in a lifetime, thus were they able to watch the Sacrifice and receive the Body and Blood of Christ.

Not only in those days of persecution, or the great days of pomp, but whenever in those older days of the faith men went out on their voyages of discovery, they landed first to hoist the Cross as the symbol of their conquest and then the priest would step ashore, fasting, that the first act of these white men might be the sacrifice, the eternal sacrifice, on the as yet unblessed new land. Thus under Columbus the wine and flour was brought from their far land of sunshine, that here on the soil of America the Spaniards might offer the sacrifice of the Body and Blood of Christ to make it a home for themselves and their children that would come after them in all the future years. No longer were they strangers here once they had him in their midst. Over all Christendom he has been the people's home. Wherever they have gone he has gone with them, not merely with that universal presence of his Godhead, but with this more homely, friendly presence of his sacred humanity, holding all the world together in the width and the depth of his love.

You know there are tribes still living, wanderers, that have forgotten the art of making fire. Once upon a time all men were like that; then they learned how to make it, or once upon a time somehow they found fire—perhaps dry branches rubbing in the wind in some wide forest—and with that a fire began to be cultivated in the life of the tribe. Out of the fire has come the civilisation of mankind. Round the fire he sheltered. Once he had a fire, he had a home. Up till then he was a wanderer. After that, he was a home-dweller. The fire tethered him, for even when he wandered, in the centre of the tribe was still carried the smouldering fire. When they stopped, they blew on it with their breath, they kindled it. When this was done they spread their meal. There they warmed themselves. Round the fire was their home. We still on Holy Saturday bless it as something sacred, as though it were the centre of our culture still. The new fire is blest, and once again the home fires are lit from it. So too he came to be a fire, a centre, something that should never be extinguished, something always in our midst, to be the centre of our life and our home. Indeed, literally, as especially you know in this parish, it is true of him that he is the home's centre, for it is with the nuptial mass that the home begins. Here you have continued without exception whenever it be allowed by the rubrics that blessed tradition. All honour to you and to those that taught it to you, that whenever the ceremonial allowed it, you should come to be married during the sacrifice of the Mass and that the Nuptial Mass, should be God's blessing on you in your home; that, plighted with its mystic significance, your human love should be made eternal by his love divine. Year by year, too, on the anniversary of that first pledge before the altar, on the anniversary day of the marriage of father and mother till death breaks it, the whole family should gather to renew again its vows. Year by year in the convents and the cloister, on the anniversary of their profession, religious in memory of their once-and-forever plighted word renew the solemnity of their vows. Here at the altar rail, do you renew, or rather let God renew in you out of Himself, by his coming, the love that he asked each of you to pledge the other. He called you to this. Thus then will your vocation be made whole. It may even be that God will give you the blessedness that one of yours should one day stand at the foot of the altar confessing for you and for himself the sins of the home; that he should mount the altar and profess for all of you the gospel-preaching and the creed; that the hands that you have fashioned should lift the Body and the Blood eternal; that he should turn around and give you the Body and Blood again. The son's first Mass, his blessing at the end of it, ah, what more beautiful symbol of the blessing of the home! Again, in that last ending, as each of the family in turn lies waiting for the last summons to leave all to go, he will come at last, the Friend of the family; He that has held them together, will come into the darkened, hushed, silenced room. They bid those that enter walk quietly and speak quietly. No one must disturb the dying. Then someone comes and brings the Master, as in Bethany, to a home where friendship has been all for him, exquisitely royal and tender. Thus he comes at death and robs death of its horrors, breaks the bonds of loneliness, gathers in that home under its shadow of sorrow a sense of peace. "You have come in time, father. He is still there waiting," and so into that darkened chamber steps the Lord of life. Into that chamber of death he comes who is light and life at once.

Thus is he by the several sacraments the centre of man, of all man's wandering. He is the centre of the family. He is the home's home. So he comes, so he has always come. If you go into the great basilica of St. Peter's at Rome and see the tabernacle on the altar of the Blessed Sacrament, carved by the greatest artist of his age, you will find that the design he has used for his tabernacle is like a wide-spread tent. Man is ever a wanderer, but while he has been always gone wandering over the wide heaths of the world he has carried his tent with him. Here in the tabernacle is the home-tent that man has always carried. He that goes hungry and thirsty needs his food and drink. He that goes cold needs fire. He that is dying needs life. Here in this tent, primitive man, forever a wanderer, has found a symbol of what has been in all the wild his home. In America you build so high that in your spirit of humour you have said of the buildings that they scrape the sky. Here in the Eucharist is your high home too, scraping the sky, the heavens. You are nearer to God, as you come to him, all together—at once, finding in his dwelling your home.

All through the pathos, lamentation, the tender cry of the Passion-music, that exquisite chanting you have heard, all through that lilting story, all through that wail as of hearts that are near to the drawn thin cry of loneliness, all through the mourning song of the passion has been echoing through it the golden note of his coming in beauty and peace; all through it his rythym, his melody have been echoing through. Tomorrow as you share in the banquet he so blessedly instituted, think in your prayers of every home, your own and others, over the world. The home is in peril everywhere. He alone can make it safe everywhere. Everywhere man's selfishness threatens it. Man's difficulty to be loyal threatens it. All that is mean and petty and pitiful threatens it. All that is worldly, all that seeks its common ease, all men's littleness, threatens the home. God's greatness alone can restore it where it should stand, as a symbol of unselfishness, of unity, to a world that with its public lips is crying for peace. Not by scrapping your weapons of warfare, but by lighting again your fires of love, shall you find the peace for which you cry; not by taking weapons out of men's hands will you heal war, but you must take hatred out of their hearts, or rather, you must put in its place that generous passion that all the world has known as love. 290 He will give it. Homes and towns and cities and nations and all God's world shall under his blessing be united states, in him surely alone finding their union; in him whom you say that you trust; in him. May he then bless all you and the homes beyond you in this great city towering to the sky! May he that came to link all mankind in this wonderful banquet of desire, whereby he desired to establish the brotherhood of the world, may he give his blessing on you and your people gathered in his love to his feast, you, your dead, and your living, who through him are made one with you! There is no human medium that will bring you messages from the tomb or from the spacious realms of the shadow. There is only this divine medium into whose Being the dead look now with eternal eyes. In him and from him may peace be on all people in memory of this Sacrament that he gave! Out of darkness to us who live in darkness he came with his marvellous light. To us that lay in the shadow of death he came, that was life itself. To us, bruised, harassed by hatred, he came of his infinite love to gather our loves to Himself and to give them back to us, that even human love should be made immortal, undying, enduring with his own sacred fire of love.

GOOD FRIDAY DISCOURSES

The Opening Discourse on Three Hours of Agony

IT IS FOR THIS DAY, my dear brethren, of Good Friday that all our Lent has been preparing, with its spirit of solemn austerity, those sombre vestments of purple, and the silent organ—it is as though while you were waiting for the opening of a drama the lights were lowered and instantly the chattering of the audience was hushed. Not just silence follows, but expectant silence, alert, tense, waiting for something to begin.

So is it with the spirit, also, as with our body. You must hush all chatter if you would hear the drama, follow it and understand. You must guard your heart if you would hear the voice of God speaking to you. He is speaking even though you may not hear. You can only hear if your heart is really silent and tranquil. Even if you are expecting God's voice, you cannot hear it in storm. So here we begin, then, our contemplation of the drama or tragedy of Calvary, which is the drama of the failure of love: God pursuing man, God appealing to man in the one way that might have been thought to have made most appeal. He came, the most beautiful of the sons of men, with exquisite external beauty, chastely fashioned in a virgin's womb. He came with beauty, not only without but within—gentle, patient, tender, forgiving, open, fearless, strong, exactly the type of character that you would have thought would have appealed to everyone. He came, he worked his miracles, he spoke his still living word. Yet he was rejected of men, and he died at last on a cross, lonely, desolate—faithful to him just a handful of women, one rescued from the streets, just that one disciple that was most of all a poet, a dreamer, who years afterwards on an island dreamed his gorgeous dream. Christ alone, on his cross, save for the women, a dreamer, the rescued sinner, and, oh! His mother, of course. They were under the Cross. He looked for man and there was no one to be his companion, his fellow. He suffered as he had loved, utterly alone. But then having suffered he has so much confidence in our fidelity that he turns round to us and says, "Follow me," not blind-eyed, but with eyes open, knowing where the road ends. In his magnificent confidence he thinks each of us to be big enough to walk his way, not of course as well as he went it, but the same way he went and in some fashion meeting the same ending, whatever men may think or say, the same ending within if not without. We must be prepared ourselves to see our life a failure, to come to its end and find it empty of result. It will seem to us then that there has been so little done. Of all our activities so little left us, dreams of childhood and in old age we shall have such withered dreams. But out of the things he suffered he learned obedience. Wisdom incarnate, wisdom infinite, learnt obedience out of suffering, failure, pain. Now that is our following of Christ. You will never escape suffering, failure, pain. You will have exactly that measure of them that God, who knows you, knows you are great enough to bear. You will have the chalice measured to your capacity. You are great enough to drink it without bitterness, to receive it, to go on tasting it to the end. The story of love, love's failures, love's tears, and yet of the loyal following of the heart, of the spirit, alone matters. The rest will be absorbed into the glory of God. Lonely and desolate, denied, betrayed, sold, falsely accused, he draws all men's hearts to Himself—compassionate, merciful, forgiving, fearless, open, strong.

He asks of us, then, as we contemplate the story of his love's suffering, that we should learn what Scripture tells us he taught, too, the beauty of pain, the beauty of suffering, the beauty of the things that men are irked by and all the world avoids. They have beauty, real exquisite beauty. You will see it unveiled as you watch him die. Never so great as his will be your suffering. More squalid yours will be, more simple, smaller, not on so big the scale. Yet you will be his follower, watching, learning, imitating him. Beauty can be won from the heart of pain; so he who loved and lost his life loving, bids us watch him, with wide open eyes, knowing the price that we must pay for our faithful following in the way God would have us go. Don't ask for suffering. Accept patiently what God gives you. Watch. Love. Learn, if you can, a little of his great love showing on Calvary, manifest to us after the lapse of the forgotten years.

Discourse on the First Word

"Father, forgive them, for they know not what they do."

As we watch the drama of Calvary, as we listen to the words that come from his lips, we know, out of his kindness and mercy, what was passing in his heart. And the first word which he spoke is the first rule that all those must learn who would find, if they can, beauty in the pains of life. He began with forgiveness. Had he not intended to forgive mankind, he would never have come. He came to forgive. But it was not merely that he forgave humanity. Almost, anyone can forgive. Almost everyone must have often forgiven. There is nothing so wonderful in that. But he said that which shows out of what spirit sprang his forgiveness: "They know not what they do." He had had suffering and pain. He had been through the agony of the garden; He had been beaten to the ground by it. He had been in such dreadful agony that in his human will he would even now have avoided death if he could. But after that long wrestle in the garden, he rose from his knees—"Not my will, but thine." His forgiveness saw, behind what was done by the soldiers, the divine will: "They know not what they do." He saw not just soldiers driving nails into his hands and feet; He saw them as instruments of the divine love, divine power, divine will. Can you go as far as that? Can you take your life, whatever it be, its pain that at times seems so wantonly inflicted by others, by their thoughtlessness or their lack of gratitude—what you will—can you take your life as you find it fashioned for you, can you look on it as he looked on his, just as the working out of the divineWill? He forgave them because he saw behind them power and love, his Father's power and his Father's love; He forgave them because they were but instruments, unknowing, unaware, of some plan designed by love and power divine. It means that in the garden when he surrendered to the power of his father he had already faced the whole meaning of the passion, that is the drama of the Cross. He had surrendered to his Father: "Not my will, but thine." He had learned obedience, he that was wisdom shows us ever more wisdom. Always he was wise, but his wisdom grew more manifest. He grew in wisdom as he grew in age.

That then is the first lesson, that we must surrender to God. If you have pain and can find no beauty in it, the fault is not because of pain. It is because of you. It is because you have missed, misunderstood, got awry the lesson somehow. You haven't seen the beauty. Somehow, for you it is veiled; it is veiled of course by self. You must surrender to God, if you would see as this great Lover saw, behind all his pain, his Father's hands. You must go on surrendering. There is never an end to it. You must give all. This is a command, not something which is merely suggested to you as a higher counsel. It is actually the only command he gave: "Thou shalt love the Lord, thy God, with thy whole heart, whole soul, whole strength, whole spirit." You will be unhappy till you do that. You will miss the beauty of life, God's nearness to you. You will miss him where he hides. His disguises are many. The hurts that come to you; the ills of life that meet you through the failure of others; be it brutality or be it misunderstanding direct pain inflicted on you or mere thoughtlessness. Those that order your life; those that you take care of, do they hurt you? Is there pain in what they do? It is hardly wise to complain of their ill conduct; it is hardly wise to lament because of what they have done. At least, it is wiser to see, if you can, the beauty that inevitably is there. This is God's world, divinely planned by God. "Father forgive them." Not that merely, not merely that we should go through life just forgiving whatever befalls us, not that! "Father forgive them for they know not what they do." They are blind. They are unaware. And behind them is the immense majesty of God. If you have learned that, there is hardly more for you to learn. Till you have learned that, you have missed his following. That is the first step. So while they nailed him and his fingers quivered, while his whole body shuddered in his pain, even so he looked at these young men and, looked beyond them, and he saw filling his horizon the power and the love of God. "Father—most tender—Father—merciful, majestic, strong, Father forgive them, they know not what they are about. Thou knowest. Behind them, I see thee." Oh, you who suffer everywhere, if anything in your life has gone as you would not have it go, learn to see in those human instruments of your pain, those who hurt you, who turn the knife in you that pierces, the awful power that lies behind them. Dare to see behind them the wonderful power of God. If you can do that, you will taste something of Calvary. You will see something of the beauty that he saw. You will make your life beautiful as his was, although it looked squalid, racked by pain. Though the mob jeered, though this Lover was rejected, yet in his own heart was the greatest beauty love could ever give. We too have to see love everywhere in everything, to laugh at it, seeing it play its jests in life, is to see God and to forgive the world, because you know that God is greater than the world. Behind the world always must be God's power and God's love. Forgive whosoever pains you, finding in those that inflict it God Himself.

Discourse on the Second Word

"Amen, I say to thee this day thou shalt be with me in Paradise."

HIS WAY IS NOT MERELY THE WAY OF FORGIVENESS. He dares even more. It is not merely to see God's power, God's action, God's love behind whatever happens; and to forgive the human instruments because they are, as far as you are concerned, mere instruments, for you can know nothing of their will, of the state of their soul, of whether they intended to hurt you or not. You only carry your wounds, and you look beyond these that inflicted them and forgive them because of what you see. You see them to be instruments of God. But now he goes beyond mere forgiveness of injuries. He welcomes those that have injured him. He gives not mercy, but love. So you must not only surrender to God, you must somehow learn how to possess God. You must surrender so absolutely that it is no longer you but He. With our Lord there was that human will of his that shrank and shuddered on the very edge of death. For he was sensitive because so innocent; His body was the most sensitive of anybody to every type of pain. He shuddered and surrendered, but God was in him and he possessed God. There are folk you meet who possess their knowledge or their sense of art or beauty. It is not just something they remember and can talk to you about, but something that fills their very lives. It seems almost part of their nature. It is interwoven, now, with their whole character. They are delicate, refined, cultured, not by a pose, but simply because they possess this marvellous sense of beauty. So was it that he possessed God. He didn't just surrender. God was in him. God walked with him. There was no will except his will attuned to God's will and God holding all, God possessing him because one with him, and owning him and urging him. He was somehow transfigured and radiant because of God within. So transfigured was he that this robber, this boy on the cross by him pierced through the uncomeliness that now was on Him—scourged, crowned, spat on, looking dreadful as he hung there—this boy with all his past of sin about him, with all that had gone before (whatever it was—his family? his childhood?—whatever had twisted his life and sent it astray), with, so it would seem, nothing to guide him, and yet saying truly, "King, remember me when Thou shalt come into thy Kingdom." Mocked, rejected, ill-used—this boy hailed him as a King. He was looking, perhaps, as boys will, for a hero, for a king, even on his deathbed. Had there already been a leader in the band, had there been someone, some elder, who led him astray because of his boyish worship of him? So it happens in life, over and over again. But here was someone hanging neighbourly to him, also in dreadful pain, and his eyes pierced through all the uncomeliness that veiled him hideously and he saw Love crowned. "Thy Kingdom! Ah, remember me. You, Love, you are unforgetting. me, even me, when you come at last to your crown." We must somehow aim at those heights. Not just to forgive people, not just to look out at the world and see it as far as we are concerned as an instrument of God; we must take pain and suffering and death and poverty and disgrace and all those things that in little or great come to us and not merely look behind them and see God's power fashioning our life through them, but we must take all men to our hearts, not by way of forgiveness merely, but by way of love. It is his way. It is the way he would teach us. To do it especially because God possesses our souls. That is the point; that God should use us ourselves as instruments of his love. Here was this most loved Son, whose whole life was obedience, surrender, acceptance. "Not I. I work no works. The Father worketh in me. I say nothing of myself. I say what I have heard," He said. He was wisdom, yet said he nothing except what he had been taught. He was the Word; no echo of God, but was possessed by God, radiant with God; He was God. He attracted those about him in whom there was anything Godlike. They came to him. He drew them. "He that is of God knoweth the works of God; knoweth his word; knoweth his Son." We watch the beauty of his suffering, watch how he treated the world, as it dealt with him, for we have here no idle drama. It is nothing that you may watch and then go your way unmoved. It should move your life, or rather your attitude to life. Love will follow if you see it truly as he saw it. Life's beauty depends upon the eye. An artist is just someone who sees. Artistry is not in the hand; it is in the eye. The artist sees beauty where you and I pass by it. He sees things. His eyes are open. With us too we see truly in proportion to the way God has entered into us; in proportion to the way that we surrender to him. in proportion to the way that he possesses us and our lives. Now we are none of us great. We are just ordinary people, and our lives are petty and small. Rather they seem so. They are magnificent. God liveth in us. That is a truth of our faith. That is no mere reward hereafter. That is true now. In our heart we carry God. Give yourself to God. Let him govern you. You must know there is a price to pay for this. But it is his way. If you refuse to surrender, if you hold back what you know he now asks of you, self is intruding. God by that much loses his hold on you. Give yourself absolutely to him, with utmost trust and confidence. If you can dare to do so, see him as your King, betrayed and denied as he was, as he still is. See that your faith be unsullied, though its beauty be betrayed by those that should hold it dear. Don't judge the world or the faith by those you see misusing it, for you can't see them properly. You don't see into their souls. You have no right to judge. See God in them, in everyone, bestowing, not forgiveness only but something finer—love. God didn't forgive merely, God lifted us, else we should never be here. He passed by. We were wounded. We shall never know till we see him how deep were the wounds we had. He passed by. He stopped and healed us. And when this Good Samaritan poured in the wine that hurt, the oil that healed the pain, he did so because he loved us. Again he lifted us and made us his friends, and he calls us, as he called this robber, this thief hanging by his side, calls us to paradise even in our pain. That boy, because he saw this was the King, was in paradise. Men have looked on death as something of which they could be proud if they died by the side of a king, if someone was there that led them, someone whom they loved, someone who inspired them, someone who seemed to make all life about them great and big. Ah, you meet them sometimes in a lifetime, and you are glad to be of any service to them, to help them to their dreams. Let him be your King. Know that he is a King whatever disguise hangs about him. He forgave. Now turn, not just be forgiven, you must turn, turn to him with your heart, with your life, with all you have to give. It is little. Ah, no! It is great! It is all you have. "Others," He said as he sat and watched those that gave their gifts, "Others give out of their abundance. This woman has given all the living that she had." Have you given? What have you left? What do you still cling to? What is the will after? Give all you have. Remember he is your King. He will remember. He is unforgetting. You may forget. Pain … Oh, that shouldn't make you forget. That should make you remember. It is his livery; it is his pain. He wore wounds. That is the badge of his fellowship. "Lord, remember me." "I will not forget. Though a mother forget the child that she bore, I forget never." Forgive. Let God hold you. Go God's way. Turn to him. You are not merely forgiven; you are lifted into the Kingdom of the Son of his love.

Discourse on the Third Word

"Woman, behold thy son. Behold thy mother."

300

UNDER THE PRESSURE OF THE PASSION, under this suffering, the obedience of Christ to his own vision, to the purpose of his coming, stands out clear. "Art thou a King?" "For this was I born. For this came I into the world," He told Pilate. He was to be a King, yet it looked as though his kingship were but a sorry kingship. It looked as though he had failed. He had preached, he had worked miracles, he had forgiven sin. He had had a crowd following him, and now he had none—except the robber and just this handful under the Cross. He is King. But of such a tiny kingdom! A robber, and then the Mother, the Beloved Disciple, and the rest. Now he looks at this little kingdom. His mother, of course she believed in him, and St. John and just those few. It had shrunk to that, but he believed—ah no, he knew that he was the King of the world. It made no difference to him, this apparent failure. He saw beyond down all the world, us he saw. First he lifted men by forgiveness and then out of forgiveness into a welcome for his Kingship, and now he makes them somehow one with Himself. That was his magic, that is what he came for, that is his Kingdom, that he and everyone, somehow, should be one. So he said to his mother as she stood by his side, pointing to St. John—Ah, not with his poor hands! They couldn't point! But with his eyes, all that was left, and his lips by which he could speak to her. He had no gesture, except by his eyes, and the words that fell from him. He said, "This is your son. He must take my place. For you he is I. Find me in him." Such a Mother! Such a Son! Now the Son was taken, and John was all the world to that Mother of Christ. She had still years to live after he had gone. After the pain of his parting she had still to live, and this was all that was given to her: "Now, everywhere, in everyone, find me. You are the Mother of all living, of all the dead. Gather them. They are yours. Each one of them is me." So to John he said, "This is your Mother. You are her son because she is the Mother of Christ. Look for me in your own heart. Be me to her." Behind is John's own mother, the mother of the sons of Zebedee. For her this ended her motherhood of this son. He was no longer her son. He had been given to another mother; her heart robbed—ah, not robbed! She, a mother now, had Christ for her son. That strange paradox spoke he, as he went out of life, to this little huddled kingdom gathered at his feet. "Mother," He says, "look for me everywhere." All mothers must find him in all sons. All the world must find him, he would say to us everywhere. Not she alone but everyone must find him in everyone, because he is in everyone. That is part of the Incarnation; that is what we learn from the sacrifice of the Mass and from the whole story of his passion. He is mankind, its mystic body. In him we are one. He on the Cross and we in some fashion with him. He is the head. We are one with him. It is this vision of the world that the mystic has bought by his own pain, or bought by the pain of this other, to learn from the discipline of the school of pain, that all the world was Christ, and that he himself somehow had Christ within. All the combat of the saint is to let Christ live in his heart; as though round about this imprisoned God within us were something heavy that impeded his birth within us, as though our will impeded his gesture or his movement, hampered his great possession of our soul. He is within us, and all about us and in our heart and in every soul alive. "Thou shalt find him in every soul." He only knows God truly who knows God everywhere. He only really follows this Master who has learned that lesson: God in every soul. Everyone is great or near to greatness. "Behold I stand at the door and knock. If any man open to me…" "Any man," just anyone. There is something foolish about love, something that seems ridiculous to those that are not loving. How they jest at young lovers! How foolish they seem! Half of comic literature is the ridicule of love, its foolishness. Of course it is foolish. That is love's way. His love was as foolish as the love of others, foolish, that is, unless you happen to be in love yourself and then you see it not foolish, but wise: "The folly of the Cross."

They said it that knew him. Just folly it seemed, human folly, yet

the wisdom was divine.

"Any man, open." That is what you have to do, all you have to do. Open! He is pathetic, he just stands, and knocks. He is not rude, discourteous. He won't break in on you. Don't be afraid. If you shut your door against him, he will stand outside waiting, waiting until you open. That is his foolishness. It is so foolish to have to stand at a doorway if they won't let you in. You see people coming back and forth and looking at you, and you feel so foolish waiting there, as though nobody wanted you. Oh, these people didn't want you. It is almost a shame that they would not answer. Ah! But you, God is knocking. God stands without so foolish. You have made him a fool. He loves you. Don't you see that? He is in love with you, any man, whoever you are, he is in love with you. That is the folly of the Cross. That is the ridicule of his love, that he just squanders it, that he throws it away on people, who aren't worth while. He is the only one that loves those that are not worth while; and by his love he works on them strange miracles and changes them into Himself. Fairy stories are only a dim presage of the greater work he would do, the magic of his way, by which he turned people, not into princes or princesses, but into Himself. So Mary is now your Mother because you now are Christ to her. She loves you because she sees in you all that she saw in him. You are her child, because you are the Christ that was begotten of her. You, even you. "If any man open, I will come in," He said. "I will sup with him." A half lit room and the door opening, and he enters. Kneel as he passes you by. He will go to the table that is spread. He will share his meal with you: "My food is to do the will of him that sent me." It is a price that you must pay, if you will sup with love. Surrender possession to him, accept identification with him. Your love at your table. He eating with you under your roof: "Lord, I am not worthy." Nobody ever could be worthy. Because we are all unworthy, that is why he came. He came because mankind was not worthy of God, and he came to make mankind worthy, even of God. "And God is not ashamed," says Scripture, "to be their God." God not ashamed to be our God! Ours, because of that miracle that if we will he works in us. That, is all he asks, that we should will it. Do you want him. Do you want to have this Lover? Do you want to share life with him. Do you want really to be his friend and to go his way always, eyes wide open, knowing where the road leads? Now will you have him. Let there be no faltering. "Lord, that I may love thee always, and then do with me what thou wilt," so glibly on our tongue. Supposing he took us at our word? "Lord, that I may love thee always, and then do with me what thou wilt." You see what love may one day do with you? You see what it did with him. Suffering, loneliness, bought, false accusations, and the rest of it? Here on the Cross he speaks and he manifests us great enough to listen and to follow. That is the splendour of his love, that he thinks us great enough to go his way. He thinks us big enough to walk with him on that rugged pathway, to go as he went, with pierced feet, pierced hands, pierced open heart. He thinks us big enough to bear the crown of thorns, to mount the throne with him, to have the agony of parting, to lose all things but him, because we believe, so to say, his faith in us. Ah, big enough if we will! But you must open to him. Open to him. Keep nothing back from him. And as he enters, give him all. "But I shall lose so much." Oh, but you have gained so much, more than all the world beside. Once a man sold all his treasures for this hidden treasure. What God hides is indeed well hid. Once someone sold all their pearls for this most precious pearl, out of the treasury of God. At least know the way that he wants you to follow. Have your eyes open to it. Don't complain if he takes you at your word. Leave him, or follow him but if you follow bear the hurts of love.

Discourse on the Fourth Word

"My God, My God, why hast thou forsaken me?"

304

In that drama of his sacred Passion he now enters into that portion of it in which he seems most lifted above all men, as though perhaps the mercy of God veiled the world from him. The world seems forgotten and he alone with God. The darkness and the mob blurred by it, and even those that love him seemingly hid by the darkness from him. Not they are in his thoughts, but God. Thus he turns from the world. Death is always like that, a severance from the world about. Between us and the world we are leaving an angel with a flaming sword comes, impenetrable, as death gathers its forces. Isolation hems you in, the world about you far off, forgotten. It is a greater business that you must be about. There is something you long to tell those that are about you, but your lips falter and are dumb. You have come out of this little world rounded by sleep; you are getting out of your sleep into waking. It has always been so: that after a long sleep to wake up is agony, almost agony. He wakes from earth to his Father. The loneliness of dying has come on him and the greater loneliness of love. So strange a thing is it that he should have sought all mankind and loved them, and would have all the world to love Him—so strange, to us that are irked by the love of those for whom we hardly care. He wanted all men's love, any man's, so wide, so wonderful, so foolish this strange love of God. No wonder they flung the garment of a fool around him. That is the judgment of man about God. That is what makes faith so hard. God seems so strange. Well, if we only knew what fools we were, it would prove God to be God. If we only knew how blind we were, how small, our very judgment that God seemed foolish would prove him wise. Love is like that because God is love; and God's behaviour will seem foolish to you unless you happen to be in love with God. To the saints, to this great Lover it was wonderful, bewildering and yet wonderful, to see the wisdom of the high ways of love. That is the beauty of that cry: "Why hast thou forsaken me?" Here is mortal love dying. Above it is immortal love that cannot die. Here is humanity fashioned by God. There is the God that fashioned him. Humanity is climbing higher, leaving all things behind, yet God is hidden from it and veiled. If you would love God, and if you would serve God, and if you would pay the price of your service, notice that this is the way he went; and if you call yourself a follower, this is the way you too will go. If you follow God, you lose the little things. You lose things visible. He dwells in inaccessible light. His light blinds you till you think it darkness. It is not darkness, it is only too strong a light. To us with eyes that dare not look at the sun, for us to see God in his beauty, unveiled, would be, says Scripture, to die. Our sight would be shattered with the glory that we should encounter; our hearts broken by the torrent of love. Men have died through love, human love. Men have died too from the love that is divine. The saints, some of them were shattered by it. They carried the torrent of love in an earthen vessel. With the pressure of the swelling tide of love, it broke. It was earthen but what it held, divine. His way is a way in which as he lifts he carries you till the lesser things are left behind. In the valley, in the valley are the houses and the laughter and the children and human love; in the valley the noise of that traffic, of that commerce. But if you climb, you must go above their roofs, above the little smoke, blue smoke that comes curling up; you must get above that, and lose all the beauty of the world—that is, if beauty for you means colour or scent. Down below are the flowers, their beauty, their fragrance; you must come up out of these if you would dare the hills. Come up, climb up, out of this colour and fragrance and all that men call beauty. Below you are the living things. A few sparse flowers may still follow your footsteps and go for a while ahead of you, and then at last you come to the pines. They are the outposts of life on the hillside. Where they end, all life ends. Below you the birds, the clouds even. You are now above the clouds. If you look to the valley, you long for the valley and your heart is torn. If you look to

the hills, you step out fresh again. That is where you want to be,
306 on the peaks of the hills. You get up out of movement and colour, and you stand up high. Rock is about you, bare bleak rock, with hardly a colour, and then above that is the width of snow. Silence ... Stillness.... Immensity... Not hills but the peaks of hills. No valley is in sight. Your valley even is hidden from you, and beyond it never a valley, just hills and the summit of hills, going on to the skyline. No colour. This vast spread of the still, silent snow. It sparkles. As it sparkles, it hurts your eyes. But life, you feel life, the live air just lifting you, as though it were life itself. Men can die at a height. You, if you would go with God, you must pay the same great price. You must leave that little valley. Are you prepared? Don't complain about it afterwards. "Ah, if my prayers were comforting, if I only got some sort of consolation out of them, I shouldn't mind." Oh, that is cheap. That is not service. At least, it seems that you are looking for pay. There is no love in that. God's way is unselfish. You have surrendered. That is the beginning. Now go up on the hills, and pay the price if you really would serve God. Don't ask consolations. "Why hast thou forsaken?" He wasn't forsaken, he knew, else, why did he speak to God? He spoke to God because he knew that God was near him, that God was hearing him. Up on those hills above the skyline when you stand, there is no life about you. Oh, yes, there is life. Where shall I look for it? Shall I look about on the hillside for it? No. Where then? Look within, for you are alive. Don't look for God elsewhere. Look in your heart. But I don't see him. No, no. You are still thinking of the valley, its colour, fragrance, sight. Anybody would serve God if they were always to taste the beauty of God's presence. That would be cheap. That would only attract the crowd. That would not be generous. That is not for the young who love generosity. It is the young for whom he calls; for those at least whose hearts are young, daring, generous, attracted by sacrifice. Those are the ones he wants. "Why hast thou forsaken me?" He never forsakes. He hears. To that height

he calls you. That is where he wants you. Perhaps it is where you are, but you don't notice it, it seems so dull. Climbing is tiring. It is wearying, and colour and fragrance are no longer with you. They must be left below you if you want to enjoy the hills. And your eyes will be hurt. You are on the summit. This is what God asks you to know. Here you are. Prayer so desolate, but you are trying, and you have turned self aside, and you are holding to the garment of God. That you have climbed at all is only because you have held his hand and he has lifted you. He has been Father and guide to you. Go his way untroubling. Ask no payment, no consolation, no reward. That men should leave you perhaps has never troubled you. That God has, may perhaps once have seemed to shatter your faith in him. Believe, unseeing, unhearing, untasting. If you must cry, cry not to men but to God. Don't look about. Look within. Within is light inaccessible. Only you must serve this love without payment; aloof, remote, intimate, exquisitely near to you. The mysteries of God are in your heart's shrine.

Discourse on the Fifth Word

"I thirst."

This great Lover of God, and because of God, a great Lover of mankind, has reached that bleak place whence all else than God is banished. No consolation is left him, nothing but God. The light inaccessible has been reached at last. Bright clouds distant, as it seems, are intimate, near. And our Lord, who taught obedience by the things that he suffered—out of pain we have the beauty of his life—here in the darkness, in the desolation in the utter loneliness, briefly says, "I thirst." It is the test of his love that though he has gained nothing, though despite his continued enjoyment of the beatific vision from birth to death, here he tastes nothing of God's nearness or God's beauty, he still desires. It is always the test. So many come to that part of the road that is bleak and barren, that is empty of anything that would give pleasure to a soul, so many reach that far and are hurt, and turn and go back to the valley. God gives us only what we can bear. God knows our capacity more than we do. What God asks, we can always give. He is just, but he is all-knowing, and he asks only what is within the competence of him from whom he asks. That is God's way. Bleakness, coldness, piety losing its pleasures—sometimes people are hurt by all this. The young, so full of adventure, and generous, are hurt by that part of the road. They have tried with all their childish enthusiasm and generosity to live up to Christ's idealism, and can remember how they have prayed; yet somehow they have fallen somewhere on the road. "I have done everything, and still somehow I don't seem to get anything out of it. I have been to Mass but it seems to mean nothing to me. I have been and received the sacrament of love and it just makes no difference. It has become a routine. It means no more to me than that, and so, reluctantly, I must let it go." How blind they are! How much they have misunderstood! How little they know of love's language: for it has none. Silence is its speech. To love and to serve simply because love is pleasant to you, because love gives—that is the beginning. That is not the end. Pain comes, and pain cleanses and purifies and burns out the dross in us: "Some will be saved yet so as by fire." If your soul has any greatness, that is its way. Don't be hurt if God seems to leave you. He is testing you. Are you big enough still to desire? Can you still want him, though he means nothing? Is your faith big enough and your hope, your confidence and your love? Are you shrunken and small, and just out for what you can get from him, and not for what you can give? His way is that way of hard service, testing you, seeing if once you have got to those hills, once you have found everything bleak, once you have left that valley with all its pleasures, such as it has that appeal to you, that please you, that rest you, you will come up to these bleak heights, without feelings—and still hold on, still desire, still long for him. That is the test. It isn't love (though you may have thought it love), it isn't love until it can get to that height, till it can go blind, and yet accept what comes to it, lose all and yet believe in God's love and desire naught but it. To have them removed, one by one, from you, the things on which you had set your heart, and still to say to God, "I want you, and only you." Ah, those others are frightened of God! He is jealous, he says it Himself. Whomsoever you work for, remember that man is ungrateful and God is austere. If you work for men your reward will not be much from them. If you work for God, he is austere. He says it in the gospels. "Out of your mouth, I will convict you. I am austere." That is the way of this service. Our Lord wishes that we should come to it open-eyed. Don't complain afterwards. Don't turn round on him. Don't say that he tempted you by any false description of the way. Faith is asked of you and that is what faith means; faith is nothing unless it has love's flame in it. Without love it won't lift. Its wings won't lift. It can't fly. You have to trust God absolutely. Whatever he seems, indeed, whatever he does, you just have to trust him absolutely. Now can you, whatever he does, still want him, though he seems humanly unwantable, something too much for us, too much above us, too austere? There is a type of beauty that almost frightens us. It is not pretty, but it is beautiful. It almost holds us off. That is God. Which of you can live with a consuming fire? God is that. He will burn out all that is little, all that is dross, burn it, and make you what his eyes see you could be. Will you, dare still desire him. Will you dare? Then, if you will, you must indeed want him. you must thirst. His way, you see, is a high way. It is a long way. It is a bleak way. It is lonely. No, there is God! Invisible, intangible but God. You shall not hear him. Above you he is, but also within you. If you still want God, you also are a lover. His love has lit your flame. While we talk, he is dying. Lesser things don't concern a man in death; realities only matter, nothing then can matter that is less than God. Darkness, desolation troubled him dying, and yet he had a thirst for the strong, living God. To that greatness he calls our little souls. He will help us to reach it. He died to help; not to set an example merely, but to give us help. Divine the love that ran through him dying. He died to be nearer to us. May we be near him then, lonely, not conscious of his presence, yet still believing, hoping, loving, desolate but athirst.

Discourse on the Sixth Word

"It is consummated."

After his desolation, he still had his undaunted desire, and beyond desire there comes, now, silence. "It is finished," He said. Not finished, really, for what he did is still being done. He ever liveth, to show forth the death of the Lord until at last he come. It is not finished, but all that love could do is done. He has come to the end of it. There at the foot are the few that are faithful, and beyond, the great world goes on its own way. Darkness, so near him, and beyond the darkness the souls he came to save. "I have done everything. It is finished," He said. "I have finished," He said in the supper place, "the work thou gavest me to do. It is finished. I can do no more." He had given, you see, his Body and Blood to feed mankind in the supper place. He had given that. He had done that. Now he has tasted everything: man's ingratitude, and the austerity of God. He is still undaunted in his desire. He is still the great Lover, and it is we whom he loved, we and God. Here and now, at that height, above the desolation, above even desire, he comes into silence, which is love's language. There is nothing that love can say. When it, speaks you know it has not reached its height. When men are so ready to speak, you never believe them. When they pour their compliments out, it does but embarrass your soul. Love has no language but silence, for words are too small for the long thoughts of love. Here he, this Lover with his love incarnate, even he comes at last to silence: "It is finished." What love could do is done. Love is always stammering, trembling, tongue-tied, hesitant, because it is trying to say what cannot be said. You cannot convey love by speech. You touch it somehow by silence. In silence souls meet. In silence he saw the God he thirsted for, the God that seemed aloof, desolating, forsaking, and who yet hadn't forsaken, for when he cried with a loud cry that pierced the clouds God heard. He thirsted for God, and now there is nothing he can say. Now all that is left him is waiting and looking. He has reached contemplation, which is a sight, a looking out at God, a gazing, nothing to be said, just to look and to see. That is his height of prayer. You see, all the while we have been describing his prayer on the Cross; the seven words are the words of his prayer; and as you listen to them you see the wings of prayer lifting him. Now he has gone beyond desire. He has gone into that higher silence, where is naught but he and God. He just looks at God: "It is finished." Here speech breaks down, even his speech, that was so wise. Just as love that is so bold stops on the edge of speech, after stammering, and can only say "But I love," and beyond that all words are spent; so is he silent, happy. It may have happened that love has silenced you sometimes because love has lifted you where you are with that which you love. The saints have shown us how at times they have reached that wonderful place, and they have felt then—no, not felt, known by faith that God was there, and have just looked for him that haply they might find him. By faith they knew he was present, and they rested with God. Our Lord, not by faith but by vision, has reached that point in his prayer which is the death of the soul in love. He has reached the point beyond darkness, beyond desire. He has come into the place of silence. Some souls, perhaps all souls, he calls to that height. If you have desire in spite of your desolation; if beyond the darkness you can still desire, then this is higher still. If in spite of that lack

of sense and consolation, that dryness, that dreariness, that drift of
312 distractions over you that might else discourage you were you not in love, if in spite of that, you still desire God, whatever he costs you, if you still desire, you will come up into this place of silence; don't look for speech. Seek no more the gates but enter. You are there. You have reached silence…unutterable silence… This is the inaccessible light. This is where the high souls go. As in the olden Scripture but once a year the high priest entered within the shrine, the Holy of Holies, and stepped into it alone, so is it still "a seldom pleasure" to gaze in silence on Beauty half-unveiled. Yet this is the ultimate place of love. Hands hold on to it, nestling under his wings.

"It is finished," He said. The work's done. All the business, all the action, all the courage, all the infinitude of desire is over. Just silence now. No seeking of words. There are none, merely he is content in silence to be with God. It may be that he has called you to sorrow somewhere. Perhaps, nobody knows, perhaps it is human love that wounds you, your child, someone you love. It may be death that has hurt you. You have looked behind and tried to see in whatever did hurt you the instruments of the divineWill, but you cannot bring yourself to speak, to say to him, "I accept it." How much pain is there not that you can bear if nobody speaks to you? Sorrow you can hold, however desolating, if nobody speaks to you. If they speak, you break down. You cannot speak. You dread their coming. Almost like a hurt dog you would creep under the bushes and die alone. You say, "But I couldn't say anything to him. I can take his will, but I can't speak." Don't. There is no need to speak. This is love. He loves you. He knows you. He understands. Don't speak. Know that he is with you. Beyond desire, comes silence…be there with him in the intimate, ultimate silence. That is the speech of love. Don't speak. Look. He is there.

Discourse on the Seventh Word

"Father, into thy hands I commend my spirit."

AND SO IT IS, MY DEAR BRETHREN, that by his own deliberate Will he dies. He has done all that love could do: "It is finished." There follows silence, and then, seeing that all things were accomplished, he cried, gathering his strength in that last cry, still a King, still in his Kingdom, still complete master of Himself, of all the world—and then crying with this loud voice he dies. He bows his head. "Into thy hands, Father, into thy hands I commit my soul." Acquiescence, in the Father's hands! He had lived through so much. It was so long ago since he had begged forgiveness for the soldiers, so long since he had been spoken to by the robber by his side. He had passed through so much, and all else had been tasted by him, he had taught obedience by what he suffered. Blessed Master that would teach us his own blessed way, out of pain to teach obedience! Love, else, is but a vain desire. Love that will not obey is self-love. It is the intuition of self clinging to its wings. Love that obeys is real love. Love that holds nothing back, that has no prejudice, no desire of its own, that desires only what love desires, no more, no less. The infinite Lover loved mankind because he loved God. He comes to the end, and he finishes it with that thought, "Into thy hands, O Father, I commit my spirit," and unto God he goes—water mingling with water, sunlight with sunlight, fire with fire, snow with snow. "As thou, Father, in me, and I in thee." Love merging into love. "Into thy hands." He sees his Father's hands in all life, in death. They are the hands of God, pure, wise, loving, the delicate hands of an artist fashioning something of beauty, slim, slender, sensitive. These were his Father's hands. Out of pain fashioning beauty; for pain is the price you must pay for beauty. The beauty of an art work depends on the pain of fashioning the material. It must be carved or chiseled or burnt. Or the fingers may be like the fingers of those that fashion machinery. Clever fingers, feeling at once where that machine has faltered, gone wrong. Swift fingers that go to the root of trouble, smeared with the grease of the engine and yet not slender only, but strong. The hands of God are the hands of an infinite artist, of an artificer working until now: "Into thy hands, O Father." He has tasted all our sorrows. He has carried all our griefs. He has gone beyond desire into silence. It is finished, and now death at last, and death is even that. He and the Father held separate, in a sense, by life, are linked now with death. "Till death do us unite" is the pledge of this sacrament of dying. It has its own ritual and its own way. Love, our love, must run the way his did, and we must just put ourselves into the divine hands. When he went on earth he touched men, and, touching, healed them. He made clay with his fingers and plastered the wound with the clay, and men were healed because of what he had done. He touched them and life ran through his finger. They were sick; but then they were healed, they said. He had touched them and something had happened. His were healing fingers, fingers that brought peace. The sick were tossing with fever, and he just soothed their tortured, fevered, exaggerated view is begotten of fever, and smoothed them away. He healed what he touched, and his fingers thrilled with love. John, who leant back on the bosom of his Master at the supper place, says boldly, "Our hands have handled the Word made flesh." Love had awakened in him in his boyhood by the lakeside as he touched hands with Christ. Something happened, some fire broke out and kindled life in him and love ran between. So they that listened knew what the words meant as he spoke them. They, still standing under the Cross, they knew what his hands v meant to them. The mother knew the hands that were her own; she knew the hands that had patted her in his babyhood; that had helped her in eager boyhood; that had waited on her with the energy of youth; the hands that had held her hands as he went out of the supper place into the darkness. She knew what sort of hands were the hands of God. The Son's hands were human. God's would be more wonderful, more full of life, more full of love, more healing, more peace-giving, infinite hands. She knew what he meant when he said that he gave Himself into his Father's hands, but we, not knowing, have yet to do as he did and give ourselves into the hands of God. In those hands we are. Beneath us are the everlasting arms. Go fearlessly the way you know he calls you. Go, he holds you, he will not let you fall. As you cross the street with a child, its hand finds your hand; linked in your hand it isn't afraid. Hold his hand. Go his way. Let him deal with you. He surely must have proved to you by this time that he is worthy of trust. This is death, his death. This is the day that we keep to the memory of it. On such a day, you shall not be afraid. Commit your way as he committed His. Silence may lead you there, hold you there by faith and hope and love. We stand in the hands of God, too powerful to be escaped from, to be avoided. If you love the hands, you will go in quietness and peace. Here is this Lover. As he ends he puts Himself into his Father's hands. With all the pain they have given him, he knows them as his Father's. Pain has blossomed into beauty under his hands, and all his soul becomes radiant now because he has put Himself into his Father's hands. God upholds all souls. Those are happy that go the way God wants them to go. The unhappy are those that seek their will. They shall not find it. He is too powerful, too wise, too much in love.

Closing Discourse on the Seven Words

AND NOW WE END THE MEMORY of his suffering, his death out of love for us. Let us remember that we must forgive because we see God's will behind all the hurt that is done us, looking behind the instruments to God that wields them in our lives. But we must do more. We must welcome with love all the world to us, robbers, thieves, whomsoever comes to us—at least for forgiveness and love. And we must do it because we see him everywhere. "My mother, my brethren," He said pointing with his hand to the crowd. And again we must go often into that way of desolation. That is the way of all souls who dare hold a love that will not doubt; and beyond that we must still have unbroken desire, in spite of the bleakness of our prayer; and again, beyond desire we must be glad to rest tranquil in utter silence. "It is finished," He said. It is never finished. Dying, and behold, we live! So we ask him, this strong Son of God, that he would lift us to his own blessed heights; that he would help us to see clearly the beauty pain has for those that will look for it, the beauty in the little small disappointments or failures, or whatever goes awry; that he would lift us to that height, and that we should bear whatever comes from our own folly and blindness and our lack of generosity (which lies at the back of so much that we call grandly our pain and our failure) and carry our griefs like men. Shall we ever reach there? Oh, that matters nothing. Go his way.

Say not the struggle naught availeth,
The labour and the wounds are vain;
The enemy faint not nor faileth,
And as things have been, they remain.

For while the tired waves vainly breaking
Seem here no painful inch to gain,
Far back, through creeks and inlets making,
Comes silent, flooding in, the main.

May he that is our Teacher, our Friend, our Lover, do his work with us in his own blessed way! May he teach us obedience through what he suffered! He that is our teacher, may he teach us that! He that is our Friend, may he help us to be ourselves, to go the way he would have us go, because we are his friends, because he is neighbourly to us! May he that is our Lover burn us, purge us, cleanse us with the flames of his love, for we are poor and small in our souls, yet we wish to be more than that! He will help us. But don't cry out at the way he deals with you. If you love you must trust, and if you trust, all is well. Lifting us, teaching us, helping us, loving us, may he make us, because we have striven to love him, still for all our failure look for beauty in the heart of pain.

SERMON FOR GOOD FRIDAY

All Ye That Sorrow

On this evening of Good Friday, we stop to think, not of the Passion of the Son, but rather of the Passion of his Mother. For him all the suffering is over; for her suffering remains. For him, death was indeed suffering; for her, death, his death, has made that suffering more intense. We call her the Queen of Martyrs, for she was among all martyrs their queen. She suffered nothing herself in the way that the martyrs suffered. No violence was done her, except the violence done to her heart. She did not suffer for him, as the martyrs suffered. That was her trouble. She could only suffer with him. Thus she watched him suffer and she could do nothing to help. That is the awfulness of watching people we love in pain. We can do nothing, nothing at all. We can just watch, perfectly helpless, but their suffering, as we watch, becomes our own. She was the queen, then, of martyrs because she suffered with him. Every blow of the scourge she felt. Every prick of each thorn in the crown pierced her forehead. Whatever hurt him, hurt her. The nails as they were driven, clenched and unclenched her own fingers. The nails driven through his feet she carried with pain. Her heart hurt when his was opened. The death that eased him gave her no ease.

She suffered with him. In all he suffered, she suffered, and that is where we touch hands with her. We have to watch suffering, be utterly unable to ease suffering, we must think of her suffering. We must ask her to gain for us strength to bear our own. She suffered, even though she knew that death would be swiftly lifted from him, that he would come back. Just to lose him, just to know that death took him was pain enough, though she knew out of death would come forth life. A mother is hurt when her child perhaps goes away to school from her. She knows she will see the child again. That doesn't lessen the pain. The pain at least is there. It isn't that she doesn't know the child will come back to her, but for the moment all she can think of is that the child is gone. There is a place empty at the table, a bed empty upstairs. Everything is desolate, quiet. She must suffer by that.

Imagine her, robbed of him whom most she loved. He was all she had, and he was taken from her, and she stood weeping under the Cross. There is no hurt in weeping. She was crying, and no one said her nay. There is nothing wrong in feeling the hurts you suffer. He blessed those that mourn. To mourn was a blessing in his eyes. He didn't say that he did not wish people to feel suffering. He said, "Blessed are they that mourn. Blessed are they that weep, for they shall be comforted." She wept, and she had at last her comfort—we must think of that, must remember the depth of her suffering and sorrow shows the height to which her comfort lifted her, which she reached, when at last comfort came.

For all we know, he died without telling her when at last she would go to him. He may have told her, but we don't know that he did, and even so it must have been hard for her to go on living. She might have wondered why she was left. What was she to do? What was her place, now that her Child had left the earth? What was she doing on earth? Why didn't he take her? Well, once before that, when he was quite a little boy, he had gone with them to the Temple at Jerusalem, and then they thought he had gone back with them, but he hadn't. He had stayed behind. They looked for him, searched for him, and couldn't find him, and they came back sorrowful, still looking for the boy. At last they found him. There he was in the temple, dealing with the wise old men, asking them questions they couldn't answer, answering all their questions. So wise he was, even as a Child. And she came and she said to him, "Why have You done this? Why have you left me without saying a word? You need only have told me that you were going, and I shouldn't have looked for you these three days. Why did you just go away and leave us, why deliberately hurt your mother's heart? You need only have said one word, 'Trust me.'" Why didn't he say it? She pondered over it, her heart was pierced by a sword. Why did he treat her like that? Why did he deliberately hurt her when he could have saved her all that pain? You wouldn't think any boy was a good son that ran away and never told where he was going when he might have told and so saved them all their pain. Especially you wouldn't think it of one like him, that was so full of sympathy and understanding. It is so strange. But he must be about his Father's business, and her business was to trust him. So she learnt to trust him and pondered over these things. That was all when he was a little boy, and now he had grown up and there he was, hanging on the Cross, and then before night fell they had taken him down. Perhaps he had died silent, saying nothing to her, just leaving her to trust. She knew, as all the disciples knew, that he had promised after three days he would come back. She knew that, but she didn't know about herself, how long she was to go on waiting after it was all done. And perhaps he never told her, or perhaps he just had said she was to wait for him. Evidently that must have been how he treated her. He said nothing. He asked her to have perfect confidence in him. We may be sure she had. Now, that is how she bore sorrow. This is the way of our Queen.

Now you and I, whoever we are, whatever our luck in life is, are sure to have all sorts of troubles, and we may sometimes wonder why God leaves us, why all we ever loved or worked for, sometimes at least, may be taken from us, and we left sorrowing and alone. It may well seem strange to us, we being so small, so bewildered, what God does must seem strange, not because it is strange, but because we have such little sight, such little understanding, and God is so infinitely great. What we have got to remember is just how he treated his mother when he was a little boy, and how when he was a grown man he left her standing, lonely. He went away from her, who had suffered with him, for him, heart in heart. Remember both his silence and her perfect confidence. Thus was she the Queen of Martyrs, but her heart at peace, tranquil, resting in confidence on God. And so you and I tonight have the thought of her suffering, the dreadfulness of that first night with him dead—not dead only, but buried. How relentless burial seems! As though the dead, while they were unburied, were still in your midst, almost alive. But when they were buried—that seemed the end of things. The earth falling on them; they hid from us. So now he was hidden from her by a great stone rolled. And as she stood, receiving the body in her arms, and then seeing it carried and placed in the tomb, and then the great stone rolled across the front, that must have seemed to make him doubly dead. To that sorrowing mother's heart, came only silence, and no words spoken, but she rested on her confidence, on her faith in him, on his love of her.

We are all children of sorrow. For all of us this is the valley of tears. Everyone, somehow, must sorrow—grown-up people, children, everyone. But there is no hurt in sorrowing. It is a blessing. In proportion to your sorrow will consolation come. So it becomes a blessedness. One day he will repay you, and now you must just wait. So we turn to her, this sorrowful mother for all that are sorrowful must come to her, and we ask that she would turn her eyes of mercy towards us, she so compassionate at heart, so understanding, who had tasted the depth of sorrow herself, had lost the best of all sons, her Child and the God who made her, the Child that her womb had fashioned, the God that had fashioned her womb. She had lost him, and life was a blank for her, and all her life would now be empty as she turned from the tomb and the closed door. All ye that sorrow declare if there be sorrow like her sorrow, or love or loss like hers? It was God's will. She bore her sorrow and she will help us to bear ours, every one of them, sorrows that others know we carry, and those more hidden sorrows that no one knows but we. She will help us. She has tasted bitterness. She carried her sorrows. She walked tranquil because she loved. Her tears were not bitter tears. Behind her tears was perfect trust in him. Our Mother will put her mantle about us, and when we stand under our cross, we know that she will stand by us. "Turn then thine eyes of mercy towards us, and after this, our exile"—it is an exile. It was meant to be an exile. Here we are wanderers. Here we have no home. "After this, our exile, show unto us the fruit of thy womb, O clement, O loving, O sweet Virgin Mary."

SERMON FOR EASTER SUNDAY

Death

The feast of Easter, my dear brethren, is above all things a feast of hope and of courage. We celebrate the triumph of our blessed Lord over death. Man has and shall vanquish and conquer many enemies; the only enemy he can never conquer is death. Yet even death, through the triumph of our blessed Lord, is to be finally conquered, not only his death, but ours. You have just listened to the choir singing beautifully that sequence which speaks of the war, the wonderful war between life and death, out of which life emerged triumphant, Christ the victor, risen from the dead. He is a conqueror of death because he can make each of us, if we will, also conquerors. It is thus that he has taken the horror out of death. He has made it something no longer to scare people, but to encourage them. It is no longer a ruin but a sacrifice that every soul can make. Each man dying is a priest, and can offer a sacrifice like his Master. Each, like his Master, is victim and priest beside. He can offer himself in memory of that offering Christ made; offer it undefeated even by death.

Again, for us death is not the end of the roadway. It is only a turn in the road. We hold it not as though it were the journey's end.

The journey ends not in death, but life. Indeed the journey has no ending. Death is merely a cliff that hides from us the full tide of life. People sometimes talk in their foolishness of such a one cut off in the prime of life. He is not cut off. Rather he is, if one could vary the metaphor, hurried into the prime, the fullness of life. He is lifted out of this life of ours, which is but a waiting till death shall find us. He is taken out of this. He is set in life itself. He has escaped, this man of whom they say to us that he is stricken in the midst of years. Too young to die, they say. Too young? Nay, rather he is blessed in being so young thus to be made swiftly an immortal. He has escaped the tremulous hands of age.

One of those great explorers who founded those early colonies that are now your states, was upon a charge of treason, brought back home to England at last to die. As he lay in prison he finished the last pages of his Universal History. He wrote them under the shadow of the axe and the block. On the eve of death he ends that history in which he had reviewed, as in a pageant, though it be in an unfinished way, all those historic times through which himself he had lived. He ends, knowing that death will come in the morning, with a great apostrophe to death. "Oh just, eloquent and mighty death!" is how he begins his appeal to that that is to release him. "Just, eloquent, mighty" is surely true of death!

It is the gateway of all knowledge. Men live and toil to discover knowledge and learning. They go as boys to school to learn all the world has to teach them. In their old age, when death comes, they are still learning. So slow is the amassing of our little knowledge. Then death comes, and suddenly they know all. It is the gateway of knowledge. It is no less the gate of peace through which after this fever men find their fulfilment and their rest. It is the gate even of mystic knowledge whence men, passing through it, receive at once all those gifts for which the saints in their lifetime have toiled.

Thus did Christ our Lord vanquish death. He taught us how to vanquish it by not being afraid to die. And death being vanquished, what other evil can we ever really fear? Death, the long undefeated foe of man, God made Man has conquered for Himself and all the world. It is because of that, my dear brethren, because death has been met and answered, that every Christian soul should know that there is nothing that cannot be firmly and properly dealt with. No problem can utterly be insoluble. There is a remedy for all things. To all things there is an end.

Men talk, and rightly, I suppose, of the problems of our time, and wonder how they are to be solved and dealt with. In consequence, people looking out into the future are a little afraid. How is this problem to be solved, they ask? What is to be the end of that? Now it is part of the spirit of the followers of Christ never to be afraid of the future, or of whatever the future may bring. There are dark clouds and difficulties beyond us always. Yet there must always be victory for good, for the good is God. God is triumphant. Life is triumphant. Every lesser thing shall fail.

Men say to us, "There is this problem of the family. How are we to preserve it? It seems to be dissolving before our eyes." That has been true perhaps always and everywhere. Everywhere good things have seemed to be going. Yet everywhere they are merely struggling to their new birth. There is always a movement. There are always difficulties. There is always a crisis. Yet here is always an answer, for this is God's world, and death has been defeated by life. What the answer is to be to any particular difficulty, who can tell? At least we know that it can be answered if it be met by courage, by daring. Thus, for instance, we are sure that a new form will be given to the family to suit the new ways. The family, in its organisation, has been always changing. It has varied with social custom, yet is of itself undying. It renews age by age the ways and the fashions that suit its own time. Of course, there are laws for the family, there are limits, a horizon set to it which it may not alter. What alone alters is what all men see. That which is invisible abides.

My brethren, it is to you, the laity, that we priests dare look for the solution of the problem. Not from us who teach, but from you who live is the answer to come. It is not to be solved by the words of a preacher. It is to be solved by living. It is not to be met by theories. It is to be met by the good Catholic life. The problem is largely of your own creation here in this land. It is here, and by your hands (or the hands, rather, of those that went before you) that the doors were flung open to the flood of divorce. It was here, I suppose, that on any large scale was first propagated all those degrading practices that have followed on the heel of divorce. Surely the land that set the problem is the land that should meet the problem. All it needs is courage, boldness and the vision, which are all the gifts and qualities of youth.

In a world that is jealous of success, those that succeed will never be popular. That is always the lesson of all human life. Men the world over now criticise you. Always they criticise the great. But no one has ever denied your daring. No one has ever denied that you are bold. Indeed, all that which is great among you is the result of boldness and daring. These are the causes of your real achievements. Thus your architecture that soars is fine because it is bold, and therefore expressive of your people. It is not copied. It is not the trick of an age that is over. It is born of the soaring spirits of you who planned it. Again, you have been bold in the organization of your industry, bold in this as in all you have done. People deny you many things when they speak of you, but no one denies your boldness or your daring. You have courage. Surely you will use it in the things of the spirit as well as the things that pass. You are young enough to have that daring, young enough not to be imprisoned in the mere memory of experience, yet old enough to look wisely and with care before you act. You have been visionary enough to plan a scheme of daring that should make the world temperate by law. You are great enough, I think, to see that you have failed in the fulfilment of the vision that was conceived in idealism and begotten in hope, great enough to change what you meant to achieve, a noble object, great enough now to reach it by a nobler means than force. You have courage. You have boldness. You have the visionary spirit. You have the greatness to admit failure when you see it clear before your eyes. These things men expect from you. Today we ask you to do a more wonderful thing, to rebuild the family.

You see, this is the feast of the unquenched spirit. It is the feast of the triumph of that which was unknown over experience. It is the triumph of life over failure and death. So men turn to you and hope that as from you came the evil, so from you will come the healing of that ill. May he that came and lived and died and rose again, he that though born as a child was yet the ancient of days before he came, he that was young and yet eternal, who was born and is unbegotten, who died and is undying, who is age and youth at once, wise and eager, may he bless you to give our world the vision of the new social order and the courage to fulfil it and the greatness to start again if at first you fail. You have that gift in other ways. God will surely bless you, God who promised to his Church that age after age she should gather the past and see the future, that she should hold in her hands all the wisdom of the ages that are dying or are dead and hold as well the wisdom of the ages that are daily born. This he promised. Our hope lies in his promise, the unending promise of old things and new. The old are new, the new are old on Easter Day. Life is triumphant. Life is eternal. The life he brought us shall never die.

CLUNY MEDIA

Designed by Fiona Cecile Clarke, the Cluny Media *logo depicts a monk at work in the scriptorium, with a cat sitting at his feet.*

The monk represents our mission to emulate the invaluable contributions of the monks of Cluny in preserving the libraries of the West, our strivings to know and love the truth.

The cat at the monk's feet is Pangur Bán, from the eponymous Irish poem of the 9th century. The anonymous poet compares his scholarly pursuit of truth with the cat's happy hunting of mice. The depiction of Pangur Bán is an homage to the work of the monks of Irish monasteries and a sign of the joy we at Cluny take in our trade.

"Messe ocus Pangur Bán,
cechtar nathar fria saindan:
bíth a menmasam fri seilgg,
mu memna céin im saincheirdd."

Printed in Great Britain
by Amazon

38985594R00195